CHEKHOV

THE MAJOR PLAYS

CHEKHOV

THE MAJOR PLAYS

English Versions by

Jean-Claude van Itallie

APPLAUSE
NEW YORK • LONDON

Library of Congress Cataloging-in-Publication Data

Chekhov, Anton Pavlovich, 1860-1904.
[Plays. English. Selections]
Chekhov : the major plays / English versions by Jean-Claude van Itallie.
p.   cm.
Includes bibliographical references.
ISBN 1-55783-162-9 : $7.95
1. Chekhov, Anton Pavlovich, 1860-1904--Translations into English. I. Van Itallie, Jean Claude, 1936- . II. Title.
PG3456.A19   1994
891.72'3--dc20   94-27070
CIP

British Library Cataloging-in-Publication Data

A catalogue record for this book is available from the British Library.

Applause Books
211 West 71st Street
New York, NY 10023
Phone (212) 496-7511
Fax: (212) 721-2856
Printed in Canada

406 Vale Road
Tonbridge Kent TN9 1XR
Phone 073 235-7755
Fax 073 207-7219

CONTENTS

Acknowledgments

I want to thank friends of these versions of Chekhov's plays, so many friends that I know I won't remember them all. They include performers, directors, producers, assistants, students, readers, editors, and other creative spirits who have helped in different ways over the years. A partial list includes Dan Seltzer, Leueen MacGrath, Joe Chaikin, Ellen Stewart, Andrei Serban, Irene Worth, Joseph Papp, Lynne Meadow, Robert Brustein, Vitaly Voulff, Tina Shepherd, David Wolpe, Didi Goldenbar, Louise Smith, Shanti Mohling, Lillian Butler, Laurie MacLoed, Alex Gildzen, Glenn Young, Wendy Gimbel, Lawrence Sacharow, Madeline Puzo, Cynthia Harris, Rosemary Quinn, Deborah Katz, Bill Coco, David Threlfall, Braham Murray, Judd Hirsch, Evangeline Morphos, Lynn Lorwin, Kim Mancuso, Janet Roberts, Gilbert Parker, Richard Gilman, Joyce Aaron, Eric Bentley, Gordon Rogoff, Gwen Fabricant, Stephanie Sills, Carol Fox Prescott, Peggy Ann Lloyd, Elizabeth Mailer and Craig Kayser.

Introduction

English has subtly evolved since I began my association with Chekhov two decades ago. Probably every translation should be revised every twenty years, so I've reworked the English of these versions for the new millennium and the Applause edition. I've polished the phrasing as if these were my own plays, being faithful to the rhythm of the characters' voices in my mind's ear. I believe I'm a better writer now. I've reduced subtle colloquialisms which I hadn't noticed before (such as "a lot of"). I hope the language flows more smoothly.

Vitaly Voulff, the renowned Russian Chekhov scholar, and translator of Tennessee Williams into Russian, has kindly scoured each line of these versions for accuracy to the original. I am impressed that Vitaly actually knew Chekhov's wife, the actress Olga Knipper.

I was teaching at Princeton in 1972 when Dan Seltzer, then Head of the Drama Department and the McCarter Theater, asked me to render a new version of *The Sea Gull* for a production at the McCarter (in which Dan was to play Sorin). I immediately voiced two objections: there were many existing translations, and I neither speak nor read Russian. Dan pushed a pile of books at me saying, "Read some of these translations before you decide." Some, like the excellent one by Stark Young, were dated. Some were too literally British for an American production. Others, while faithful to the exact translation of each word, paid scant attention to rhythms of speech, making Chekhov seem obscure, pedantic, and, worst, unactable, the very opposite of what he is. Dan wanted a new version by an American playwright to be performed by Americans for a contemporary American audience. I agreed, provided Dan supply me with a literal translation by a Russian native. The father of Lou Criss, the director, ably obliged.

I found myself approaching my task like an actor. My objective was to imaginatively 'become' Chekhov, to enter his frame of mind in order to 'speak' his words in English. First I had to demystify him. If Chekhov and I were to collaborate, I had to remove him from his remote tower of genius, to see him as a friend. I needed to meet the person before I could work with the artist.

When, as an undergraduate at Harvard in the late fifties, I was introduced to Chekhov by reading him in what must have been an old and stilted translation, I found him barely accessible. Drawn to a more explosive kind of theatre, in the sixties I became a playwright in the new Off-Broadway movement. By the time Dan asked me to work on *The Sea Gull*, however, I was able to read Chekhov with a different eye. I looked to him now as a teacher, a co-laborer in the field. I remade his acquaintance by reading some of his letters. Finding him charming, full of common sense, compassionate and human, I encouraged myself to identify with him. Chekhov loved trees and living in the country (as do I). He found living in the country cheaper than living all year in Moscow. He loved to hear and tell stories about people he knew. Many of his friends were in the theatre. He had an aversion to dry intellectuality. A country doctor, he had to cope with a cholera epidemic. He spoke some French.

Now I read Chekhov's plays as if they were the work of an avuncular friend, like Dr. Dorn who in Act One of *The Sea Gull* encourages Treplev's writing, and sympathises with Masha's tale of unrequited love.

I worked on *The Sea Gull*, and later the other three plays, with a specially-made literal English translation and a selection of French translations.

There is no single objectively 'right' way to say anything, of course. Meaning changes with choice of words and subtly spoken language. Working with more than one language reaffirms that while words point toward a reality, they aren't it. French was my first language. It has a feminine quality of playful intimacy. Having a smaller vocabulary than English, phrases are "sung" for subtle meaning. Samuel Beckett wrote in French or English, then translated into the other language. He may have used translation as a sieve, distilling meaning to arrive at a poetically economical text.

My process was to read to myself a single phrase in both English and French, let its meaning 'flow through' me (that's the image I had of what I was doing). Then, as the character, I would perform aloud a version of the phrase to my assistant (almost always an actor) who would write it down then read it back. Listening to the rhythm of the spoken phrase, I would refine it and speak it back again. We repeated the process for each speech, scene and act. My goal was to deliver Chekhov as fresh and alive as possible, without my own or idiomatic imposition. I wanted Chekhov in English to flow from the actors' mouths like clear water.

As I do for my own plays, I continued to work during early rehearsals of first productions. I listened to the actors, making small refinements in phrasing the English. When in January, 1975 Joe Chaikin directed *The Sea Gull* at the Manhattan Theater Club in New York City (with Dan Seltzer again as a superb Sorin, and my dear friend, the late Leueen MacGrath, exquisitely playing Arkadina) we found the English in a couple of Trigorin's monologues laborious, so I combed out some of the knots I had inadvertently placed there. On the other hand, when the incomparable Irene Worth played Ranevskaya in Andrei Serban's production at Lincoln Center in 1977, she'd say to me, "I need another vowel here so I can make the *sound* of the emotion." She was always absolutely right. In returning to the Russian we discovered that the extra beat had been there all along.

Chekhov wrote of *The Sea Gull*, "I began it *forte* and finished it *pianissimo.*" His plays seem to 'breathe,' alternating times of tension and release like a satisfying piece of music. He orchestrates the order of monologues, duets, trios, and group scenes. (We know that he actually edited with scissors and paste.)

In *The Sea Gull* Trigorin confesses to Nina that despite trying to keep up with social and political issues of the day, the only things he really describes well are landscapes. Starting a play, Chekhov may have been similarly inspired by an image of a familiar home. In that home he placed characters resembling people he knew.

How are Chekhov's plays different from the melodramas of his immediate predecessors? Soap opera and melodrama also deal with suicide, mortgage foreclosure, unhappy love affairs, and evil sisters-in-law. Chekhov's intention is different. Chekhov strikes deep chords while soap opera and melodrama do not. Intending to plumb the mysterious human heart, he listens with keen attention to his characters, to the rhythms and tones of their feelings.

Chekhov is a compassionate but sharp listener. He maintains what Henry James called "middle distance" from his characters, a loving detachment (as a good doctor should). His characters are not on stage merely to prove a point. They are fully dimensional and complex. The author doesn't pretend to know everything about them. He sustains a questioning attitude, respects and *listens* to his characters rather than forcing them to speak information.

'Pause' repeatedly occurs in Chekhov's stage directions. There's that extraordinary moment in Act Two of *The Cherry Orchard* when everyone listens to what sounds like the faint chord of a broken string echoing far away. In the quiet the characters listen, and the audience listens with them. For that to happen, the playwright had to listen too. Chekhov listened to people's voices, and to the silence between them. The gaps between thoughts are filled with drama. Reality asserts itself between words, literally between the lines. To 'hear' this reality we must listen from a correspondingly deep silent place within ourselves.

When reading these plays, listen with feeling to the characters. Resist, as their author did, the temptation to judge them too swiftly or too harshly.

You may find yourself laughing and crying at the same time, not knowing what to think.

Rowe, Massachusetts
January, 1995

A Word About Names

The character lists for each play are exactly as Chekhov wrote them. He sometimes introduces someone by one name, while in the text he may call them differently. This may confuse a reader in English (although not the audience which has the advantage of seeing the live actor on stage). While "Voinitsky, Ivan Petrovich" appears in the cast list of *Uncle Vanya*, on reading it may not be immediately evident that the loquacious Voinitsky is the title character, Vanya. But Chekhov's apellations may tell us how close he felt to each character when he created the *dramatis personae* (which he apparently did before writing a play).

Introducing *The Cherry Orchard*, Chekhov writes that "the play takes place on the estate of Lyubov Andreyvna." "Lyubov Andreyvna" translates as "Lyubov, daughter of Andre." In the character list, Chekhov calls this lady "Ranevskaya, Lyubov Andreyvna." Ranevsky was her dead husband's last name. She is called Madame Ranevskaya by her servants, Lyubov Andreyevna by her friends, and nicknamed Lyuba by her brother. Each name suggests a different degree of formality or intimacy. Some upper class people enjoyed addressing others in French, as Vanya sometimes calls Yelena Hélène.

"Ivan Petrovich," means "Ivan, son of Pyotr," or "John, son of Peter." Vanya is a nickname for Ivan, as Johnny is for John. (The play's title could conceivably be translated as *Uncle Johnny*.)

The Sea Gull

In 1892 Chekhov bought his family an estate in Melikhovo where, in 1895, he wrote *The Sea Gull* in a small cottage he'd built on the property. He read the play aloud to a group of theatre artists in Moscow who reacted not unlike Arkadina to Treplyev's play; they were accustomed to more melodramatic fare. The first production of *The Sea Gull*, in 1896, for reasons having nothing to do with the script, was a flop. Appalled by reactions which he felt as personal attacks, Chekhov fled St. Petersburg, announcing, "Not if I live to be seven hundred will I write another play."

Nemirovich-Danchenko, co-founder with Stanislavsky of the new Moscow Art Theater, persuaded Chekhov to allow them to produce *The Sea Gull*. Olga Knipper, who played Arkadina, and later became Chekhov's wife, describes "the huge excitement" the actors felt when Chekhov came to an early rehearsal at the Moscow Art. Stanislavsky played Trigorin. Meyerhold, perhaps the most innovative theatre director of the Soviet era, played Treplyev. *The Sea Gull* opened in Moscow on December 17th, 1898. "When the curtain fell on the first act," Nemirovich-Danchenko writes, "...there was silence, utter silence..." The actors held their breath, afraid they had failed. The silence lasted "...quite a long time .... Then, suddenly...as if a dam had burst or a bomb exploded...there was a deafening crash of applause ...." The play was, as Chekhov read the next morning in the telegram sent to him in Yalta, "a colossal success."

The Sea Gull may be Chekhov's most personal play. It is about writing and writers, the theatre, sons, mothers and lovers. Treplyev's confrontation with Arkadina owes something to Hamlet's closet scene with his mother. Treplyev's attempted suicide is likely based on a similar attempt by Chekhov's painter friend, Levitan, whom Chekhov visited in a house in the Novgorod lake district. Chekhov's personal voice is heard in Dorn's compassion. For Nina's ill-fated relationship with Trigorin, Chekhov probably drew on his brief affair with the young Lika Misinova, a friend of his sister Maria, and on Misinova's subsequent affair with a Ukrainian writer, Potapenko, by whom she had a child. Trigorin's least likeable characteristics may be based on Potapenko. Nina's gift of a locket to Trigorin, with words from his book engraved on it, was inspired by a similar gift made to Chekhov by his friend Lydia Avilova.

It is surely Chekhov's own note-taking and writing habits that Trigorin describes. Trigorin is middleaged, a famous and prolific novelist afraid he has lost touch with a certain passion. Chekhov the writer is also present in Treplyev, the young playwright who is so sensitive and artistically uncompromising he can hardly write down a word. After struggling over a short story, Treplyev finally exclaims, "More and more I think it's not a question of new forms or old forms. What matters is to allow what you write to come straight from the heart." Treplyev's play within the play is usually directed only for farce; but as one who started writing in the theatrical avant-garde of the 1960's, I believe, with Dorn, that there is some beauty in its sad solitary questioning of the purpose of life on earth. I've rendered it as eloquently as I can.

Because Chekhov borrowed specific traits from people he knew, his characters feel like family. One feels inclined to gossip about them, to speculate, for instance, about why Masha "takes snuff, drinks vodka, always wears black," as Trigorin writes in his notebook. Chekhov provides us with a few provocative specifics while leaving space for our imagination to play, so we are drawn into the creative process ourselves (which may be partly why actors love to perform in Chekhov's plays).

The Sea Gull's principal story is of Nina, beloved of Treplyev, seduced by his mother's lover, Trigorin. Nina, however wounded, is the most hope-filled character in *The Sea Gull*. Surviving the loss of her illusions, she prepares to travel by third class rail to the dismal town of Yelets where, despite all, she will act in a play. Secondary threads in *The Sea Gull* include Masha's hopeless love for Treplyev, and her mother's long-secret affair with Dorn.

But plot in Chekhov serves merely as bedrock for a succession of intimate moments. This play, set by a "magic lake," has some of the qualities of a dream. If *The Sea Gull* were a melodrama we might learn that Dorn is really Masha's father, and that Dorn has always been in love with Arkadina. In *The Sea Gull* such suspicions remain mysterious underpinnings. What is the symbolism of the sea gull? Is the sea gull Nina shot down by Trigorin? Treplyev abandoned by Nina? Treplyev suffocated by his mother? Treplyev himself? All are possibilities.

Uncle Vanya

Uncle Vanya is based on an earlier play by Chekhov, *The Wood Demon*, written in 1889. Chekhov finished *Uncle Vanya* in 1897 and it was first produced in the provinces where it was a great success.

In *Uncle Vanya* the setting again is a home, a country estate owned by Sonya, a young unmarried woman who with her bachelor uncle Vanya works to make the estate provide a good income for her father, "a retired professor — a dried out prune, a talking parrot with rheumatism and migraine, bilious with Jealousy and envy..." and his young second wife, Yelena. The house is often visited by the virile Doctor Astrov, an ardent conservationist, with whom Sonya is secretly in love. Astrov complains of a lack of cultured companionship, but his care of and advocacy for the dwindling Russian forests vitalizes him, makes him magnetic, and his words vivid and urgent. Today he would be an active protestor of the destruction of the rain forests.

Sonya, who does not consider herself pretty, confesses her love to the beautiful Yelena, who in turn uses Sonya's confession to encourage Astrov herself. Yelena seems trapped by her own indolence, and, as Astrov tells her, she constitutes a glamorous delusive trap for others. Vanya, educated and remarkably intelligent, has lived his life on the estate with his niece and his old mother (who loves only to read literary articles), devoting himself to the support of the professor. Now that he realizes that the professor is a fraud, Vanya despairs that his own life has been wasted. He blames the professor and tries to kill him. Finally, uncle and niece are left much as they were, working together on the accounts.

At the end of *Uncle Vanya*, just as at the end of *Three Sisters* (Nina speaks of it, too, toward the end of *The Sea Gull*), when all other hope is lost, some characters feel there is still salvation in work. The characters who say so are all, like Chekhov himself, childless. As for any artist, work is also a child. An old Sufi saying proclaims: "Unfortunate is the person who faces death without work to do." To Vanya and Sonya their work, however monotonous and mundane, is valuable because now, all illusions lost, they consciously choose to do it. Like Astrov, they give meaning to their lives by devoting themselves to being useful. However unglamorous, this ending is more bittersweet than tragic.

Three Sisters

Three Sisters was written in 1900 in the warm climate of Yalta where Chekhov, having had to sell his Melikhovo estate, and realizing that tuberculosis would likely cut short his life, had bought land and built a house. *Three Sisters* was written for the Moscow Art. There were many rewrites, including added lines for Masha who was to be played by Olga Knipper.

Three Sisters opened at the Moscow Art on January 31st, 1901. Meyerhold played Tuzenbach. One week before opening, Stanislavsky decided to play Vershinin, and Stanislavsky's wife, Maria Lilina, played Natasha. On May 25th, 1901, Olga Knipper and Anton Chekhov were married.

The Moscow Art production of *Three Sisters* came to New York in 1923 where, along with other plays in the Moscow Art repertory, it was greatly appreciated, and provided the impetus toward a more realistic "truer" acting style in the American theater.

In the cast of characters Chekhov lists the three sisters by their first names. In creating each of Olga, Masha and Irina, Chekhov probably borrowed some traits from his wife and some from his sister Maria. Olga, Masha and Irina touch us intimately. Each is a complex good person. Olga, the eldest sister, is hardworking, idealistic, self-sacrificing, and, at twenty-eight, reconciled to remaining unmarried. She remembers childhood days when the family lived in Moscow, a Moscow that shines brightly in her memory. (Chekhov, his ill health confining him to a warmer climate during Moscow's artistically active season, may, in this play, be parodying his own yearning to be in Moscow.) Forced to be a breadwinner, Olga becomes principal of the local girls' high school, a job which gives her a constant headache. Masha, the middle sister, is romantic, bright, sensitive, brusque, cultured and unhappily married to a comically conventional schoolteacher. She deserves better, but when "better" comes along in the shape of the eloquent Colonel Vershinin, he is already unhappily but irrevocably married, and is eventually transferred away. Irina, the youngest, like Nine in *The Sea Gull*, embodies radiant hope at the start of the play. Sleeping late, she dreams of a happy life full of good works. The Baron, an army officer, bright and kind but physically unattractive, is in love with Irina. Although she doesn't love him, Irina eventually promises Olga she will marry the Baron, abandoning hope of a prince charming in Moscow. Fate, however, snatches away even this compromise with happiness. The Baron is killed in a duel with Solyony, who lives only in his head, and has a borrowed literary personality instead of true feelings.

Andrei, the brother, is weak. He marries the coarse Natasha, who is as close to a villain as the play offers (except for her lover, the bureaucrat Protopopov, whom we never see). Natasha, although a comical figure, is a cruel personification of the dark relentless ignorance slowly engulfing the sisters. By the end of the play she's virtually evicted them from their home, and is about to have the property's old trees cut down. (In *Uncle Vanya* Astrov makes clear Chekhov's feelings about forests and trees.) The sisters are cultured people condemned to a provincial backwater. Chekhov may have based the place on the garrison town of Voskressensk, near Moscow, where he spent summers with his family at his brother Ivan's apartment, until Ivan was appointed headmaster of a school in Moscow).

The sisters are condemned by their father's death, their brother's weakness and by his wife's opportunism. At the end of the play the army officers, the only other cultured people in town, are transferred away. With them leaves any hope of a return to Moscow (a move the sisters can't afford on their own). Chekhov depicts specific characters trapped in a specific circumstance. But we all experience an equivalent "trap." We're here on a temporary visa. Sickness, old age and death lie in wait. Our choices are in how we behave along the way. The sisters are not morbid (except sometimes Masha who has a flair for the dramatic). The sisters are not benumbed or bitter. In each moment they remain full of feeling, and full of love for each other.

The Cherry Orchard

Chekhov, now quite ill, completed *The Cherry Orchard* after many revisions in 1903. He wrote the play with certain of the Moscow Art actors in mind. Olga Knipper, his thirty-four year old wife, was originally to play Varya. But Knipper was determined to play the leading role of the much older Ranevskaya instead. Chekhov finally agreed, confident that Knipper's sensitivity and humor would prevent the character from being played as a stereotypical 'loose woman.' He delivered the manuscript by mailing it from Yalta to Olga Knipper in Moscow with an accompanying casting note — "You play Ranevskaya, for no one else can do it as well. She's clever, kind, absent-minded, affectionate to everyone, with always a smile on her face." In addition to the inaugural production, Knipper continued to play Ranevskaya for over forty years.

When Stanislavsky wanted to play Gaev instead of Lophakin, he wrote to Chekhov for approval of the change. Chekhov worried that the new Lopakhin, the actor Leonidov, would make the character appear merely greedy and vulgar. Chekhov wrote to Stanislavsky -"Lopakhin mustn't be played by a shouter... He is a soft person."

The Cherry Orchard premiered at the Moscow Art in 1904 on January 17th, Chekhov's birthday. The ailing author arrived during the third act. Chekhov died at the German spa of Badenweiler on July 2nd, 1904 at the age of forty-four, telling stories to his wife, and drinking champagne.

Chekhov planted his own orchard of fifty cherry trees at Melikhovo in 1892. These trees were cut down in 1899 by the lumber dealer who had bought the estate. Later at Yalta Chekhov planted trees from all over Russia, and tenderly cared for them. Before the destruction of the forests in the 1880s, Chekhov spent holidays as a child in the Ukraine, and was familiar with homes there that boasted cherry orchards. Chekhov visited the country estates of many friends, including one near Kharkov.

The Cherry Orchard is about home and all that 'home' implies (including its opposite, homelessness). Home implies habits of thinking, beliefs, and extended family. But home is never static. Wherever we feel at home — in our dwelling, our country, with our friends, in our economic situation, our bodies — there is bound to be change. Chekhov when still a child witnessed the traumatic effect of bankruptcy on his father. The cherry orchard is threatened by the axe at a time when every aspect of Russian life, including the class and belief system buoying up a genteel life, is shaking underfoot. Written fourteen years before the Russian revolution, *The Cherry Orchard* records the warning tremors of that impending earthquake as it manifests in the lives of the characters. Our own time is one of ever more frequent violent social, ecological and political change. Change is often painful, a violation of what we believed to be secure. On becoming aware of change, our first responsibility may be to acknowledge that it's happening. Only then can we begin to know how to respond. While offering no solutions, the play, if only by its existence, stands against denial and ignorance.

Each inhabitant of *The Cherry Orchard* feels and behaves differently toward home. Lyubov Andreyevna Ranevskaya adores her home but from a distance. (She lives in Paris.) Her weak-minded brother, Gaev, is dependent on home, a baby in its maternal embrace. For Varya, the adopted daughter, home is a place to caretake, a place in which she is accustomed to feeling secondary. When she has the chance to marry Lopakhin and change her status, she cannot. Trofimov, student of revolution, feels at home only in the future. Anya, like Nina in *The Sea Gull*, is the most hopeful character. When her home starts to change, she starts to change too. Lopakhin, the self-made successful man, truly loves the Cherry Orchard. He wants to hug it to death, so to speak. Lopakhin dreams of possessing the Cherry Orchard in order to destroy it. Firs, the old retainer, *is* the house almost literally. He's inseparable from it. (The old nannies in *Three Sisters* and *Uncle Vanya*, who are earthy and loving, resemble Firs.) When at the end of the play the axe blades are heard hacking into the cherry trees, it's as if Firs' old bones themselves were being cut. When the house dies, Firs dies, and the old order is dead. For better or for worse something new is happening in Russia.

The settings of *The Cherry Orchard* move musically, like a ghostly farewell dance, from the inner sanctum of the nursery from which we can see the cherry blossoms in spring bloom (Chekhov on a snowy February day in the Crimea writes to Stanislavsky how he wants this scene to look — "...an utterly white orchard, and the ladies in white dresses."), to the characters listening to music sitting on old tombstones near the orchard by the side of a road leading from the house toward a new factory faintly visible in the distance, then back to the house for a frenzied midsummer ball, and finally, in autumn, for the last time to the nursery in the house about to be destroyed.

In Chekhov's plays, as in life, the best times feel sad and funny at once. Stanislavsky, on reading the script, had communicated to Chekhov that *The Cherry Orchard* was a "truly great tragedy." Chekhov, not wanting his play painted merely in dark colors, responded that it was a farce. Comic characters populate Chekhov's world. But they are not merely comical. They are complex characters, frequently touching, and inextricably woven into the fabric of a play. They don't so much provide 'comic relief' as contribute small human moments that are funny and poignant at once.

In a melodrama Lopakhin would be the villain foreclosing on the mortgage. Chekhov did not want him played that way. Lopakhin does what comes naturally to a successful man born a peasant. He loves Ranevskaya. She doesn't hate him nor do we. We see good and bad in Lopakhin, as we see weakness and lovingness in Ranevskaya. Each character struggles with themselves and with circumstance. Chekhov invites us to listen to them as he does, with clarity and compassion.

THE
SEA GULL
A COMEDY IN FOUR ACTS

Jean-Claude van Itallie's English version of Anton Chekhov's *The Sea Gull* was first produced at the McCarter Theatre, Princeton, New Jersey (Daniel Seltzer, artistic director), in October, 1973, directed by Lou Criss, with Daniel Seltzer as Sorin, and Irene Dailey as Arkadina.

It was produced in New York City at the Manhattan Theatre Club (Lynne Meadow, artistic director) in January, 1975, directed by Joseph Chaikin, costumes by Gwen Fabricant. The cast included Leueen MacGrath as Arkadina, Tina Shepherd as Nina, Margo Lee Sherman as Masha, and Daniel Seltzer as Sorin.

Some other productions of the van Itallie version of Chekhov's *The Sea Gull* include those at the Goodman Theatre, Chicago, in October, 1977, with Ruth Ford as Arkadina; New York Shakespeare Festival Public Theater, New York City, directed by Andrei Serban, with Rosemary Harris as Arkadina, Christopher Walken as Trigorin, and F. Murray Abraham as Dorn; Circle Repertory, New York City, in October, 1983, directed by Elinor Renfield, with Judd Hirsch as Trigorin, and Richard Thomas as Treplyev; the Guthrie Theater, Minneapolis, Minnesota, in November, 1983, directed by Lucian Pintile; River Arts Repertory, Woodstock, New York, in July, 1985, directed by Lawrence Sacharow with Joanne Woodward as Arkadina; Great Lakes Theater Festival, Cleveland, in October, 1989, directed by Gerald Freedman, with Anita Gillette as Arkadina; the Guthrie Theater in October, 1992, directed by Garland Wright; the premiere reading of the revised version by the Actors Company Theater at the Players Club, New York City, directed by Scott Evans, with Cynthia Harris as Arkadina.

CAST OF CHARACTERS

ARKADINA, IRINA NIKOLAYEVNA (married name Trepleyev), an actress

TREPLYEV, KONSTANTINE GAVRILOVICH, her son, a young man

SORIN, PYOTR NIKOLAYEVICH, her brother

ZARECHNAYA, NINA MICHAILOVNA, a young girl, daughter of a rich landowner

SHAMRAEV, ILYIA AFANASYEVICH, a retired army lieutenant, manager of Sorin's estate

PAULINA ANDREYEVNA, his wife

MASHA, his daughter

TRIGORIN, BORIS ALEXYEVICH, a novelist

DORN, YEVGENY SERGEYVICH, a doctor

MEDVEDYENKO, SEMYON SEMYONOVICH, a teacher

YAKOV, a worker

COOK

MAID

The action takes place on Sorin's country estate.

Two years elapse between Act III and Act IV

Part of the park in Sorin's estate. A broad avenue leads away from the audience deeper into the park towards a lake, but the avenue and view of the lake are blocked by a temporary stage being built for an amateur performance tonight. From behind the closed curtain of the temporary stage, YAKOV and other workers are heard coughing and hammering. Bushes on the right and left further conceal the lake. A few chairs and a small table. The sun has just set. MASHA and MEDVEDYENKO enter from the left, returning from a walk.

MEDVEDYENKO: Why do you always wear black?

MASHA: I'm in mourning for my life. I'm unhappy.

MEDVEDYENKO: *(wondering)* Why? I don't understand. You're healthy. Your father's not rich, but he's not poor. My life is much harder than yours. I earn only twenty-three rubles a month, and from that they deduct for the pension fund. But I don't wear mourning. *(They sit.)*

MASHA: It's not a matter of money. Even a poor person can be happy.

MEDVEDYENKO: That's a nice theory, but in practice it doesn't work. Take my case—there's me, my mother, my two sisters and my little brother. On my salary of twenty-three rubles a month we all have to eat and drink, to buy sugar and tea and tobacco and so on and so on and so on.

MASHA: *(looking toward the stage)* The play will begin soon.

MEDVEDYENKO: Yes. Nina Zarechnaya is to perform in a play by Konstantine Gavrilovich. They're in love. Tonight their souls will mingle in art true to both of them. But my soul and your soul have no such common ground. I love you so much I can't stay home alone. Each day I walk six miles here, and six miles back—to meet nothing but indifference on your part. I suppose it's to be expected. I have no private means, and a big family. Who'd want to marry a man who can't provide?

MASHA: Nonsense. *(taking snuff)* I'm touched by your love. But I can't return it. That's all. *(She offers him the snuff box.)* Here—have some snuff.

MEDVEDYENKO: No, thank you. I don't feel like it. *(pause)*

MASHA: The air's heavy. We'll probably have a storm. All you do is philosophize, or talk about money. You think there's nothing worse than to be poor. But I'd a thousand times prefer to be a beggar in rags than to—oh, you wouldn't understand.

(SORIN *and* TREPLYEV *enter from the right.*)

SORIN: *(leaning on a cane)* For some reason—who knows why, my dear— the country's just not my style. It's not, and it's too late to change me. Last night I went to bed at ten. This morning I woke at nine. All that sleep—it's glued my brain to my skull. It has. *(laughing)* Then I fell asleep again after lunch. And now I'm a wreck—still in a nightmare. Do you know the feeling?

TREPLYEV: You should be living in town. *(seeing* MASHA *and* MEDVEDYENKO) And you two shouldn't be here. You'll be called when we're ready, but please leave now.

SORIN: *(to* MASHA) Maria Ilyinitchna, please ask your father not to tie up the dog at night. It kept my sister awake again.

MASHA: You'll have to ask him yourself. I won't ask him, and please don't ask me to ask him. *(to* MEDVEDYENKO) Let's go.

MEDVEDYENKO: *(to* TREPLYEV) Don't forget to call us when the play starts.

(MASHA *and* MEDVEDYENKO *go out.*)

SORIN: That means the dog will howl again all night. You see how it is? I never get my way in the country. When I came here on twenty-eight-day leave to rest and so on, as soon as I'd arrive, they'd pester me with all sorts of nonsense. So of course right away I'd want to leave. *(He laughs.)* Leaving was always the best part. Anyway, now I'm retired—nowhere to go, and so on. So, like it or not—I'm here.

YAKOV: *(to* TREPLYEV) Konstantine Gavrilovich, we're going for a swim.

TREPLYEV: Alright, but be back in ten minutes. *(looking at his watch)* It's almost time.

YAKOV: Yes, sir. *(He leaves.)*

TREPLYEV: *(inspecting the stage)* This is our theatre. Curtain, the wings, and beyond—empty space. No scenery. All you'll see is the lake and the horizon. The curtain goes up at half past eight, just when the moon is rising.

SORIN: Perfect.

TREPLYEV: If Nina's late, of course, the whole effect will be spoiled. She should be here by now. Her father and stepmother watch her like hawks. It's as hard for her to escape from home as from a prison. *(He straightens his uncle's tie.)* Your hair and beard are a mess. You should have them trimmed.

SORIN: *(combing out his beard)* It's the bane of my life. Even when I was young, I always looked drunk or something. Women were never attracted to me. *(sitting)* Why is your mother in such a bad mood today?

TREPLYEV: Why? She's bored. *(sitting by his uncle)* And she's jealous. She's angry about my play because Nina's acting in it, and she's not. She hasn't seen or read it, but she hates it.

SORIN: *(laughing)* Is that really true?

TREPLYEV: Yes, she's angry in advance because, even though it's just on this little stage, it will be Nina's success and not hers. *(looking at his watch)* She's a psychological case, my mother. Certainly talented and smart—she can cry over a book, and recite the whole of Nekrassov by heart. And when you're sick, she'll nurse you like an angel. But just try praising Duse around her. Oh no, not that. You may praise only Mother, write only about productions that Mother's in, rave only about Mother's performance in *Camille* or *The Fumes of Life*. And since she finds no intoxicating adulation in the country—Mother's bored. She's cross, we're all her enemies—it's our fault. And she's superstitious—afraid of of three candles on a table, and the number thirteen. And she's a miser. She has seventy thousand in the bank at Odessa. I know that for a fact. But ask her for a loan, and she bursts into tears.

SORIN: You think your mother doesn't like your play, or something. Don't worry. Your mother adores you.

TREPLYEV: *(pulling petals off a flower)* She loves me, she loves me not, she loves me, she loves me not, she loves me, she loves me not. *(He laughs.)* You see—my mother doesn't love me. Why should she? She wants excitement, romance, and pretty clothes. I'm twenty-five now. That reminds her she's no longer young. When I'm not around, she's thirty-two. When I am, she's forty-three. She hates me for that, and because I don't believe in The Theatre. She adores The Theatre. She believes she's serving Mankind and the Sacred Cause of Art. I think theatre today is boring and trite. The curtain goes up on three walls within which our famous actors are carefully lit. Our high priests of art strut about, showing us how to eat, drink, love, walk and dress. The playwright squeezes out a moral, a smug cozy little moral, fit for home consumption. Each play repeats the same formula with tiny variations. That's why I flee from The Theatre—like Maupassant fled from the Eiffel tower, knowing it would cheapen his mind.

SORIN: But we must have a theatre.

TREPLYEV: What we need is a new kind of theatre. We need new forms. And if we can't have them—let's have no theatre at all. *(He looks at his watch.)* I love Mother, I love her very much, but she leads a stupid life—always fussing about that writer of hers, always wanting her name in the paper. It's boring. Maybe I'm selfish, but I wish she weren't a famous actress. I'd be happy if she were just an ordinary mortal. Can you imagine what life is like with her, Uncle—the house always full of famous actors and writers? Can you imagine how I feel? The only nobody there is me. And who am I? Her son. That's the only reason they talk to me. I left University my third year due to circumstances, as they say, beyond my control. I haven't a kopeck. And no talent. According to my passport, I'm a "bourgeois of Kiev." That's my social position. My father was a "bourgeois of Kiev" too, but he was a famous actor. When my mother's famous actor, writer, and musician friends deign to notice me, I feel them measuring my insignificance. I imagine their thoughts. It's humiliating.

SORIN: By the way, tell me—what sort of man is her writer? I can't make him out. He never opens his mouth.

TREPLYEV: He's intelligent, simple, rather melancholy. He seems decent. He's under forty and famous. He has everything he wants. As for his writing—well, you could say it's charming and clever. But after reading Tolstoy or Zola, you'd hardly want to read Trigorin.

SORIN: I love literary people, my boy. In my life I wanted two things passionately—to marry and to become a writer. Neither happened. So, to be even a second-rate writer sounds pretty good to me.

TREPLYEV: *(listening)* Someone's coming. *(He embraces his uncle.)* I can't live without her... Even the sound of her footsteps is beautiful. I'm wildly happy! *(going to meet* NINA ZARECHNAYA *as she enters)* My darling one, my dream.

NINA: *(agitated)* I'm not late? I hope I'm not late.

TREPLYEV: *(kissing her hands)* No, no, no...

NINA: I worried all day. I was so afraid Father wouldn't let me come. He and my stepmother just went out. I raced the horse. The sky's already red. The moon will be up soon. *(laughs)* But I'm happy now. I'm here. *(She takes SORIN's hand.)*

SORIN: *(laughing too)* You've been crying. I can tell by your pretty eyes. That won't do. It really won't.

NINA: I'm alright now. I'm just out of breath. Please let's hurry. I have to leave in half an hour. I have to. Please don't ask me to stay longer. I can't. My father doesn't even know I'm here.

TREPLYEV: It's time. I'll call them.

SORIN: I'll go. I'm going now. *(He goes off singing "The Two Grenadiers.")* "To France we're returning, two Grenadiers..." *(He stops, turns back toward them.)* Once when I started to sing like that, an assistant prosecutor said, "Your Excellency has a strong voice." Then he stopped to think, and added, "Strong, but not very good." *(He goes out laughing.)*

NINA: My father and his wife forbid me to come here. They say it's Bohemia. They're afraid I'll become an actress. But I'm drawn here, to the lake—like a sea gull... My heart is filled with you. *(She looks around.)*

TREPLYEV: We're alone.

NINA: Is that someone over there?

TREPLYEV: No, no one. *(a kiss)*

NINA: What kind of tree is that?

TREPLYEV: An elm.

NINA: Why does it look so dark?

TREPLYEV: It's evening. Everything looks darker now. Don't go away early. Please don't.

NINA: I must.

TREPLYEV: Then I'll follow you home. I'll stand all night in your garden looking up at your window.

NINA: No, don't. The watchman would see you. And Tresor doesn't know you yet—he'd bark.

TREPLYEV: I love you.

NINA: Ssh!

TREPLYEV: *(hearing footsteps)* Who is it? Is that you, Yakov?

YAKOV: *(from behind the curtain on the stage)* Yes, sir.

TREPLYEV: Go to your places. It's time. Is the moon up?

YAKOV: Yes, sir.

TREPLYEV: Do you have the mentholated spirit? Is the sulphur ready? When the red eyes appear, there must be the smell of sulphur. *(to* NINA*)* You'd better go. Everything's ready. Are you nervous?

NINA: Yes, terribly. I don't mind your mother so much—I'm not afraid of her. But Trigorin will be here. I'm terrified of acting in front of him... A famous writer... Is he young?

TREPLYEV: Yes.

NINA: He writes wonderful stories.

TREPLYEV: *(coldly)* I wouldn't know. I haven't read them.

NINA: You know, your play is hard to perform. There are no people in it.

TREPLYEV: Why should there be? I don't want to show life as it is, or tell people how things should be. I want to show life in dreams.

NINA: But almost nothing happens. It's just talk. And I think there should always be lovers in a play...

(They disappear behind the stage. PAULINA ANDREYEVNA *and* DORN *enter.)*

PAULINA ANDREYEVNA: It's getting damp. Go back and put on your galoshes.

DORN: I'm too hot.

PAULINA ANDREYEVNA: You don't take care of yourself—so stubborn. You're a doctor, you know perfectly well damp air is bad for you. But you want me to suffer. You sat on the terrace the whole of yesterday evening on purpose.

DORN: *(singing)* "Oh, never say your young life's ruined..."

PAULINA ANDREYEVNA: You were so busy talking to Irina Nikolayevna you didn't even notice the cold. Admit you find her attractive.

DORN: I'm fifty-five.

PAULINA ANDREYEVNA: So what? For a man that's not old. You're still handsome. Women like you.

DORN: What do you want me to do?

PAULINA ANDREYEVNA: Men always throw themselves at the feet of an actress. Always.

DORN: *(singing softly)* "Once more, once more, I stand before you, love." Everyone loves actors. We think of them differently than, say, shopkeepers. It's natural. It's idealizing.

PAULINA ANDREYEVNA: Women fall in love with you, always. They throw themselves at you. Is that idealizing too?

DORN: *(shrugging)* Maybe. There's some good in the feelings women have for me. What they love is that I'm a good doctor. Ten or fifteen years ago I was the only good midwife in the county. And I'm a decent person.

PAULINA ANDREYEVNA: *(taking his hand)* And a dear one, my darling!

DORN: Careful. Someone's coming.

(ARKADINA *enters on* SORIN's *arm, with* TRIGORIN, SHAMRAEV, MEDVEDYENKO *and* MASHA.)

SHAMRAEV: At the Poltava Fair in 1873 she was fantastic, just fantastic—a sheer delight. *(to* ARKADINA*)* And do you happen to know where the actor Chadin is—Pavel Semyonovich? His Raspluyev was even better than Sadovsky's. It was, dear lady, I assure you. Where is he now?

ARKADINA: Stop asking me about actors from before the flood. How should I know where he is? *(She sits.)*

SHAMRAEV: *(sighing)* Aah, Pavel Chadin. There's no one like him now. The theatre's not what it was, Irina Nikolayevna. There were mighty oaks in those days—now there are only stumps.

DORN: There may not be many great talents, but the general level of acting is higher.

SHAMRAEV: I can't agree, sir. But, it's a matter of taste—*De gustibus aut bene aut nihil.*

(TREPLYEV *comes from behind the stage.*)

ARKADINA: Dearest son, when will it start?

TREPLYEV: In a moment. Please be patient.

ARKADINA: *(reciting from* Hamlet*)*

　　"Oh, Hamlet, speak no more.

　　Thou turn'st mine eyes into my very soul,

　　And there I see such black and grained spots

　　As will not leave their tinct."

TREPLYEV: *(paraphrasing from* Hamlet*)* Nay, but to live in wickedness, to seek love in the depths of sin... *(From behind the stage, we hear a horn blowing.)* Ladies and gentlemen, your attention please. The play is about to begin. *(pause)* It begins now. *(He thumps with a stick three times. He speaks in a louder voice.)* Oh, ancient shades that by night fly over this lake, lull us to sleep now. Bring us dreams of what will be in two hundred thousand years.

SORIN: In two hundred thousand years what will be is nothing.

TREPLYEV: Then let them show us that nothing.

ARKADINA: Yes, let them. We sleep.

(The curtain rises revealing a view of the lake. Just over the horizon is the moon, its reflection in the water. NINA ZARECHNAYA, dressed in white, sits on a rock.)

NINA: Human, lion, eagle, quail, deer, goose, spider, the silent fish dwelling in the deep, starfish, tiny creatures invisible to the eye— these and every form of life, every form of life, have ended their round of sorrow, and become extinct. For thousands of centuries the earth has borne no living creature. In vain now does the poor moon light her lamp. Cranes no longer wake and cry in the meadow, and, in the linden groves, the hum of beetles is no longer heard. All is cold, cold, cold, empty, empty, empty—desolate, desolate, desolate. *(pause)* The bodies of all beings are dissolved into dust. Eternal Matter has changed them into stone, water and cloud. Their souls are merged into one, into me. I am the Spirit of the World. In me lives the soul of Alexander the Great, of Caesar, Shakespeare, and Napoleon, and of the lowest worm. In me lives the awareness of all humans, and the instincts of all animals. I remember everything, everything, everything. Each being lives in me. *(The will-o-the-wisps appear.)*

ARKADINA: *(in a whisper)* This is something decadent.

TREPLYEV: *(reproachfully imploring her)* Mother.

NINA: I'm alone. Every hundred years I open my lips and speak, but my voice echoes sadly in the void. No one hears—not even you, pale flames. The decay of the marsh spawns you late in the night, and you flicker 'til dawn without thought, will, or feeling. But, afraid of what might be born from you, Satan, Father of Eternal Matter, continuously changes your atoms. You, the stones and water continuously change. Only I, Spirit of the World, remain unchanged.

I am eternal. *(pause)* I am like a prisoner down a deep, empty well. I don't know where I am, or what awaits me. I know only that in the savage struggle with Satan, Prince of Matter—I shall ultimately win. Then, when Spirit and Matter merge harmoniously, become one—the reign of Universal Will shall begin. But that will be only after countless millennia, when the moon, the bright Dog Star and the earth have turned to dust... Until then—horror, horror... *(A pause. Two red spots appear over the lake.)* Satan, my mighty enemy, approaches. I see his terrible blood-red eyes.

ARKADINA: I smell sulphur. Is that part of the play?

TREPLYEV: Yes.

ARKADINA: *(laughing)* Oh, I see. A scenic effect.

TREPLYEV: Mother!

NINA: Without humans, Satan is lonely.

PAULINA ANDREYEVNA: *(to* DORN*)* You've taken your hat off again. Put it on, or you'll catch cold.

ARKADINA: The doctor has taken his hat off to Satan, the Father of Eternal Matter.

TREPLYEV: *(angry, in a loud voice)* The play is over. That's enough. Curtain!

ARKADINA: Why are you angry?

TREPLYEV: That's enough! Curtain! Close the curtain! *(He stamps his foot.)* Curtain! *(The curtain closes.)* Forgive me. I forgot that only a chosen few are permitted to write plays, or act in them. I've infringed on a monopoly. You—I— *(Instead of saying more, he makes a gesture of dismissing the whole thing, goes out.)*

ARKADINA: What's the matter with him?

SORIN: Irina, you can't hurt a young man's pride like that.

ARKADINA: What did I say?

SORIN: You hurt his feelings.

ARKADINA: He said the play was to be for our amusement. I simply took him at his word.

SORIN: Yes, but...

ARKADINA: And now it seems he's written a masterpiece. Good Lord, he's concocted this whole performance, fumigating us with sulphur, not as an entertainment but as a lesson. He wants to teach us how to write, how to act. I'm sick of it. It's boring. His perpetual fury at me would wear out the patience of a saint. He's nothing but a capricious, conceited boy.

SORIN: He only wants to please you.

ARKADINA: Is that so? Then why can't he write an ordinary play, instead of forcing us to listen to depraved rubbish? I don't mind listening to rubbish occasionally, if it's entertaining. But this has pretensions to being a new form of Art, to ushering in a new era in Art. Well, I see nothing new in it. I see nothing in it but the expression of a spiteful mind.

TRIGORIN: Everyone writes what he wants and what he can.

ARKADINA: Well, let him write what he wants and what he can—but don't ask me to listen to it.

DORN: Great Jove is angry.

ARKADINA: I'm not Great Jove. I'm a woman. (*She lights a cigarette.*) And I'm not angry—I'm just sorry to see a young man waste his time. I didn't mean to hurt his feelings.

MEDVEDYENKO: There's no scientific basis for dividing Sprit from Matter. After all, Spirit may just be a different combination of atoms. (*brightly, to* TRIGORIN) I wish someone would write a play about a schoolteacher. We have a very hard life, very hard.

ARKADINA: Of course you do, but let's not talk about plays or atoms on such a beautiful evening. Listen, do you hear? They're singing. (*She pauses to listen.*) It's lovely.

PAULINA ANDREYEVNA: It's from the other side of the lake. (*pause*)

ARKADINA: (*to* TRIGORIN) Sit here by me. Ten or fifteen years ago we had music and singing on the lake every night. In the six big houses along the shore there was always laughter, noise, people firing guns and endlessly making love. And the *jeune premier* of it all, the idol of six houses, was our friend here. (*She nods toward* DORN.) Doctor Yevgeny Sergeyvich. He's charming now, but then he was simply irresistible. My conscience is beginning to bother me. Why did I hurt my poor boy's feelings? I feel badly. (*She calls.*) Kostya! Darling! Konstantine!

MASHA: I'll go look for him.

ARKADINA: Would you, my dear?

MASHA: (*going out*) Yoo-hoo. Konstantine Gavrilovich!.. Yoo-hoo.

NINA: *(appearing from behind the curtain)* I guess we're not going on—so I can come out. Good evening. *(She kisses* ARKADINA *and* PAULINA ANDREYEVNA.*)*

SORIN: Bravo, bravo.

ARKADINA: Bravo, bravo. Enchanting. Such beauty, such a lovely voice. It's a sin to bury yourself here in the country. You have talent. Believe me. You must go on the stage.

NINA: That's the dream of my life. *(sighing)* But it'll never happen.

ARKADINA: Who can tell? Let me introduce Boris Alexyevich Trigorin.

NINA: Oh, I'm so happy... *(embarrassed)* I read everything you write...

ARKADINA: *(making her sit down beside her)* Don't be shy, dear. He has a simple soul for such a famous man, don't you, dear? See how shy he is?

DORN: Can we open the curtain now? It's oppressive this way.

SHAMRAEV: *(loudly)* Yakov, my boy, open the curtain.

(The curtain is opened.)

NINA: *(to* TRIGORIN*)* It's a strange play, isn't it?

TRIGORIN: I didn't understand it. But I enjoyed watching you in it. You were sincere. And the scenery was lovely. *(pause)* I suppose there are many fish in this lake.

NINA: Yes.

TRIGORIN: I love to fish. There's nothing I'd rather do than sit by the water at sunset watching the cork float.

NINA: But surely for one who's experienced the joy of creation, no other pleasure can exist.

ARKADINA: *(laughing)* You mustn't talk to him like that. He doesn't know what to say when people compliment him.

SHAMRAEV: I remember one evening at the Moscow Opera, the great Silva hit low C. By sheer coincidence the bass from our church choir was in the second balcony, and suddenly we heard "Bravo, Silva."—a whole octave lower! Like this. *(in a deep bass, loudly)* Bravo, Silva. The audience was thunderstruck. You could have heard a pin drop. *(pause)*

DORN: An angel of silence has flown over us.

NINA: I must go. Goodbye.

ARKADINA: Where must you go? Why so soon? We won't let you go.

NINA: Papa's expecting me.

ARKADINA: What a man he is, really... *(kissing her)* Well, we can't help that. It's sad to lose you.

NINA: If you only knew how much I want to stay!

ARKADINA: Someone must see you home, darling.

NINA: *(alarmed)* Oh, no, no.

SORIN: *(imploring her)* Don't go.

NINA: I must, Pyotr Nikolayevich.

SORIN: Stay just one more hour. Come now. Do.

NINA: *(hesitating, tears in her eyes)* I can't. *(She shakes hands, hurries out.)*

ARKADINA: That poor little girl! They say the mother left everything to the father, down to the last kopeck. And now he's willed it all to his second wife. Nina will be left with nothing. It's shocking.

DORN: The truth is her father's an impossible scoundrel.

SORIN: *(rubbing his hands together to warm them)* What do you say we go in? It's getting damp. My legs ache.

ARKADINA: Your poor legs—stiff as wood. Here, let me help you. Come along, poor old patriarch. *(She takes his arm.)*

SHAMRAEV: *(offering his arm to his wife)* Madam?

SORIN: There's that dog howling again. *(to SHAMRAEV)* Please tell them to unchain the dog, Ilyia Afanasyevich.

SHAMRAEV: Can't be done, Pyotr Nikolayevich, or we'll have thieves in the barn. I have the millet stored there. *(to MEDVEDYENKO who's walking beside him.)* A whole octave lower. "Bravo Silva!" And he wasn't a concert singer, mind you—just an ordinary choir person.

MEDVEDYENKO: How much does an ordinary choir person earn?

(They all leave except DORN.)

DORN: *(alone)* I don't know. Maybe I'm stupid, maybe I'm crazy—but I liked his play. There's something fresh and direct about it. When she spoke of loneliness, and later when the red eyes appeared—my hands trembled. I think he's coming. I want to say nice things to him.

TREPLYEV: *(coming in)* So, they've all gone.

DORN: I'm here.

TREPLYEV: Mashenka's stalking the woods for me. What an annoying creature.

DORN: Konstantine Gavrilovich, I liked your play, very much. It's strange, and of course I didn't hear the end, but it made an impression on me. You have talent. You must write more. *(TREPLYEV shakes his hand warmly, impulsively embraces him.)* How nervous you are, my friend—tears in your eyes. What was I saying? You chose an abstract topic. That's good. Art should express great ideas. Nothing can be beautiful if it's not serious. You're looking pale.

TREPLYEV: Do you think I should go on?

DORN: Yes, but write only what's true and timeless. I've had a good life, varied—I've made good choices. But if I'd had the luck to experience the ecstasy of creating, I would have soared above the earth, been carried off to the heights —

TREPLYEV: Excuse me, but where is Zarechnaya?

DORN: One more thing. A work of art must have a clear, concise purpose. You must know why you write. If you merely wander down an aesthetic path with no definite aim, you'll lose your way—and your talent will be your downfall.

TREPLYEV: *(impatiently)* Where's Nina?

DORN: She's gone home.

TREPLYEV: *(in despair)* What shall I do? I want to see her... I have to see her... I'm going after her.

(MASHA enters.)

DORN: Calm down, my friend.

TREPLYEV: I'm going after her. I must.

MASHA: Please come inside, Konstantine Gavrilovich. Your mother's worried about you. She wants to see you.

TREPLYEV: Tell her I've gone. And please, all of you, leave me alone— just leave me alone. Stop following me around.

DORN: Calm down, Kostya. Don't get so excited. It's not good for you, my dear.

TREPLYEV: *(with tears in his eyes)* Goodbye, Doctor. Thank you. *(He leaves.)*

DORN: *(sighing)* Ah, youth, youth.

MASHA: When people have nothing else to say, they say "Ah, youth, youth." *(She takes a pinch of snuff.)*

DORN: *(taking* MASHA's *snuff box, throwing it into the bushes)* Disgusting habit. *(pause)* There's music at the house. We should go in.

MASHA: Wait.

DORN: What is it?

MASHA: I want to tell you something. I've wanted to tell you before. *(very disturbed)* I have to tell someone. I don't love my father... But you and I—I feel we have something in common. I don't know why, but I feel close to you. Please help me. Help me, or I'll do something silly—I'll make a mess of my life, I'll ruin it... I can't go on...

DORN: What's the matter? What can I do?

MASHA: I'm suffering. No one knows my suffering. *(She puts her head on his chest, speaks softly.)* I love Konstantine.

DORN: What bundles of nerves you all are. And so much love... Oh, magic lake. *(tenderly)* But what can I do, my dear? What? What?

Curtain

A croquet lawn. Flowerbeds. In back, on the right, is the large porch of the house. On the left is the lake, the reflection of the midday sun sparkling on the water. It's hot. To one side ARKADINA, DORN, *and* MASHA *sit on a garden bench in the shade of an old linden tree.* DORN *has an open book on his lap.*

ARKADINA: *(to* MASHA*)* Come, stand next to me. *(They stand together.)* You're twenty-two, and I'm nearly twice your age. Yevgeny Sergeyvich, which of us looks younger?

DORN: You, of course.

ARKADINA: *(to* MASHA*)* There. You see? And why? Because I work, I feel, I move all the time. You stay put, you don't really live... I make it a rule never to worry about the future. I don't think about aging or dying. What will be, will be.

MASHA: And I, I drag my life along like a dress with an endless train. I feel a thousand years old. And often I wish I were dead. *(She sits.)* Of course it's all nonsense. I have to shake it off—pull myself together.

DORN: *(singing softly)* "Tell her, oh, tell her, my flowers sweet..."

ARKADINA: I'm as particular about myself as an English duchess. I hold myself together, as they say. My clothes and hair are always *comme il faut.* I would never leave the house in a dressing gown, my hair a mess—even to come into the garden. I look young because I'm not sloppy with my body. I don't let myself go—like some people do. *(She walks up and down the croquet lawn, her hands on her hips.)* There. You see? I'm light as a bird—ready to play a fifteen year old any time.

DORN: If you don't mind... *(He takes up the book.)* We stopped with the corn merchant and the rats.

ARKADINA: And the rats. Yes. Go on. *(She sits.)* Or I'll read. Give it to me. It's my turn. *(She takes the book, scans the page looking for the place.)* And the rats. Here we are. "Thus, although it's as dangerous for Society people to entice novelists into their homes as it is for corn merchants to breed rats in their granaries—nonetheless writers are in great demand. When a woman chooses a writer she wishes to capture, she lays siege to him with all manner of flattery and favors." Well, that may be true in France, but certainly not in Russia. We're not that calculating. Here a woman is in love with a writer before she tries to capture him. Look at me and Trigorin for example.

(SORIN enters leaning on a cane, with NINA beside him. MEDVEDYENKO pushes a wheelchair behind them.)

SORIN: *(fondly, as if talking to a child)* Yes? So we're happy today? We're happy at last. *(to his sister)* Such fun. Our father and stepmother have gone to Tver. We're free for three whole days.

NINA: *(sitting by ARKADINA, embracing her)* I'm so happy. Now I'm yours.

SORIN: *(sitting in the wheelchair)* She's looking very pretty today.

ARKADINA: Neatly dressed, and interestingly. What a clever girl. *(She kisses her.)* But we mustn't praise her too much. It may bring bad luck. Where's Boris Alexyevich?

NINA: Down by the lake fishing.

ARKADINA: I'm amazed he's not sick of it yet. *(She prepares to go on reading.)*

NINA: What are you reading?

ARKADINA: Maupassant's *On The Water*, dear. *(She reads a few lines to herself.)* Well, the rest is dull—and completely untrue. *(shutting the book)* I'm anxious, I'm troubled. Tell me, what's the matter with my son? Why is he so moody, so bad-tempered? He spends whole days by the lake. I hardly ever see him.

MASHA: He looks worried. *(to NINA, timidly)* Would you recite from his play?

NINA: *(shrugging)* If you'd like, but it's so uninteresting.

MASHA: *(restraining her excitement)* When he reads aloud, his eyes shine, and he turns pale. He has a wonderful sad voice. He looks like a poet. *(We hear SORIN snoring.)*

DORN: Sweet dreams.

ARKADINA: Petrusha.

SORIN: Eh?

ARKADINA: Are you sleeping?

SORIN: No, I'm not. *(pause)*

ARKADINA: So foolish of you, dear, not to take medicine.

SORIN: I want to take medicine. The doctor won't give me any.

DORN: Cure-alls at sixty!

SORIN: Even at sixty, one wants to live.

DORN: *(annoyed)* Oh, alright, take some valerian.

ARKADINA: I think he should go to a spa.

DORN: Well, let him go to a spa if he wants. Or not, if he doesn't.

ARKADINA: What does that mean?

DORN: Just what I said. It's clear. *(pause)*

MEDVEDYENKO: I think Pyotr Nikolayevich should give up smoking.

SORIN: Nonsense.

DORN: No, it's not nonsense. Alcohol and tobacco rob us of our selves. When you drink and smoke, you're not just Pyotr Nikolayevich anymore—you're Pyotr Nikolayevich plus someone else. You begin to think of yourself not as me but as him, a third person.

SORIN: *(laughing)* It's easy for you to talk. You've had a good life. I've spent twenty-eight years in a law court. I haven't lived, I haven't experienced a thing. You're satisfied, you've had it all. You can be detached, it's easy for you. But I have to enjoy myself now. That's why I drink sherry after dinner, smoke cigars, and so on. That's why.

DORN: The will to live is good. But wanting to go to spas, to take cures at sixty, and complaining you didn't enjoy your youth—well, that, forgive me, is just silly.

MASHA: *(rising)* It must be time for lunch. *(walking slowly, limping)* My leg's asleep. *(She leaves.)*

DORN: She'll have two vodkas before lunch.

SORIN: She has no other pleasure in life.

DORN: Nonsense, your Excellency.

SORIN: You talk like a man who's had everything.

ARKADINA: Oh, what could be more boring than this boring country life? It's hot and humid. No one does anything, everyone philosophizes... It's lovely being with you my friends, of course, and lovely to hear you talk. But—how much more lovely to be alone in my hotel room studying my part.

NINA: *(ecstatically)* Oh, yes—I know just what you mean!

SORIN: Of course it's better in town. You sit in your study, a servant announces your visitors, you have a telephone, there are taxis in the street, and all that.

DORN: *(humming)* "Tell her, oh tell her, my flowers sweet ..."

(SHAMRAEV enters followed by PAULINA ANDREYEVNA.)

SHAMRAEV: Here they are. Good morning to you! *(He kisses ARKADINA's hand, then NINA's.)* Delighted to see you looking so well. *(He speaks to ARKADINA.)* My wife tells me you wish her to drive into town with you today. Is that true?

ARKADINA: Yes, we're going into town.

SHAMRAEV: Hm! Very nice, but how do you propose to go there, dear lady? We cart rye today. The men are busy. What horses can I spare?

ARKADINA: What horses? How should I know what horses?

SORIN: The carriage horses, of course.

SHAMRAEV: *(excited)* The carriage horses? And where am I to find collars? This is extraordinary! Amazing! Dear lady, forgive me—I kneel before your talent, I'd gladly give you ten years of my life—but I can't give you horses!

ARKADINA: But if I have to go into town? Isn't that a bit odd?

SHAMRAEV: Dear lady, you don't realize what it is to run a farm.

ARKADINA: *(flaring up, angry)* It's the same old story. Well, then—I return to Moscow today. Send to the village to hire horses, or I walk to the station.

SHAMRAEV: *(also flaring up)* Then I resign. Find yourself another manager! *(He leaves.)*

ARKADINA: It's the same old story every summer. Every summer I'm insulted! I shall never set foot here again.

(She leaves going toward the lake. A moment later she's seen going toward the house followed by TRIGORIN carrying fishing rods and a pail.)

SORIN: *(angry)* The nerve of that man. I've had enough. I want all the horses brought here right now!

NINA: *(to PAULINA ANDREYEVNA)* To refuse the famous actress Irina Nikolayevna! It's incredible. Her slightest whim matters more than all your silly farming.

PAULINA ANDREYEVNA: *(in despair)* What can I do? Put yourself in my place. What can I do?

SORIN: *(to* NINA*)* We'll go find my sister. We'll plead with her not to leave, won't we? *(looking toward where* SHAMRAEV *went out)* That man is impossible—a tyrant.

NINA: *(preventing him from standing)* Don't get up. Sit. We'll push you. *(She and* MEDVEDYENKO *push the wheelchair.)* Oh, this is terrible.

SORIN: Yes, yes it's terrible, but he won't get away with it. I'll give him a piece of my mind.

(They leave. DORN *and* PAULINA ANDREYEVNA *remain.)*

DORN: People are tiresome. Your husband, of course, should have been fired years ago. But in the end it'll be that old woman, Pyotr Nikolayevich, and his sister who'll apologize. You'll see.

PAULINA ANDREYEVNA: He sent the carriage horses into the fields of course. Every day it's something else. If you only knew how it makes me feel. It makes me ill. Look, I'm trembling. I can't bear his coarseness. *(imploring)* Yevgeny, my darling, my dearest darling, please take me away with you. Our time is passing. We're not young anymore. If only before our days end we could stop hiding, stop lying... *(pause)*

DORN: I'm fifty-five. It's too late for me to change how I live.

PAULINA ANDREYEVNA: *(suddenly hurt, sarcastic)* I see. Of course. There are other women. Of course, you can't take us all home. You can't live with us all. I'm sorry if I bother you. You must be very tired of me.

*(NINA *appears near the house picking flowers.)*

DORN: No. It's alright.

PAULINA ANDREYEVNA: *(relenting)* I'm always jealous—I suffer from jealousy. I know a doctor can't avoid women. I understand that.

DORN: *(to* NINA *as she comes to join them)* What's happening in there?

NINA: Irina Nikolayevna is crying, and Pyotr Nikoleyevich is having an asthma attack.

DORN: *(getting up)* I'll go give them some valerian.

NINA: *(handing him her flowers)* For you.

DORN: *Merci bien.* *(He goes toward the house.)*

PAULINA ANDREYEVNA: *(going with him)* What pretty flowers. *(When they are far enough from* NINA *she hisses in a whisper.)* Give me those flowers. Give them to me! *(He gives them to her. She tears them up, throws them away. They go into the house.)*

NINA: *(alone)* How strange a famous actress should cry over such a small thing. How strange a famous writer—everyone's favorite, mentioned every day in the papers, his picture everywhere, his books translated—should spend whole days fishing, and be happy to catch two fish. I thought the famous were proud and unapproachable, that they had contempt for everyone else—that they used their fame to revenge themselves on the world for having placed rank and wealth ahead of them. But they seem to cry, fish, play cards, laugh and lose their tempers just like everyone else.

(TREPLYEV enters without a hat, carrying a gun and a dead sea gull.)

TREPLYEV: Are you alone?

NINA: Yes. *(TREPLYEV lays the sea gull at her feet.)* What does that mean?

TREPLYEV: I was vile enough to kill this sea gull today. I lay it at your feet.

NINA: What's the matter with you? *(She picks up the sea gull, looks at it.)*

TREPLYEV: *(after a pause)* I'll kill myself the same way soon.

NINA: I hardly recognize you.

TREPLYEV: I hardly recognize you. You've changed toward me. Your eyes are cold. My presence seems to embarrass you.

NINA: You're so irritable lately. And you talk in riddles. Like this. This sea gull—what is it? A symbol? I'm sorry, but I don't understand it… *(She puts the sea gull on the bench.)* I'm afraid I'm too simple to understand you.

TREPLYEV: It all began the night my play failed, didn't it? Women don't forgive failure. I burned the play, down to the last page. If you only knew how unhappy I am. Your being cold to me is terrible, it's unbelievable. It's as if I'd woken up and found the lake dry, or sunk into the earth. You say you're too simple to understand me. But what is there to understand?! My play failed, so now you don't like my work, you think I'm worthless and unimportant just like everyone else does… *(He stamps his foot.)* I understand that. I understand it only too well! It's like a nail pounding into my head. To hell with it. And to hell with my pride which sucks my blood like a leech. *(He sees TRIGORIN walking toward them reading a book.)* Here comes real genius. He walks like Hamlet, and with a book too. *(mockingly)* "Words, words, words…" This sun has but to appear, and you're smiling. The coldness in your eyes melts in its warmth. I won't stand in your way. *(He goes out quickly.)*

TRIGORIN: *(making notes in a notebook)* Takes snuff, drinks vodka, always wears black. Schoolmaster in love with her.

NINA: Good morning, Boris Alexyevich.

TRIGORIN: Good morning. Events have taken a turn. I'm afraid we're leaving today. You and I are not likely to meet again. I'm sorry. I don't often meet young charming girls. I've forgotten what it is to be eighteen or nineteen. I can't picture it. That's why young women in my stories and novels are unconvincing. I'd like to be in your shoes for just an hour, to see through your eyes—know what you think, know what kind of person you are.

NINA: I'd like to be in your shoes.

TRIGORIN: Why?

NINA: To know how it feels to be a famous writer. What is it like to be famous? How does it make you feel?

TRIGORIN: How? I don't know. I've never thought about it. *(reflecting)* One of two things—either you exaggerate my fame, or I don't feel it much.

NINA: How do you feel when you read about yourself in the newspaper?

TRIGORIN: When they praise me, I'm pleased. When they hate me, I feel badly for a day or two.

NINA: It's an amazing world. If you only knew how I envy you. People's fates are so different. Most people live miserable, anonymous lives—each just like the next, all terribly unhappy. While some, like you, are one in a million. It's your fate to live a bright, worthwhile fascinating life... You must be very happy.

TRIGORIN: Me? *(He shrugs.)* Hmm. Fame, happiness, a fascinating life... Forgive me, but those words are about as meaningful to me as sugar plums—which I don't eat. You're very young and very kind.

NINA: You have a beautiful life!

TRIGORIN: What's so beautiful about it? *(He looks at his watch.)* I have to go back to work. Excuse me. I'm going in— *(He stops himself, laughs.)* You stepped on my toes, as they say. You've made me angry and excited. So let's talk. Let's talk about my bright beautiful life... Where shall we begin? *(He reflects a moment.)* You know how it is with an obsession. The moon, for instance—day and night someone thinks only of the moon. Well, I have a moon. Day and night I'm obsessed—I must write, I must write, I must write. I barely finish a novel when I must write another, then a third, then a fourth. I write without stopping, at lightning speed. It's the only way I can write. What's bright and beautiful about that? I talk to you, I'm excited, but at the same time I can't forget the unfinished story waiting on my desk. I see that cloud. It's shaped like a grand piano. Instantly I take note—a cloud sailed by like a grand piano. The smell of heliotrope. I take note—a sickly smell, the widow's color. I'll use it to capture a summer evening. I capture every word we say, and lock it in my literary storeroom. Who knows when it'll be useful? When I've finished work, I race to the theatre, or go fishing—hoping to find rest. But no. A new idea drops into my head like a cannon ball, and I'm back at my desk—writing, writing, writing. I have no rest. I consume my life. To obtain honey for strangers, I rob my best blossoms of their pollen, tear them up, trample them. You think I'm crazy? Well, do people talk to me as if I were sane? What are you writing now? What masterpiece will you give us next? I think all that attention and praise is like speaking kindly to a sick person, to deceive and soothe him before stealing up to carry him off to the madhouse, like Poprischin. And as for my young years, my best years—life was a torture. A beginning writer, especially an unlucky one, feels awkward and unwanted—the world doesn't need him. His nerves are frazzled, he's always on edge. But he can't resist being around people in the arts and literature. They, of course, are not interested in him. They ignore him, while he's too shy to even look at them. He's like an incurable gambler with no money. I'd never met my readers, but I pictured them angry and suspicious. I had a deathly fear of theatre audiences. They terrified me. When a new play of mine was produced, I felt the dark-haired people in the audience were hostile, and the blondes cold and indifferent. It was horrible—torture.

NINA: But when you're inspired and creating, you must have moments of great ecstasy.

TRIGORIN: Yes, I enjoy writing, and reading proofs. But as soon as something's published, I hate it. I see it's not what I meant—and I feel angry, I feel bad. (*He laughs.*) Then other people read it. Yes, they say, charming and clever, but a long way from Tolstoy. Or—it's good, but Turgenev's *Fathers and Sons* is better. Until I die they'll say—charming and clever, nothing more. And on my tombstone they'll write—Here lies Trigorin—a good writer, but not as good as Turgenev.

NINA: Forgive me, but I refuse to understand you. I think you've been spoiled by success.

TRIGORIN: What success? I've never liked myself, and I don't like my work. And the worst of it is I live in a daze. I write about things I don't even understand... I love this lake, the trees, the sky—nature stirs a passionate irresistible urge in me to write about it. But I refuse to be just a landscape artist. I'm a citizen. I love my country and its people. A writer should write about his people, about their suffering, their future, about science, and the rights of Man, and so on and so on. So I write about all that—but too hurriedly. And then I'm attacked from all sides. People are angry at me. I run like a fox pursued by hounds. Science and society move on, while I fall more and more behind. I feel like a peasant trying to run as fast as a train. I think in the end all I can really write about are landscapes. About everything else, I'm false, false to the core.

NINA: You work too hard. You don't have the time, or the wish, to realize the importance of what you write. Of course, you may not be satisfied with yourself, but others consider you a great man. If I were a writer like you, I'd give my life to the people. I'd know they could be happy only by raising themselves to my level. I'd permit them to pull my chariot.

TRIGORIN: A chariot? You see me as Agamemnon?

(They both smile.)

NINA: For the glory of being a writer or an actress, I'd endure anything—the disapproval of my family and friends, poverty, and disappointment. I'd live in a garret, eat dry bread, and agonize over my limitations. But in return I'd demand fame—real, resounding fame. *(She buries her face in her hands.)* Oh, my head is spinning.

VOICE OF ARKADINA: *(from inside the house)* Boris Alexyevich!

TRIGORIN: She's calling me. It's time to pack. But I don't want to leave. *(He looks toward the lake.)* Look, how beautiful the lake!... Glorious!

NINA: Do you see the house with the garden on the other side?

TRIGORIN: Yes.

NINA: That was my mother's house. I was born there. I've spent my life by this lake. I know every little island on it.

TRIGORIN: It's charming. *(He sees the sea gull.)* What's that?

NINA: A sea gull. Konstantine Gavrilovich shot it.

TRIGORIN: A beautiful bird. I don't want to leave. Try to persuade Irina Nikolayevna to stay. *(He makes a note in his notebook.)*

NINA: What are you writing?

TRIGORIN: Just a note. An idea for a short story flashed into my mind. *(He puts away his notebook.)* A young woman, like you, has lived all her life by a lake. She loves the lake as a sea gull loves it. She's happy and free as a sea gull. But by chance a man comes by, sees her, and, having nothing better to do, destroys her like this sea gull. *(pause)*

ARKADINA: *(appearing at a window of the house)* Boris Alexyevich, where are you?

TRIGORIN: Coming. *(As he walks toward the house he looks back at NINA. Then he turns to ARKADINA still at the window.)* What is it?

ARKADINA: We're staying. *(TRIGORIN goes into the house.)*

NINA: *(comes forward, pauses a moment)* It's a dream!

The dining room in Sorin's house. There are doors to the right and left, a sideboard, a medicine cupboard, and, in the middle of the room, a table. A small trunk and cardboard hat-boxes show signs of preparation for leaving. TRIGORIN *eats lunch.* MASHA *stands by the table.*

MASHA: I'll tell you this because you're a writer. You can use it if you want—it's the truth. If he'd died when he shot himself, I wouldn't have lived another moment. But I'm becoming braver. I've made up my mind. I shall uproot love from my heart.

TRIGORIN: How will you do it?

MASHA: I shall marry Medvedyenko.

TRIGORIN: The schoolmaster?

MASHA: Yes.

TRIGORIN: I don't understand. Is that necessary?

MASHA: Loving and hoping, loving and hoping year after year—what's the point? When I'm married, there'll be no time for love. New worries will make me forget. Anyway, it'll be a change, won't it? Shall we have another?

TRIGORIN: Haven't we had enough?

MASHA: No. *(She fills a glass for each of them.)* And don't look at me like that. More women drink than you think. Most of them don't do it openly, as I do—that's all. They drink in secret. Yes, and always vodka or cognac. *(They clink glasses.)* Your health! You're nice—easy to get along with. I'm sorry you're leaving.

(They drink.)

TRIGORIN: I don't feel like leaving.

MASHA: Then ask her to stay.

TRIGORIN: No, she won't do that. Her son behaves tactlessly. First he tries to shoot himself, and now it appears he wants to challenge me to a duel. Why? He sulks, snorts and preaches about new art forms. There's room for all forms of art, old and new. Why push and shove?

MASHA: He's jealous, of course. But that's none of my business. *(A pause.* YAKOV *crosses with a piece of luggage.* NINA *enters, stands by the win-*

dow.) My schoolmaster's not smart—but he's kind and he's poor. He loves me, he needs me. I feel sorry for him, and for his old mother. Well, I wish you luck. Think kindly of me. *(She shakes his hand warmly.)* I'm grateful for your friendship. Send me your books. Don't forget to autograph them. But please don't write 'with best wishes.' Write—to Masha, who doesn't know where she's from, or why she's alive. Goodbye. *(She goes out.)*

NINA: *(holding out her closed hand to* TRIGORIN*)* Odd or even?

TRIGORIN: Even.

NINA: *(sighing)* No—there's only one pea in my hand. I wanted to know my future. Shall I become an actress, or not? I want someone to tell me.

TRIGORIN: Only you can tell you. *(pause)*

NINA: You're leaving. We'll probably never see each other again, so I'd like to give you this little medallion. I had your initials engraved on it, and on the other side the title of your book—*Days and Nights.*

TRIGORIN: What a beautiful thing to do. *(He kisses the medallion.)* A beautiful present.

NINA: Think of me sometimes.

TRIGORIN: I will. I'll think of you on that sunny day a week ago—do you remember—wearing your white summer dress? We talked. There was a white sea gull on the bench.

NINA: *(thoughtfully)* Yes, a sea gull. *(pause)* Someone's coming. Let me see you for just two minutes before you leave. Please.

(She goes out left as ARKADINA *and* SORIN *enter.* SORIN *is in full civil uniform with the star of an order on it.* YAKOV *enters behind them, busy packing.)*

ARKADINA: Stay home, my dear. With your rheumatism, you shouldn't be running about, paying visits. *(to* TRIGORIN*)* Who just went out? Nina?

TRIGORIN: Yes.

ARKADINA: I'm sorry. We intruded. *(She sits.)* I think I've packed everything. I'm exhausted.

TRIGORIN: *(reading the inscription on the medallion)* *Days and Nights,* page 121, lines 11 and 12.

YAKOV: *(clearing the table)* Shall I pack your fishing rods, sir?

TRIGORIN: Yes, I'll want them. But give away the books.

YAKOV: Yes, sir.

TRIGORIN: *(to himself)* Page 121, lines 11 and 12. What are they? *(to ARKADINA)* Do you have my books in the house?

ARKADINA: In my brother's study—the corner bookcase.

TRIGORIN: Page 121. *(He goes out.)*

ARKADINA: Really, Petrusha, you should stay home.

SORIN: You're leaving. It's lonely without you here.

ARKADINA: But what is there to do in town?

SORIN: Nothing, of course. *(He laughs.)* But they are laying the corner-stone of the new Council House, and all that. I've been lying around here like an old pipe. I have to shake myself out sometimes. I've ordered the horses for one—and we're leaving together.

ARKADINA: *(after a pause)* Alright, but don't be too bored when you return. You have to go on living here, you know. Try to avoid catching cold. And take care of Konstantine. Advise him. *(pause)* I'm leaving, and I don't even know why he tried to kill himself. I suppose it was jealousy. The sooner I take Trigorin away, the better.

SORIN: I don't know... There may have been other reasons too. He's a bright young man living in the country with no money, no position and no future. He has nothing to do. He's ashamed of that, and frightened of it. I love him very much, and I think he loves me too, but he feels superfluous in this house—like a dependent, a poor relation. We can understand that, you and I—it's pride...

ARKADINA: That boy is such a worry to me. *(thinking)* He should get himself a job in the civil service or something.

SORIN: *(whistles a bit, then speaks casually)* It wouldn't be so bad if you were to—give him a little money. You see, I think he should have some decent clothes. He's worn that same old jacket for three years, and he doesn't have an overcoat. *(He laughs.)* And it wouldn't be so bad for a young man to have a little fun, maybe go abroad for a while... That wouldn't cost much, would it?

ARKADINA: I don't know. I suppose I could manage a new suit. But going abroad is out of the question... I don't even think I can afford the suit. *(firmly)* I don't have any money. *(SORIN laughs.)* I don't!

SORIN: *(whistling again)* Yes, well, don't be angry with me, my dear. I believe you. You're a generous warm-hearted woman.

ARKADINA: *(crying)* I don't have any money!

SORIN: Of course, if I had some I'd give it to him. But I don't—not a kopeck. *(He laughs.)* Shamraev grabs my pension, and spends it all on the farm raising cattle and bees. That's where my money goes. Then the cows die, the damn bees die, and when I want a carriage, the horses are being used elsewhere…

ARKADINA: Of course I have some money. But I'm an actress. Just the cost of my costumes is enough to ruin me.

SORIN: You're a generous warm-hearted woman, my dear… I respect you—I do… I'm afraid I don't feel so well. *(swaying)* My head is swimming. *(He supports himself on the table.)* I feel funny. Something's coming over me.

ARKADINA: *(alarmed)* Petrusha! *(She tries to support him.)* Petrusha darling!… *(She calls.)* Help me! Help! *(TREPLYEV and MEDVEDYENKO come in. TREPLYEV's head is bandaged.)* He's feeling faint.

SORIN: It's nothing. Really… Nothing… *(He smiles, drinks some water.)* It's going away… It's over.

TREPLYEV: *(to his mother)* Don't worry, Mama. It's not serious. Uncle often has these attacks now. *(to his uncle)* You must go lie down, Uncle.

SORIN: For a little while, yes… But then I'm going to town… I'll lie down, but then I'm going to town… Is that clear? *(He goes out leaning on his stick.)*

MEDVEDYENKO: *(offering SORIN his arm)* Have you heard this riddle, sir? What is it that goes on four legs in the morning, two at noon, three in the evening —

SORIN: *(laughs)* And at night lies on its back. Yes, I've heard that riddle. I can manage alone, thank you.

MEDVEDYENKO: No need to stand on ceremony with me, sir!…

(SORIN and MEDVEDYENKO go out.)

ARKADINA: Oh, he frightened me!

TREPLYEV: It's not good for him to live in the country. He doesn't feel well here. If you suddenly felt generous, Mama, and loaned him a thousand or two, he could spend a whole year in town.

ARKADINA: I don't have any money. I'm an actress, not a banker. *(pause)*

TREPLYEV: Will you change my bandage for me, Mama? You do it so well.

ARKADINA: *(taking iodine and bandages from the cupboard)* The doctor's late today.

TREPLYEV: Yes, he said he'd be here at ten. It's noon.

ARKADINA: Sit down. *(She takes off his bandage.)* You look like you're wearing a turban. Yesterday in the kitchen someone asked your nationality. The wound's almost healed. Just a little scar. *(She kisses his head.)* You won't do anything silly again while I'm gone, will you?

TREPLYEV: No, Mama. It was just a moment of crazy despair. I couldn't control myself. It won't happen again. *(He kisses her hands.)* You have golden hands, Mama. When I was little, and you were still playing in the public theatres, there was a fight once in our courtyard. One of the other tenants, a washerwoman, was beaten almost to death. Don't you remember? She was unconscious when they picked her up. You nursed her, brought her medicine, and washed her children in a tub. Don't you remember?

ARKADINA: No. *(She puts on a fresh bandage.)*

TREPLYEV: Two ballerinas lived in that house too... You invited them for coffee...

ARKADINA: I remember that.

TREPLYEV: They were awfully pious, weren't they? *(pause)* These past few days, Mama, I've loved you as innocently and fully as a child. I have only you now. But why do you allow yourself to fall under the spell of that man?

ARKADINA: Konstantine, you don't understand him. He has a noble character.

TREPLYEV: When he heard I was going to challenge him to a duel, that noble character turned into a coward. He's leaving. An ignominious retreat.

ARKADINA: Nonsense. I asked him to leave.

TREPLYEV: A noble character. You and I almost quarrel about him here, and he's probably making fun of us in the drawing room or in the garden—expanding Nina's mind, convincing her he's a genius.

ARKADINA: You enjoy saying disagreeable things to me. I've told you I respect him, and I'll thank you not to speak badly of him in my presence.

TREPLYEV: Well, I don't respect him. You want me to think he's a genius. Well, I'm sorry, I can't lie about it—his books make me sick.

ARKADINA: That's just envy. People who have only pretensions to talent always insult genius. It must be comforting to you.

TREPLYEV: *(ironically)* Genius. *(angrily)* I have more genius than any of you, if it comes to that. *(He tears off his bandage.)* You and he and your boring old ideas—you control the arts. You won't recognize or tolerate anything but your own superficial notions. You sit on and suppress everything else. Well, I don't accept your high artistic opinions of yourselves. I don't accept his, and I don't accept yours!

ARKADINA: You're decadent.

TREPLYEV: Well then—go back to your precious theatre. Act in your trashy third-rate plays!

ARKADINA: I have never acted in trashy third-rate plays. Why don't you leave me alone? You can't even write a cheap vaudeville sketch. Little bourgeois from Kiev! Little sponger!

TREPLYEV: Miser!

ARKADINA: Beggar! *(He sits down and cries softly.)* Little nobody! *(She walks up and down excitedly.)* Don't cry! Please don't cry. *(She cries herself.)* Darling, do stop. *(She kisses him on his forehead, his cheeks, his head.)* My darling, forgive me. Forgive your wicked mother. I'm such a miserable person. Please forgive me.

TREPLYEV: *(embracing her)* If you only knew. I've lost everything. She doesn't love me now. I can't write... It's hopeless.

ARKADINA: Don't feel like that. It'll work out. He's leaving today. She'll love you again. *(She wipes away his tears.)* There, that's enough. We've made up now.

TREPLYEV: *(kissing her hands)* Yes, Mama.

ARKADINA: *(tenderly)* Make up with him too. You don't really want a duel. It's too silly.

TREPLYEV: Alright, Mama. Only don't make me see him again. That would be too much. I couldn't bear it... *(TRIGORIN comes in.)* Here he is. I'm going. *(He quickly returns the bandages and iodine to the medicine chest.)* The doctor will bandage me when he comes...

TRIGORIN: *(looking through a book)* Page 121, lines 11 and 12. Here it is. *(He reads.)* "If you should ever need my life, come and take it." *(TREPLYEV picks up the bandage from the floor, goes out.)*

ARKADINA: *(looking at her watch)* The horses will be here soon.

TRIGORIN: *(to himself)* If you should ever need my life, come and take it.

ARKADINA: Are you packed?

TRIGORIN: *(impatiently)* Yes, yes. *(musing)* Why does that appeal from a pure heart make me sad? If you should ever need my life, come and take it. *(to* ARKADINA*)* Let's stay another day. *(*ARKADINA *shakes her head, no.)* Let's stay.

ARKADINA: Darling, I know why you want to stay. But try to control yourself. You're a little drunk. Be sober.

TRIGORIN: You be sober. Be wise and understanding, I beg you. You're capable of sacrifice. Be a true friend. *(He presses her hand.)* Be my friend. Free me.

ARKADINA: *(very disturbed)* Are you that infatuated?

TRIGORIN: I'm drawn to her. Maybe she's just what I need.

ARKADINA: The love of a little country girl? How little you know yourself.

TRIGORIN: Sometimes people are talking, but they're asleep. That's how I feel now. I'm talking, but I'm asleep dreaming of her. Such sweet beautiful dreams. Please let me go.

ARKADINA: *(trembling)* No. No... I'm an ordinary woman. You mustn't talk to me like that... Don't torture me, Boris... I'm frightened.

TRIGORIN: If you wanted, you could be extraordinary. There's a kind of love, young love—all poetry and beauty—that sweeps you into a world of dreams. On this earth only that kind of love can bring real happiness. I've never known that kind of love. When I was young there was no time. I was too busy running to publishers, trying to earn a living... But now it's here. It's come. It's calling... Why should I run from it?

ARKADINA: *(angrily)* You're out of your mind!

TRIGORIN: What if I am?

ARKADINA: Why are you all conspiring to torture me today? *(She cries.)*

TRIGORIN: *(clutching at his head)* She doesn't understand! She doesn't want to understand!

ARKADINA: Am I so old and ugly that you can talk to me that way about other women? *(She embraces him, kisses him.)* Oh, you're mad! My beautiful, my wonderful... You're the last chapter of my life. *(She falls on her knees.)* My joy, my pride, my bliss! *(embracing his knees)*

If you leave me for even an hour—I won't survive, I'll go out of my mind. My wonderful magnificent one, my master.

TRIGORIN: Someone might come in. *(He helps her stand.)*

ARKADINA: Let them. I'm not ashamed of my love for you. *(She kisses his hands.)* My precious, reckless boy—you want to be mad, but I won't let you. I won't let you. *(She laughs.)* You're mine... Mine... This forehead is mine, these eyes are mine, this lovely silky hair is mine!... You're all mine! You're so talented and clever, the best of all living writers, the brightest hope of Russia... You write with such sincerity, simplicity, and healthy humor... With one stroke of your pen you go straight to the heart of a character or place. People in your books are so alive. I can't read you without rapture. You think I exaggerate, flatter you? Look in my eyes... Look!... Am I lying? You see! Only I truly appreciate you, only I tell you the truth! Oh my darling, my wonderful one—you'll come with me, won't you? You won't leave me, will you?

TRIGORIN: I have no will of my own... I've never had a will of my own... I'm flabby and weak. I always submit. How could any woman love me? Take me with you. Carry me off. But don't let me out of your sight for a moment...

ARKADINA: *(to herself)* Now he's mine. *(casually, as if nothing had happened.)* Well, of course if you want to stay, do. I'll go by myself. You can come later, in a week. After all, why should you hurry?

TRIGORIN: No, we may as well go together.

ARKADINA: Whatever you say. Together then—together. *(A pause.* TRIGORIN *writes in a notebook.)* What are you writing?

TRIGORIN: A phrase I heard this morning. It'll be useful. The chaste forest. I like that. *(He yawns and stretches a little.)* So we're going. Once more the railway carriage, the stations, the station buffets—more stews and conversations.

(SHAMRAEV enters.)

SHAMRAEV: I have the honor to announce, dear lady, with deep regret, that the horses are ready. It's time to go to the station. The train arrives at five minutes after two. And, please, Irina Nikolayevna, would you inquire after the actor Swzdaltsef? Is he alive? Is he well? We had a drink together once. He was wonderful in *The Stolen Mail*. And in the same theatre company, at Elisavetgrad, was the actor Izmaylov, also remarkable. No need to hurry, dear lady—you have five minutes. Once they played conspirators together in a melodrama. When they were discovered, Izmaylov was supposed to say, "We've been caught in a trap." Instead he said, "We've been clapped in a traught!" *(He roars with laughter.)* Clapped in a traught!

(While he was speaking, YAKOV *has been busy with the luggage. A maid brings* ARKADINA's *hat, coat, and parasol. Everyone helps her with them. The cook peers in through the door on the left, and, after hesitating, comes in.* PAULINA ANDREYEVNA, *then* SORIN *and* MEDVEDYENKO *come in.)*

PAULINA ANDREYEVNA: *(with a little basket)* I brought you some plums for the journey. They're sweet. I thought you might like them on the train.

ARKADINA: Thank you. You're very kind, Paulina Andreyevna.

PAULINA ANDREYEVNA: Goodbye, my dear. If there's been anything... not quite right—please forgive it. *(She weeps.)*

ARKADINA: *(embracing her)* Everything has been fine, just fine. Only please don't cry.

PAULINA ANDREYEVNA: Our time goes by so fast.

ARKADINA: There's nothing we can do about that.

(SORIN crosses the stage wearing his overcoat with cape and hat, carrying a cane.)

SORIN: Irina, if we don't want to be late, we have to leave. I'm going to the carriage. *(He leaves.)*

MEDVEDYENKO: I'll walk to the station. If I walk fast, I'll be there just in time to see you off. *(He goes out.)*

ARKADINA: Goodbye, my dears. God willing, we'll see each other next summer. *(The* MAID, YAKOV *and the* COOK *kiss her hands.)* Don't forget me. *(She gives the* COOK *a ruble.)* Here's a ruble. It's for the three of you.

COOK: Thank you very much, madam. We're very grateful. We wish you a good journey.

YAKOV: God bless you.

SHAMRAEV: Don't forget—drop us a line, dear lady. Goodbye, Boris Alexyevich!

ARKADINA: Where's Konstantine? Tell him I'm going. I want to say goodbye. Well, think of me kindly. *(to* YAKOV*)* I gave Cook a ruble. It's for the three of you.

They all go out on the right. The stage is empty as we hear the sounds of farewell. The MAID *comes back, takes the basket of plums from the table, goes out again.)*

TRIGORIN: *(coming back)* I forgot my stick. It must be on the terrace. *(He goes toward the door on the left where he meets* NINA *coming in.)* It's you. We're just leaving —

NINA: I knew we'd meet again. Boris Alexeyevich, I've made up my mind; the die is cast. I'm going on the stage. I won't be here tomorrow; I'm running away, I'm leaving my father and everything. I'm starting a new life. Like you I'm going to Moscow. We'll meet there.

TRIGORIN: *(Looking around)* Stay at the Hotel Slavyansky Bazaar. Let me know as soon as you get there: Molchanovka Groholsky House. I have to hurry. *(a pause)*

NINA: Just one moment.

TRIGORIN: *(in a low voice)* You're so lovely. I'm glad we'll be together again soon. *(She puts her head on his chest.)* I'll see those wonderful eyes again, that sweet tender smile, that dear face—so angelic and pure… My darling. *(a long kiss)*

Two years pass between the third and fourth acts.

*A sitting room in Sorin's house which Treplyev has turned into a study. It is
dimly lit by a single shaded table lamp. Doors on the right and left lead to other
parts of the house. At the back in the center is a French window leading to the
terrace. Apart from the usual sitting room furniture, there's a writing desk in
the corner on the right, a sofa by the door on the left, a bookcase, and books by
the windows and on chairs. Evening. From outside we hear the wind in the
trees, and the night watchman tapping on his wooden board to frighten away
thieves. The wind howls in the chimney.* MEDVEDYENKO *and* MASHA *come in.*

MASHA: Konstantine Gavrilovich! Konstantine Gavrilovich! *(looking
around)* No, he's not here. The old man wants to know every minute
where is Kostya, where is Kostya. He can't live without him.

MEDVEDYENKO: He's afraid of being alone. *(listening)* What horrible
weather. Two days now.

MASHA: *(turning up the lamp)* There are waves on the lake—huge waves.

MEDVEDYENKO: And it's pitch black in the garden. We should have told
them to pull down the stage. It's standing there bare and ugly—
like a skeleton, curtain flapping in the wind. Last night when I
passed it, I thought I heard someone crying.

MASHA: What next?... *(pause)*

MEDVEDYENKO: Masha, let's go home.

MASHA: *(shaking her head, no)* I'm staying here tonight.

MEDVEDYENKO: *(imploring)* Masha, let's go home, please. Our baby's
hungry.

MASHA: Don't be silly. Matryona feeds him. *(pause)*

MEDVEDYENKO: Poor thing. His third night without his mother.

MASHA: You're becoming a bore. In the old days at least sometimes you
liked to philosophize. Now it's all baby and home, baby and home.
That's all you talk about.

MEDVEDYENKO: Masha, let's go home.

MASHA: Go by yourself.

MEDVEDYENKO: Your father won't give me a horse.

MASHA: He will if you ask him.

MEDVEDYENKO: Alright, I'll ask him. Will you come home tomorrow?

MASHA: *(taking snuff)* Yes, tomorrow. Just stop pestering me. *(*TREPLYEV *and* PAULINA ANDREYEVNA *enter.* TREPLYEV *carries pillows and a blanket,* PAULINA ANDREYEVNA *some sheets. They put them on the sofa.* TREPLYEV *sits at his desk.)* What's that for, Mama?

PAULINA ANDREYEVNA: Pyotr Nikolayevich wants to sleep in Kostya's room.

MASHA: I'll do it. *(She makes the bed.)*

PAULINA ANDREYEVNA: *(sighing)* Old people are such children. *(She goes to the desk. Leaning on her elbow, she looks at a manuscript lying there. A pause.)*

MEDVEDYENKO: Well, I guess I should go. Goodbye, Masha. *(He kisses his wife's hand.)* Goodbye, Mother. *(He tries to kiss his mother-in-law's hand.)*

PAULINA ANDREYEVNA: Oh—just go if you're going.

MEDVEDYENKO: Goodbye, Konstantine Gavrilovich.

*(*TREPLYEV *gives him his hand without speaking to him. Medvedyenko goes out.)*

PAULINA ANDREYEVNA: *(looking at the manuscript)* Who'd have thought one day you'd be a real writer, Kostya? Now, praise God, the magazines pay you for your writing. *(She strokes his hair.)* And you've grown so handsome. Dear, good Kostya, please be nice to my little Masha.

MASHA: *(making the bed)* Leave him alone, Mama.

PAULINA ANDREYEVNA: *(to* TREPLYEV*)* She's a good girl. *(pause)* A woman doesn't need much, Kostya—a kind word, a glance once in a while. That's all she needs. I know. *(*TREPLYEV *gets up from his desk, leaves without speaking.)*

MASHA: Look, now he's angry. You mustn't annoy him like that, Mama.

PAULINA ANDREYEVNA: I feel so for you, Mashenka.

MASHA: It doesn't help.

PAULINA ANDREYEVNA: My heart aches for you. I see it all, you know—I understand it so well.

MASHA: But it's nonsense, Mama. Unrequited love is something you read about in novels—it's not real. I won't sit around brooding anymore, hoping for something that won't happen. Since I'm foolish enough to have fallen in love, I'll just have to fall out of it. My husband's been promised a transfer to another district. When we're there, I'll forget love—I'll tear it out of my heart, roots and all.

(A melancholy waltz is heard from two rooms away.)

PAULINA ANDREYEVNA: Kostya's playing. He must be feeling sad.

(MASHA waltzes a few turns silently.)

MASHA: Mama, I have to live where I can't see him. When they give Semyon his transfer, I'll forget all this in a month. It's too silly.

(The door on the left opens. DORN *and* MEDVEDYENKO *push* SORIN *into the room in his wheelchair.)*

MEDVEDYENKO: Now I have six mouths to feed. And flour's at two kopecks a pound.

DORN: So out it flows, eh?

MEDVEDYENKO: You can joke about it. You have more money than you can use. You're rolling in it.

DORN: Rolling in it? After thirty years of practicing medicine, on call day and night, do you know, my friend, how much I've managed to save? Two thousand rubles. I've just spent them on my trip abroad. I have nothing.

MASHA: *(to her husband)* Haven't you gone yet?

MEDVEDYENKO: *(guiltily)* How can I go? Your father won't let me have a horse.

MASHA: *(bitterly, under her breath)* I wish I had never laid eyes on you.

(SORIN is wheeled to the left side of the room. PAULINA ANDREYEVNA, MASHA, *and* DORN *sit beside him.* MEDVEDYENKO, *looking downcast, goes to the right side of the room.)*

DORN: I see you've made changes—turned the sitting room into a study.

MASHA: Konstantine Gavrilovich likes to work here. He can go into the garden to think any time he likes.

(The watchman is heard tapping on his piece of wood.)

SORIN: Where's my sister?

DORN: She went to the station to meet Trigorin. She'll be back soon.

SORIN: If you sent for my sister, I must be very sick. *(He thinks.)* So, if I'm very sick—why won't you give me medicine?

DORN: Well, have what you want. Valerian? Soda? Quinine?

SORIN: You're preaching again. You're so difficult! *(He gestures with his head toward the sofa.)* Is that for me?

PAULINA ANDREYEVNA: Yes, Pyotr Nikolayevich—for you.

SORIN: Thank you.

DORN: *(half humming)* "The moon drifts through the evening sky…"

SORIN: I'd like to give Kostya an idea for a story—The Man Who Wanted, *L'homme qui a voulu.* When I was young I wanted to be a writer, but I never became one. I wanted to be eloquent in court, but I'm hopeless at public speaking. *(He mimicks himself.)* And well, I mean, uh, well, I think that, uh, maybe, well, that uh. I'd go on like that for hours, in a sweat. I wanted to marry, but I didn't. I wanted to live in town, but here I am ending my life in the country, and so on.

DORN: You wanted to be a civil counselor, and you became one.

SORIN: *(laughing)* I didn't want to be a civil counselor. It just happened.

DORN: To quarrel with life when you've reached sixty-two is ungrateful, don't you think?

SORIN: You're so stubborn. Can't you understand a person wanting to live?

DORN: Yes, but it's irrational. It's the law of nature that every life must end.

SORIN: You talk like a man who's had everything. You've satisfied your appetites. You can afford to be philosophical. Even so, you too will be afraid when you're dying.

DORN: Fear of death is an animal fear. We have to overcome it. Only religious people have real reason to be afraid. They believe in life after death—they're afraid they'll be punished for their sins. That's not your case. You're not religious, and you've committed no sins, except to serve in the Ministry of Justice for twenty-five years.

SORIN: *(laughing)* Twenty eight…

(TREPLYEV enters, sits on a stool beside SORIN. MASHA doesn't take her eyes off him.)

DORN: We're keeping Konstantine Gavrilovich from his work.

TREPLYEV: It doesn't matter. *(pause)*

MEDVEDYENKO: May I ask, Doctor, what city you most preferred abroad?

DORN: Genoa.

TREPLYEV: Why Genoa?

DORN: Because of the marvelous crowds in the streets. In the evening when you leave your hotel, the streets swarm with people. You can drift among them aimlessly, live their lives. With the soul of the crowd pouring into you, you start to feel there might really be a world spirit after all—like the one Nina Zarechnaya performed in your play. By the way, where is Zarechnaya now? How is she?

TREPLYEV: I suppose she's well.

DORN: Someone told me she was leading a strange life. What did they mean by that?

TREPLYEV: It's a long story, Doctor.

DORN: Well, shorten it. *(pause)*

TREPLYEV: She ran away from home, and had an affair with Trigorin. You knew that, didn't you?

DORN: Yes, I knew that.

TREPLYEV: She had a child. The child died. Trigorin tired of her, went back to his old attachments—as might have been expected. He'd never really given them up, just went back and forth in his spineless way. As far as I know, Nina's private life was a disaster.

DORN: And on the stage?

TREPLYEV: Even worse it seems. She made her debut in a small summer theatre near Moscow. Then she toured the provinces. I never lost sight of her. Wherever she went, I followed. She always played major roles, but her acting was crude. It lacked subtlety. She tended to rant. Her gestures were stiff. At moments she showed some talent—she screamed well, and she died well. But that's all. They were only moments.

DORN: But at least she has some talent?

TREPLYEV: I don't know. It's hard to tell. I suppose she must have. I saw her, but she wouldn't see me. Her maid at the hotel turned me away. I understood Nina's feelings. I didn't insist. *(pause)* What more can I tell you? Afterward, when I came home, she wrote to me. Her letters were warm, sensible and interesting. She never complained, but I could tell she was terribly unhappy. Her handwriting revealed how tense and tired she was. She even seemed a little unbalanced, always signing herself 'the sea gull.' In Pushkin's

River Nymph the miller keeps saying he's a crow. In her letters she keeps saying she's a sea gull. Now she's here.

DORN: What do you mean, here?

TREPLYEV: She's staying in town, at the inn. She's been here for five days. I went, and so did Maria Ilyinichna, but she won't see anyone. Semyon Semyonovich says he saw her last night after dinner—in a field, about a mile from here.

MEDVEDYENKO: Yes, I saw her. She was walking toward town. I bowed to her. I asked why she hadn't come to see us. She said she'd come.

TREPLYEV: She won't. *(pause)* Her father and stepmother will have nothing to do with her. They've posted guards around their estate to make sure she doesn't come near the house. *(He goes toward the desk with DORN.)* It's easy to be a philosopher on paper, Doctor, but hard in life.

SORIN: She was a beautiful girl.

DORN: What's that?

SORIN: I said she was a beautiful girl. State Counselor SORIN himself was once in love with her for a little while.

DORN: The old rascal.

(They hear SHAMRAEV's laughter.)

PAULINA ANDREYEVNA: They're back from the station.

TREPLYEV: Yes, I hear Mother.

(ARKADINA and TRIGORIN enter, followed by SHAMRAEV.)

SHAMRAEV: *(as he enters)* We all age and fade like leaves in fall, gracious lady, except you, of course, who are always young and full of life, wearing bright-colored clothing.

ARKADINA: You dreadful man, do you want to bring me bad luck?

TRIGORIN: *(to SORIN)* How are you, Pyotr Nikolayevich? Are you still sick? That's not good. *(pleased to see MASHA)* Ah, Maria Ilyinichna.

MASHA: So you remember me? *(She shakes hands with him.)*

TRIGORIN: Are you married?

MASHA: A long time now.

TRIGORIN: Are you happy? *(He bows to DORN and MEDVEDYENKO who bow in return, then hesitantly he approaches TREPLYEV.)* Irina Nikolayevna tells me you've forgotten the past, you're not angry with me anymore. *(TREPLYEV holds out his hand.)*

ARKADINA: *(to her son)* Look, Boris Alexyevich has brought you the literary review with your new story in it.

TREPLYEV: *(taking the review from Trigorin)* Thank you. That's very kind of you.

TRIGORIN: Your public sends you greetings. In Petersburg and Moscow people are very interested in your work. They ask me about you—what's he like? How does he look? How old is he? Does he have dark hair or is he blonde? Oddly enough, most people think you're old, and no one knows your real name. Why do you write under a pseudonym? You're as mysterious as the Man in the Iron Mask.

TREPLYEV: Will you be staying long?

TRIGORIN: No, I have to go to Moscow tomorrow. I want to finish my novel, and I promised something for an anthology. It's always the same with me. *(ARKADINA and PAULINA ANDREYEVNA have set up a card table. SHAMRAEV lights candles, arranges chairs, and gets a box of lotto from a cupboard.)* The weather's not welcoming—the wind is fierce. If it dies down tomorrow morning, I'll fish in the lake. I want to walk around the garden, look at the place where your play was done—do you remember? I have an idea for a story. I want to remind myself where it takes place.

MASHA: *(to her father)* Papa, will you please let my husband have a horse. He has to go home.

SHAMRAEV: *(mimicking her)* A horse. He has to go home. *(sternly)* Can't you understand? The horses are just back from the station. They can't go out again in this weather.

MASHA: But they aren't the only horses. *(Realizing her father won't answer, she gestures impatiently.)* Oh, you're impossible!

MEDVEDYENKO: I can walk, Masha. Really.

PAULINA ANDREYEVNA: *(sighing)* Walk in this weather... *(She sits at the card table.)* Well, come everyone—let's play.

MEDVEDYENKO: Oh, well. It's only six miles. Goodbye. *(He kisses his wife's hand.)* Goodbye, Mother. *(Reluctantly, his mother-in-law holds out her hand for him to kiss.)* I wouldn't have troubled anyone if it weren't for the baby. *(He bows.)* Goodbye. *(He leaves apologetically.)*

SHAMRAEV: He'll get home. After all, he's not a general. He can walk.

PAULINA ANDREYEVNA: *(tapping on the table)* Please friends, let's not lose any more time. They'll be calling us to supper soon. (SHAMRAEV, MASHA *and* DORN *sit at the card table.*)

ARKADINA: *(to* TRIGORIN*)* During long autumn evenings here we play lotto. This is the lotto set my mother taught us with when we were children. Play with us, why don't you, until supper. *(She and* TRIGORIN *sit at the table.*) It's not a thrilling game, of course. But it's pleasant enough when you're accustomed to it. *(She deals three cards to each player.)*

TREPLYEV: *(turning the pages of the review)* He's read his own story, but he hasn't even cut the pages of mine. *(He puts the review down on the desk, goes toward the door on the left. As he passes his mother, he kisses her on the forehead.)*

ARKADINA: What about you, Kostya?

TREPLYEV: No thanks, Mama. I don't feel like it. I'm going for a walk. *(He goes out.)*

ARKADINA: Everyone must put ten kopecks into the bank. Put mine in for me, Doctor.

DORN: At your command.

MASHA: Is everyone in? I'll start. Twenty-two.

ARKADINA: I have it.

MASHA: Three!…

DORN: Here it is.

MASHA: Did you put down three? Eight? Eighty-one! Ten.

SHAMRAEV: Slow down.

ARKADINA: How they loved me in Kharkov. My head's still spinning from it.

MASHA: Thirty-four.

(A melancholy waltz is played off-stage.)

ARKADINA: The students gave me an ovation, three baskets of flowers, two bouquets—and look, this brooch. *(She takes a brooch off her dress, tosses it on the table.)*

SHAMRAEV: Very impressive.

MASHA: Fifty!

DORN: Fifty, you say?

ARKADINA: I had a fabulous costume. You must admit I do know how to dress.

PAULINA ANDREYEVNA: Konstantine is playing again. The poor boy's unhappy.

SHAMRAEV: They often attack him in the newspapers.

MASHA: Seventy-seven!

ARKADINA: He shouldn't worry about that.

TRIGORIN: He's had no luck. He can't find a style of his own. There's something vague and strange about his writing—almost like delirium. And never a single live character.

MASHA: Eleven!

ARKADINA: (*glancing at* SORIN) Petrusha, are you bored? (*pause*) He's asleep.

DORN: State Counselor Sorin is asleep.

MASHA: Seven! Ninety!

TRIGORIN: Do you think if I lived by a lake that I'd write? I would not. I'd conquer that passion, and do nothing but fish.

MASHA: Twenty-eight!

TRIGORIN: Catching a perch is my idea of heaven.

DORN: Well, I for one believe in Konstantine Gavrilovich. He has something. He thinks in images. His stories are striking, full of color. I find them moving. I'm only sorry he doesn't write with more purpose. He creates powerful emotional impressions, but that's not enough. Irina Nikolayevna, are you pleased your son's a writer?

ARKADINA: Can you imagine, I've never read anything he's written? There's never any time.

MASHA: Twenty-six!

(TREPLYEV *enters. Without speaking, he sits at his desk.*)

SHAMRAEV: Boris Alexyevich, we have something of yours here.

TRIGORIN: What is it?

SHAMRAEV: Konstantine Gavrilovich shot a sea gull once, and you asked me to have it stuffed.

TRIGORIN: I don't remember. (*thinking*) I don't remember.

MASHA: Sixty-six! One!

(TREPLYEV *throws open the window, stands by it listening.*)

TREPLYEV: It's so dark out there. I don't know why I'm so restless.

ARKADINA: Kostya, shut the window. There's a draft.

(TREPLYEV shuts the window.)

MASHA: Eighty-eight.

TRIGORIN: My game, ladies and gentlemen.

ARKADINA: *(gaily)* Bravo! Bravo!

SHAMRAEV: Bravo.

ARKADINA: This is a man who's lucky in everything. *(She gets up.)* And now let's eat. Our famous author hasn't had anything all day. We can continue our game later. *(to her son)* Kostya, why don't you stop writing and come have supper?

TREPLYEV: I don't want supper, Mother. I'm not hungry.

ARKADINA: Whatever you say. *(She wakes SORIN.)* Petrusha, supper's ready. *(She takes SHAMRAEV's arm.)* I want to tell you about the ovation they gave me in Kharkov.

(PAULINA ANDREYEVNA blows out the candles on the table. She and DORN wheel SORIN out of the room. Everyone but TREPLYEV goes out the door on the left. TREPLYEV remains alone sitting at his desk. Preparing to write, he looks over what he's already written.)

TREPLYEV: I've talked and talked about creating new forms, but little by little I'm falling into a pattern myself. *(He reads.)* "The poster proclaimed a pale face framed by dark hair." 'Proclaimed,' 'framed by dark hair'—horrible. Trite. *(He crosses it out.)* I'll start when the hero is woken by the rain. I'll cut the rest. The description of the moonlit night is too long, too precious. Trigorin's style is set—he has it easy. The broken piece of bottle lies on the dam glittering, the mill wheel casts its dark shadow—and there's his moonlit night. But I have to include the shimmering light, the soft twinkling of the stars, and the distant piano sounds dying away in the fragrant air. Horrible. This is agony. *(pause)* More and more I think it's not a question of new forms or old forms. What matters is to allow what you write to come straight from the heart. *(There is a tap at the window near the desk.)* What's that? *(He looks out.)* I can't see anything. *(He opens the French doors, looks into the garden.)* Someone's running down the steps. *(He calls.)* Who's there? *(He goes into the garden. We hear his steps as he runs along the terrace. A moment later he returns with NINA ZARECHNAYA.)* Nina! Nina! *(She leans her head on his breast with restrained sobbing. He is very moved.)* Nina! Nina, it's you. You! I knew it. I had a feeling—all day my heart's been pounding. *(He takes off her hat and cape.)* Oh, my sweet darling. She's come! Don't cry. Let's not cry.

NINA: Someone's here.

TREPLYEV: No one, there's no one.

NINA: Lock the doors, or someone might come in.

TREPLYEV: No one will come in.

NINA: I know Irina Nikolayevna's here. Please lock the doors...

TREPLYEV: *(locking the door on the right, going to the door on the left)* This one doesn't lock. I'll put a chair here. *(He puts a chair against the door.)* Don't be afraid. No one will come in.

NINA: *(studying his face intently)* Let me look at you. *(She glances around her.)* It's warm and cozy here. This was the sitting room. Am I very changed?

TREPLYEV: Yes. You're thinner. Your eyes are larger. It's strange to be actually looking at you. Nina, why wouldn't you let me see you? Why didn't you come here? You've been at the inn nearly a week. I've been there every day. I stood under your window like a beggar.

NINA: I was afraid you'd hate me. I dream every night that you look at me and don't recognize me. If you only knew. Ever since I've been back I've been walking around the lake. I've been near your house many times but I couldn't bring myself to come in. Let's sit. *(They sit.)* Let's sit and talk and talk. It's so nice, so warm and cozy here. Listen to the wind. There's something in Turgenev—"On such a night, happy he who has a roof over his head and a warm corner of his own." I'm a sea gull... No, that's not what I mean. *(She touches her forehead, rubs it.)* I'm sorry. What was I saying? Oh, yes. Turgenev. "And may the Lord help homeless wanderers." It doesn't matter. *(She sobs.)*

TREPLYEV: Nina, you're crying again... Nina!

NINA: It's nothing. It'll do me good. I haven't cried in two years. Last night I went to the garden to see if our stage was still there. When I saw it standing, I cried for the first time in two years. It was like a weight started to lift from me—I started to feel lighter. Look, I'm not crying now. *(She takes his hand.)* So, you've become a writer... You're a writer, and I'm an actress... We've been drawn into the maelstrom, both of us... I was happy as a child once. I'd wake up singing in the morning. I loved you, and dreamed of being famous. And now? Early tomorrow morning I leave for Yelets—third class… With the peasants. In Yelets the businessmen will plague me with their attentions. Life is sordid!

TREPLYEV: Why go to Yelets?

NINA: I have an engagement there for the winter. I have to go.

TREPLYEV: Nina, I cursed and hated you. I tore up your letters and photographs. But I knew I belonged to you. My heart is yours. I can't stop loving you. Since I lost you, and my work has begun to be published, life has been agony. It's as if my youth had been snatched away. I feel I'm ninety. I've called your name, and kissed the ground where you walked. Wherever I look I see your face, your smile—as in the days when I was happy.

NINA: *(a little desperate)* Why does he talk like that, why does he talk like that?

TREPLYEV: I'm lonely. I'm cold. No love warms me. I feel I'm living in a dungeon. Everything I write is dry, harsh, gloomy. Please stay, Nina. And if you won't, then take me with you. *(NINA quickly puts on her hat and cloak.)* Why, Nina? For God's sake!… *(He watches her put on her outdoor clothes. A pause.)*

NINA: I have a carriage at the gate. Don't see me off. I'll be alright. *(She cries.)* Give me some water…

(He gives NINA a glass of water.)

TREPLYEV: Where are you going now?

NINA: Back to town. *(pause)* Is Irina Nikolayevna here?

TREPLYEV: Yes. My uncle had an attack on Thursday. We telegraphed her to come.

NINA: Why do you say you kiss the ground I walk on? You ought to kill me. *(She leans over the desk.)* I'm so tired! If only I could rest—rest! *(She raises her head.)* I'm a sea gull… No. I'm an actress. Yes. *(She hears TRIGORIN and ARKADINA laughing in the dining room. She listens, runs to the door on the left, looks through the keyhole.)* He's here too… *(She returns to TREPLYEV.)* Well… It doesn't matter… He doesn't believe in the theatre. He laughed at my dreams, until finally I stopped believing in them. I lost heart… And there were the anxieties of love and jealousy, and worrying about the baby… I became narrow and trivial. My acting was bad… I didn't know what to do with my hands. I couldn't even stand properly on stage, or control my voice. You can't imagine what it's like to know you're acting badly. I'm a sea gull. No, that's not what I mean... Do you remember once you shot a sea gull? A man came along, saw a sea gull, and destroyed it for fun... That's a subject for a short story... No, that's not what I mean... *(She touches her forehead, rubs it.)* What was I saying? My acting. I'm not like that now. I'm a real actress. I enjoy it, I revel in it. I'm intoxicated on stage, and feel beautiful there. Ever since I've been home I've been walking, walking and thinking, feeling my mind and spirit getting stronger every day... I know now, Kostya, what matters in our work. What matters for a writer or an actor is not fame, glory, or the things I dreamed about, but knowing how to endure—how to bear your cross and have faith. I have faith now, and it's not so painful anymore. When I think about my calling, I'm not afraid of life.

TREPLYEV: *(sadly)* You've found your way. You know where you're going. But I'm still living in dreams and images. I can't make sense of them. I don't know what or who it's all for. I have no faith, no calling.

NINA: *(listening)* Shh—I'm going. Goodbye. When I'm a great actress, come see me perform. Promise? But now... *(She takes his hand.)* It's late. I can hardly stand... I'm feeling faint, I need something to eat.

TREPLYEV: Stay. I'll bring you supper.

NINA: No, thank you... I can't. I really can't. The horses are waiting... Don't see me off. I'll find my way. So she brought him with her? Well, it doesn't matter... When you see Trigorin, don't tell him anything... I love him. I love him passionately, desperately—much more than before... A good subject for a short story... How lovely it was, Kostya. Do you remember? How warm, pure and happy our life was. Our feelings were like sweet delicate flowers... Do you remember? Human, lion, eagle, quail, deer, goose, spider, the silent fish dwelling in the deep, starfish, tiny creatures invisible to the eye—these and every form of life, every form of life, have ended their round of sorrow, and become extinct. For thousands of centuries the earth has borne no living creature. In vain now does the poor moon light her lamp. Cranes no longer wake and cry in the meadow, and, in the linden groves, the hum of beetles is no longer heard. *(She impulsively embraces* TREPLYEV, *runs out the French doors. A pause.)*

TREPLYEV: I hope no one sees her in the garden and tells Mama. Mama wouldn't like it.

(For the next two minutes TREPLYEV *tears up all his manuscripts, throws them under the desk. Then he unlocks the door on the right, goes out.)*

DORN: *(trying to open the door on the left)* That's odd. This door seems to be locked... *(He enters, puts the chair back in place.)* It's an obstacle course.

*(*ARKADINA *and* PAULINA ANDREYEVNA *enter, followed by* YAKOV *with a tray and bottles, then* MASHA, SHAMRAEV, *and* TRIGORIN.)*

ARKADINA: Put the wine and beer for Boris Alexyevich here on the table. We'll drink as we play. Sit down, my friends.

PAULINA ANDREYEVNA: *(to* YAKOV) Bring the tea in too. *(She lights the candles, sits at the card table.)*

SHAMRAEV: *(leading* TRIGORIN *to the cupboard)* Here's what I was telling you about... As you requested. *(He takes out the stuffed sea gull.)*

TRIGORIN: *(looking at the sea gull)* I don't remember! *(thinking)* I don't remember!

(From offstage on the right comes the sound of a shot. Everyone is startled.)

ARKADINA: *(frightened)* What was that?

DORN: Nothing. My medicine case—something probably exploded. Don't worry. *(He goes out the door on the right, returns almost immediately.)* Just as I thought. A bottle of ether blew up. *(He sings softly.)* "Once more I stand before thee, love."

ARKADINA: *(sitting at the table)* Oh, I was so frightened. It reminded me of... *(She covers her face with her hands.)* Everything went black for a moment...

DORN: *(leafing through a review, to* TRIGORIN) Two months ago there was an article in this review—a letter from America. By the way, I want to ask you... *(He puts his arm around* TRIGORIN's *waist, leads him toward the front of the stage.)* Because I'm very interested in this question... *(He lowers his voice.)* Get Irina Nikolayevna away from here. The point is—Konstantine Gavrilovich has just shot himself.

Curtain

1896

UNCLE
VANYA
SCENES FROM COUNTRY LIFE
IN FOUR ACTS

Jean-Claude van Itallie's version in English of Anton Chekhov's *Uncle Vanya* was first produced at LaMama Annex (Ellen Stewart, artistic director) in New York City in September, 1983, directed by Andrei Serban, set designed by Santo Loquasto, constructed by Jun Maeda. The cast included Joseph Chaikin as Vanya, F. Murray Abraham as Astrov, and Dianne Venora as Yelena.

It was produced at the Guthrie Theater, Minneapolis, Minnesota, in April, 1989, directed by Garland Wright.

CAST OF CHARACTERS

SEREBRYAKOV, ALEXANDER VLADIMIROVICH, a retired professor

YELENA ANDREYEVNA, his wife, twenty-seven years old

SOFYA ALEXANDROVNA, SONYA, his daughter by his first wife

VOINITSKAYA, MARIA VASILYEVNA, widow of a privy councillor,
 mother of the professor's first wife

VOINITSKY, IVAN PETROVICH, her son

ASTROV, MIKHAIL LVOVICH, a doctor

TELYEGIN, ILYA ILYICH, an impoverished landowner

MARYINA, an old nanny

WORKER

The play takes place on the Serebryakov estate.

A garden. We see part of the house, and the terrace. Within the avenue of trees, a table is set for tea under an old poplar. There are chairs and benches. A guitar lies on a bench. A little to the side of the table—a swing. It's almost three. The weather is gray. MARYINA, *the old nanny, stolid 'though weighed down by age, sits by a samovar, knitting a sock.* ASTROV *paces.*

MARYINA: *(pouring a glass of tea for* ASTROV*)* Have something to eat, Batushka.

ASTROV: *(taking the glass unwillingly)* I don't want anything.

MARYINA: A little vodka, maybe?

ASTROV: No. I don't drink vodka every day. And the air's too heavy—it's too humid. *(pause)* Nanny, how long have we known each other, you and I?

MARYINA: *(thinking)* How long? Lord, let me think. You first came to our region—when was it? Sonyechka's mother, Vera Petrovna, was still alive. It was in her time. You came to the house those two winters—it was somewhere around eleven years ago. *(thinking)* Maybe even more.

ASTROV: Have I changed much since then?

MARYINA: Very much. You were young and handsome. You're not so handsome now—you've aged. Vodka, you know, after a while...

ASTROV: Yes. In ten years I've become someone else. Why? I drive myself, Nanny. From morning 'til night—no rest. Even when I'm in bed I worry I'll be pulled out from under the blankets to go see yet another sick person. Since you met me, I haven't had a day off. How could I not be aging? My life is stupid, boring, dirty, and exhausting. It wears me out. And I'm surrounded by cranks—they're all crazy. A few years with them, and you're a crank too, without noticing. You can't help it. *(He pulls on his long moustache.)* Look at this enormous moustache. It just grew by itself—a stupid moustache. I'm a crank, Nanny. I'm not yet mindless, thank God—my brain's all there—but my feelings are numb. I don't want anything, don't need anything, I don't love anyone—except you, of course. *(He kisses her on the head.)* My nanny was like you when I was little.

MARYINA: Maybe you'll have something to eat.

ASTROV: No. During Lent I go to the village of Malyitskoye. An epidemic—typhus. They're in their huts, lying on top of each other. Dirt, stink, smoke everywhere—calves wandering among the sick, and piglets. I work all day—I don't sit, I don't swallow a thing... As soon as I'm home, they bring me a railroad switchman. I lay him on the table to operate, and he dies under chloroform. That, of course, is when my feelings choose to wake up. My conscience haunts me, as if I'd killed him. I sit, I close my eyes—like this, and I ask myself—those who'll live in a century or two, those for whom we're clearing the path—will they have a good word for us? No, my dear. They'll have forgotten us.

MARYINA: People, yes—but God won't forget.

ASTROV: Well said. Thank you.

(VOINITSKY *enters. He has just taken a nap. He looks still sleepy. He sits on a bench, rearranges his elegant necktie.*)

VOINITSKY: Yes. *(pause)* Well.

ASTROV: Have you slept enough?

VOINITSKY: Yes. Thank you. *(He yawns.)* Since the professor and his wife came, everything's upside down. I sleep at strange hours, we eat fancy food, we drink wine. It's unhealthy. Before, I never had a moment free—Sonya and I worked all day. Now Sonya works alone, and all I do is sleep, drink and eat. It's not right.

MARYINA: *(shaking her head)* Chaos. The professor gets up at noon, and the samovar's been boiling since morning. Before, we ate at one, like everyone else, but now—not 'til after six. At night the professor reads and writes. Then suddenly at two in the morning he rings. Heavens! What is it? He needs his tea! Everyone wake up, heat the samovar—it's chaos!

ASTROV: Are they staying long?

VOINITSKY: *(whistling)* A century. The professor's decided to settle here.

MARYINA: And now, look. The samovar's on the table since two, and they've gone for a walk.

VOINITSKY: They're coming, they're coming. Don't worry.

(*We hear voices from the back of the garden.* SEREBRYAKOV, YELENA ANDREYEVNA, SONYA *and* TELYEGIN *are returning from a walk.*)

SEREBRYAKOV: Lovely, lovely—a lovely view.

TELYEGIN: Yes, a lovely view, your Excellency.

SONYA: Tomorrow the tree nursery. You'll go, won't you Papa?

VOINITSKY: Ladies and gentlemen, come have some tea.

SEREBRYAKOV: Please, my friends, have tea sent to my study. I have work to do.

SONYA: You'll like the tree nursery, Papa.

(YELENA ANDREYEVNA, SEREBRYAKOV *and* SONYA *go into the house.* TELYEGIN *goes to the table, sits near* MARYINA.)

VOINITSKY: It's hot and humid, but our professor goes for a walk in his overcoat and rubbers, and carries an umbrella and gloves.

ASTROV: He takes good care of himself.

VOINITSKY: She's so beautiful, so beautiful! In my whole life I've never seen a woman as perfect.

TELYEGIN: Maryina Timofeyevna, when I ride through the fields, walk in the garden, or just look at this table—I feel incredibly happy. The weather is beautiful, the birds are singing—peace and harmony. Who could ask for more? (*He takes a glass of tea.*) Thank you. Thank you very much.

VOINITSKY: (*dreaming*) Those eyes—what a magnificent woman.

ASTROV: (*to* VANYA) So tell us something, Ivan Petrovich.

VOINITSKY: (*without enthusiasm*) What should I tell you?

ASTROV: Well, what's new?

VOINITSKY: Nothing. Everything's the same. I'm the same. No—I'm worse. I let myself go. I don't do anything anymore except complain. My old crow of a mother still carries on about the emancipation of women. With one eye she peers into the grave—with the other she searches through books for signs of a new age.

ASTROV: And the professor?

VOINITSKY: In his study writing from morning 'til night. "Our brow is furrowed, our brain we wrack, we write and write, but alas no praise get back." What waste of paper. What he should do is write his autobiography. Now there's a subject. A retired professor—a dried out prune, a talking parrot with rheumatism and migraine, bilious with jealousy and envy. This old parrot lives on his first wife's estate, because he can't afford to live in town. He's always

complaining, but the truth is he's lucky. *(nervously)* He's unbeliev-
ably lucky. He was born the son of a mere deacon, but he managed
to go to seminary, obtain a doctor's degree, a faculty chair, then to
be called Your Excellency, and become son-in-law to a senator.
And what's he done? Nothing. For twenty-five years he's lectured
and written about the arts but he doesn't understand them. He's
rehashed other people's ideas on realism, naturalism and all that
nonsense, teaching what smart people already know, and others
don't care about. For twenty-five years he's done nothing. He's
held a position which rightfully should have been someone else's.
He's retired, but no one's ever heard of him—no one. And yet—
what confidence, what pretension. Look how he walks—he thinks
he's a demigod.

ASTROV: It seems to me you're jealous.

VOINITSKY: Of course I'm jealous. Look at his success with women—it's
more than Don Juan's. My sister, his first wife, was beautiful, gentle, generous, noble, pure as the sky is blue, with more admirers
than he had students—yet she loved him, as only angels can love.
My mother, his former mother-in-law, is in awe of him. He
inspires in her a sort of sacred terror. And his second wife, beautiful and intelligent—you saw her—married him when he was old.
She gives him her youth, beauty, freedom, brilliance—everything.
And for what? Why?

ASTROV: Is she faithful to the professor?

VOINITSKY: Yes, unfortunately.

ASTROV: Why "unfortunately?"

VOINITSKY: Because that sort of fidelity is wrong. It has only face value,
it makes no sense. Is it better to stifle your youth and your feelings
than to deceive an old husband?

TELYEGIN: *(in a teary voice)* Vanya, don't talk like that, please. I don't like
it. Adulterers are faithless people. They can't be trusted. They
could even betray their country.

VOINITSKY: *(annoyed)* Oh, shut up, Waffles.

TELYEGIN: Vanya, please. My wife ran off with her lover the day after we
were married—because I'm so ugly. But I've done my duty. I still
love her. I'm still faithful to her. I give her all my money to raise
the children she had with him. I've lost my chance to be happy, but

I still have my self-respect. And what does she have? Her youth and beauty are gone, her lover is dead. What does she have?

(SONYA *and* YELENA ANDREYEVNA *enter. A moment later* MARIA VASI-LYEVNA *comes in, a book in hand. She sits and reads, is served tea which she drinks without looking up from her book.*)

SONYA: (*to* MARYINA, *speaking rapidly*) Nanny dear, some peasants have come. Go talk to them. I'll pour tea.

(*She pours the tea. Nanny leaves.* YELENA ANDREYEVNA *sits on the swing drinking her tea.*)

ASTROV: (*to* YELENA ANDREYEVNA) I came to see your husband. You sent a note he was sick—rheumatism or something. He seems in perfect health.

YELENA ANDREYEVNA: Last night he felt very bad. He complained of pains in his legs. Today he's better.

ASTROV: I galloped here like a lunatic—thirty miles. Well, it's not the first time. At least I can catch some sleep. I'll sleep here tonight—*quantum satis.*

SONYA: Good. You don't come often enough. Have you eaten?

ASTROV: No.

SONYA: You'll eat with us. We don't sit down 'til after six now. (*She drinks her tea.*) The tea is cold.

TELYEGIN: The temperature of the samovar has dropped considerably.

YELENA ANDREYEVNA: So what, Ivan Ivanyich? We'll drink it cold.

TELYEGIN: Pardon me, but my name is Ilya Ilyich, not Ivan Ivanyich. Ilya Ilyich Telyegin, or Waffles, as some call me, because of my pocked face. I'm godfather to Sonyechka. His Excellency, your husband knows me very well. I live here on your estate now. You may not have noticed me, but I eat with you every day.

SONYA: Ilya Ilyich helps us so much—he's our right arm. (*tenderly*) Pass me your glass, Godfather dear. I'll pour you more tea.

MARIA VASILYEVNA: Oh!

SONYA: What is it, Grandmother?

MARIA VASILYEVNA: I'm losing my memory... I forgot to tell *Alexandre* I received a letter today from Pavel Aleksyevich in Kharkov... He sent his new article...

ASTROV: Interesting?

MARIA VASILYEVNA: Yes, but oddly enough he attacks what he advocated seven years ago. That's terrible!

VOINITSKY: There's nothing terrible about it. Drink your tea, *Maman*.

MARIA VASILYEVNA: But I want to talk.

VOINITSKY: We've been reading articles and talking about them for half a century. Isn't that long enough?

MARIA VASILYEVNA: *Jean*, why is it so disagreeable to you to hear me speak? This last year you've changed so I don't recognize you. Before, you were a man of convictions. You were an enlightened person.

VOINITSKY: An enlightened person who enlightened no one. *(pause)* Enlightened? That's a cruel joke. I'm forty-seven. Til last year I did what you do—clouded my mind with articles from academic journals to avoid seeing. I thought you were supposed to do that. But now—if you only knew. I can't sleep—I'm angry, furious that I've stupidly wasted my life. I could have had everything. Now I'm too old.

SONYA: That's not funny, Uncle Vanya.

MARIA VASILYEVNA: *(to her son)* You blame your old convictions, but it's not their fault. It's yours. You should have done something with your life.

VOINITSKY: Not everyone can be a writing machine, a *perpetuum mobile*, like your Herr Professor.

MARIA VASILYEVNA: What do you mean by that?

SONYA: *(pleading)* Grandmother! Uncle Vanya! Please.

VOINITSKY: I'm silent, I'm silent. I'm sorry. *(pause)*

YELENA ANDREYEVNA: It's not too hot today. It's nice weather.

VOINITSKY: It's nice weather for hanging oneself.

(TELYEGIN *tunes his guitar.* MARYINA *is near the house, busy calling chickens.*)

MARYINA: Here, tsik, tsik, tsik, tsik.

SONYA: Nanny dear, what did the peasants want?

MARYINA: Always the same thing—permission to farm an old field. Here, tsik, tsik, tsik.

SONYA: Which one are you looking for?

MARYINA: The speckled. She's disappeared with her chicks. And there're some crows over there.

(She goes out. TELYEGIN *plays a polka. The others listen to him silently. A* WORKER *enters.)*

WORKER: His honor the doctor? *(to* ASTROV*)* Some people have come. They need you, Mikhail Lvovich.

ASTROV: Where are they from?

WORKER: The factory.

ASTROV: *(vexed)* Wonderful. So. Have to go. *(He looks around for his cap.)* What a—nuisance. Damn it.

SONYA: Really. What a nuisance. But come back after the factory.

ASTROV: It'll be too late. Too bad... *(to the* WORKER*)* Listen, friend— bring me a vodka, will you? *(The* WORKER *leaves.)* Too bad. Can't be helped. *(He finds his cap.)* In an Ostrovsky play, there's someone with a big moustache and no brain. That's me. Well, ladies and gentlemen, I have the honor... *(to* YELENA ANDREYEVNA*)* Please come visit me, with Sonya. It would give me great pleasure. I've only eighty acres, but I have a model garden and the best tree nursery for a thousand miles. I'm next to the state forest. The forester is old and sick. I care for the trees.

YELENA ANDREYEVNA: I've heard you love to work in the woods. That's useful, of course. But doesn't your real vocation suffer? After all, you're a doctor.

ASTROV: God only knows our real vocations.

YELENA ANDREYEVNA: So, they really fascinate you...trees?

ASTROV: Yes, trees are fascinating.

VOINITSKY: *(ironic)* Oh, fascinating.

YELENA ANDREYEVNA: *(to* ASTROV*)* You're young, you're—I don't know— thirty-six, thirty-seven? I can't imagine trees are as fascinating as you say. Woods, always woods—it must be boring after a while.

SONYA: No, it's fascinating. Each year Mikhail Lvovich plants a whole new forest. He's won a bronze medal, and a citation. He won't permit them to cut the old trees, and he's right. He says the forest teaches us to appreciate beauty, it softens the harshness of the climate. In countries where the climate is milder, people don't have to fight so hard to survive—they're softer, more loving, more beautiful, they make more sense, have more hope, move more gracefully, art and science thrive, and men treat women more gently.

VOINITSKY: *(laughing)* Bravo, bravo. Very nice, but not very convincing.

I hope, my friend, *(to* ASTROV*)* you'll still allow me to burn logs in my stove, and to build my barns out of wood.

ASTROV: Burn peat in your stove, and build your barns out of stone. Of course we have to cut trees sometimes, but why whole forests? Russian forests tremble under the axe—millions of trees are lost, animals and birds have to flee, rivers dry out, beautiful landscapes are gone forever. And why? Because man is too lazy to pick up the fuel under his nose. *(to* YELENA ANDREYEVNA*)* Isn't that so, dear lady? Aren't we barbarians to burn beauty in a stove, to kill what we can't recreate? Our wit and vitality are given us to increase what there is. But what do we do? We destroy. There are less forests, waters are polluted, wildlife disappears, the climate is harsher, and each day the world is poorer and uglier. *(to* VOINITSKY*)* You're looking at me sarcastically. You don't believe a word I say. Well, perhaps I'm crazy. But when I pass a peasant's woods that I've saved from the axe, or hear leaves rustling in a tree that I've planted—I feel I've helped. If, in a thousand years people are happier, I'll have helped. When I plant a birch, see its leaves sprout, see it sway in the wind—I'm proud, and I think... *(seeing the* WORKER *bringing him a glass of vodka on a tray)* But— *(He drinks.)* Time to go. And who knows? Perhaps I'm crazy. I have the honor, ladies and gentlemen... *(He goes toward the house.)*

SONYA: *(taking his arm, accompanying him)* When will you come again?

ASTROV: I don't know.

SONYA: Will we have to wait another month?

*(*SONYA *and* ASTROV *go into the house.* MARIA VASILYEVNA *and* TELYEGIN *remain at the table.* YELENA ANDREYEVNA *and* VOINITSKY *go toward the terrace.)*

YELENA ANDREYEVNA: And you, Ivan Petrovich—you've been impossible again. Why irritate your mother with words like *perpetuum mobile?* Then at lunch another argument with Alexander. So petty.

VOINITSKY: I hate him.

YELENA ANDREYEVNA: Why do you hate him? He's the same as other people. He's as good as you are.

VOINITSKY: If you could only see your face, your gestures—so languid. You look tired of living, tired of being alive.

YELENA ANDREYEVNA: Yes—well I'm bored, I have nothing to do.

Everyone speaks badly of Alexander, and they pity me—poor woman, she has an old husband. You all say the same thing. I know what you really want. Astrov is right. You destroy. Soon there'll be no forests. You'll have destroyed everything good—no more fidelity, purity, or devotion. Why can't you look at a woman who's not yours without desire? He's absolutely right, that doctor. There's a destructive demon in men. You have no pity for forests, birds, women, or each other.

VOINITSKY: "And the meek shall inherit the earth." I don't like that kind of thinking. (*pause*)

YELENA ANDREYEVNA: The doctor has an interesting face—a tired nervous face. I think Sonya's attracted to him. It doesn't surprise me. This is his third visit since we've been here, but I can't really speak to him. I want to be pleasant but I'm shy. He must think I'm mean. You and I are friends, Ivan Petrovich, because we're both of us weak and boring. Yes, boring. And don't look at me like that—I don't like it.

VOINITSKY: How can I look at you differently? I love you. You're my happiness, my life, my youth. I don't expect you to love me back. I'm not asking for that. I just need to look at you, to hear the sound of your voice.

YELENA ANDREYEVNA: Shhh! Someone will hear you.

(*They go toward the house.*)

VOINITSKY: (*following her*) I need to tell you I love you. That's all. Don't send me away. Just that will make me happy.

YELENA ANDREYEVNA: This is unbearable.

(*They go into the house.* TELYEGIN *strums a polka on the guitar.* MARIA VASILYEVNA *scribbles in the margin of her pamphlet.*)

Curtain

The dining room in Serebryakov's house. It's night. We hear the night watch-
man tapping in the garden. SEREBRYAKOV *dozes in a chair near the open win-*
dow. YELENA ANDREYEVNA *sits next to him, also dozing.*

SEREBRYAKOV: *(waking up)* Who is it? Sonya?

YELENA ANDREYEVNA: It's me.

SEREBRYAKOV: Ah, Lenochka. It's you. I have a terrible pain.

YELENA ANDREYEVNA: Your blanket fell. *(She wraps up his legs.)* I'll close
the window, Alexander.

SEREBRYAKOV: No, don't—I'm suffocating. I dozed off. I dreamed my left
leg wasn't mine, and then I woke with a terrible pain. It's not gout.
Maybe it's rheumatism. What time is it?

YELENA ANDREYEVNA: Twenty after twelve. *(pause)*

SEREBRYAKOV: We must have Batyushkov in the library. Bring him to me
in the morning.

YELENA ANDREYEVNA: What?

SEREBRYAKOV: In the morning—bring me the books of Batyushkov. I saw
them in the library. Why am I having such trouble breathing?

YELENA ANDREYEVNA: It's fatigue. You haven't slept for two nights.

SEREBRYAKOV: They say Turgenev's gout turned into angina. I think that's
what's happening to me. Damn old age. I hate it. I'm old, I disgust
myself and everyone else. You all find me disgusting, don't you?

YELENA ANDREYEVNA: You talk about your age as if it were our fault.

SEREBRYAKOV: I disgust you, don't I? *(YELENA ANDREYEVNA moves away,*
sits farther from him.) Obviously. It's understandable. I'm not stupid. You're young, healthy, beautiful—you have your life to live.
And I'm half dead. I know. I understand. Too bad I'm still alive,
right? Well, don't worry—you won't have long to wait. Just be
patient.

YELENA ANDREYEVNA: For God's sake, stop it. I can't bear any more. Stop it.

SEREBRYAKOV: It's my fault your youth is wasted, isn't it? You're bored,
but I'm having a wonderful time, I'm happy. That's it, isn't it?

YELENA ANDREYEVNA: Stop it. You exhaust me.

SEREBRYAKOV: I exhaust everyone, obviously.

YELENA ANDREYEVNA: *(through tears)* I can't bear it. What do you want from me?

SEREBRYAKOV: Nothing.

YELENA ANDREYEVNA: Then be quiet. Please.

SEREBRYAKOV: Isn't it strange? When Ivan Petrovich opens his mouth, or that old fool his mother—everyone listens. But when I say something, it's disaster. The sound of my voice repels you all. Well, so I'm disagreeable, an egotist, a tyrant. At my age isn't that allowed? Don't I have the right to some attention, some respect? Don't I deserve it?

YELENA ANDREYEVNA: No one's denying you anything. *(A window bangs in the wind.)* It's the wind. I'll close the window. *(She closes it.)* It's going to rain. No one's denying you anything. *(A pause. Outside, the night watchman taps and sings.)*

SEREBRYAKOV: To give your life to scholarship, to pen, to podium, to share it with respectable colleagues—and then, suddenly, for no reason, to be buried alive here with common people talking drivel... I want success, fame, excitement. I'm in exile—yearning for the past, reading of other people's success, afraid of dying. I can't bear it—I don't have the strength. And now, even my age is held against me.

YELENA ANDREYEVNA: Be patient—another five, six years, and I'll be old too.

(SONYA comes in.)

SONYA: Papa, you sent for Dr. Astrov. Now he's here, and you refuse to see him. That's not kind. Why disturb him if you don't need him?

SEREBRYAKOV: I don't want your Astrov. He knows medicine as well as I know astronomy.

SONYA: We can't call in a whole medical college for your gout.

SEREBRYAKOV: I won't talk to that fool.

SONYA: Whatever you say. *(She sits.)* I don't care.

SEREBRYAKOV: What time is it?

YELENA ANDREYEVNA: Almost one.

SEREBRYAKOV: The weather's too humid. Sonya, give me the drops on the table.

SONYA: Here. (*She gives him the drops.*)

SEREBRYAKOV: (*irritated*) Not those! Can't you do anything?

SONYA: No scenes please. Some people may like them. I don't. I have too much work to do. Tomorrow I'm up early. It's haycutting time.

(VOINITSKY *enters in a bathrobe, a candle in his hand.*)

VOINITSKY: There's a storm coming. (*Lightning is visible.*) Did you see that? *Helene*, Sonya—go to bed. I'll stay with him.

SEREBRYAKOV: (*frightened*) No, don't leave me alone with him! He'll talk me to death!

VOINITSKY: They haven't slept for two nights. They need to rest.

SEREBRYAKOV: Well, then let them go rest. But you leave too, please. No, don't protest. Please! In the name of our past friendship. Please. We'll talk some other time.

VOINITSKY: (*with an ironic smile*) Our past friendship? Past?

SONYA: Enough, Uncle Vanya.

SEREBRYAKOV: (*to his wife*) My dear, don't leave me alone with him. He'll talk me to death.

VOINITSKY: This is ridiculous.

(MARYINA *enters with a candle.*)

SONYA: You should be in bed, little nanny. It's late.

MARYINA: How can I go to bed? The samovar's still on the table.

SEREBRYAKOV: Of course. No one's in bed—everyone's exhausted. Except me, of course—I'm having a wonderful time.

MARYINA: (*approaching* SEREBRYAKOV, *affectionately*) Now, *Batyushka* — now, now. Your legs hurt? Mine too. Your legs have hurt for years, haven't they? Mine too. (*She arranges the professor's blanket.*) Sonya's poor mother, Vera Petrovna, spent whole nights worrying about you—no sleep. She loved you so much... (*pause*) Old people are like children. We want everyone to feel sorry for us. No one does. (*She drops a kiss on* SEREBRYAKOV's *shoulder.*) Come *Batyushka*, come to bed. I'll make you some linden blossom tea, warm your feet. I'll pray for you.

SEREBRYAKOV: (*moved*) Yes, Nanny.

MARYINA: Poor legs. They hurt, they hurt. (*She takes him out,* SONYA *supporting his other side.*) Sonya's poor mother, Vera Petrovna, was always crying, always worried about you. Sonyuchka, you were so little, so silly. Come, *Batyushka*, come now.

(SEREBRYAKOV, SONYA *and* MARYINA *go out.*)

YELENA ANDREYEVNA: He's exhausted me. I can hardly stand.

VOINITSKY: He's exhausted you, and I've exhausted myself. I haven't slept for three nights.

YELENA ANDREYEVNA: Things aren't going very well in this house. Your mother hates everything but her latest article and the professor. The professor's irritable, doesn't trust me, is afraid of you. Sonya's angry at her father, and hasn't spoken to me for two weeks. You hate my husband, and have contempt for your mother. My nerves are raw. I've nearly cried twenty times since this morning. No, things aren't going very well in this house.

VOINITSKY: Who cares about all that?

YELENA ANDREYEVNA: Ivan Petrovich, you're smart, you're well-educated. You know that the world falling apart is not due to crime or gunfire. It's due to hatred and pettiness—little intrigues. Surely you know that. Instead of always complaining, why don't you help make peace among us?

VOINITSKY: Why don't you help me make peace with myself? My dearest. *(He presses her hand to his lips.)*

YELENA ANDREYEVNA: Leave me alone. *(She pulls her hand away.)* Go away.

VOINITSKY: The storm is almost over. All nature will breathe again, be refreshed—except me. I won't be refreshed. My life is wasted. That thought haunts me like an evil spirit. I wasted the past stupidly, and the present is frighteningly foolish. So there's my life. And my love for you—what good is it? Wasted feelings—what to do with them? Bury them? I'm lost, I'm dying.

YELENA ANDREYEVNA: When you talk about your love for me, I become numb. I have nothing to say. I'm sorry, I have nothing to say. *(She starts to leave.)* Good night.

VOINITSKY: *(blocking her way)* If you only knew how it hurts me that in this house, so close to me, another life wastes away—yours. Why wait? Why be bound by convention? You must know... You do know...

YELENA ANDREYEVNA: *(looking at him attentively)* Ivan Petrovich, you're drunk.

VOINITSKY: Possible. That's possible.

YELENA ANDREYEVNA: Where's the doctor?

VOINITSKY: In there, sleeping in my room. Possible. That's possible. Everything's possible.

YELENA ANDREYEVNA: You're drunk. Why get drunk?

VOINITSKY: To pretend to live. Don't ask me to stop, *Helene.*

YELENA ANDREYEVNA: You didn't drink before, and you didn't talk so much before. Go to bed. You bore me.

VOINITSKY: *(leaning over her hand.)* My dearest one, my wonderful one.

YELENA ANDREYEVNA: *(irritated)* Leave me alone. You disgust me. *(She goes out.)*

VOINITSKY: *(alone)* Gone. *(pause)* Ten years ago when I first saw her at my poor sister's, she was seventeen. I was thirty-seven. Why didn't I fall in love with her then? Why didn't I propose then? It would have been easy. She'd be my wife now. The storm would have woken us, she'd be frightened of the thunder. I'd hold her. I'd say, don't be afraid, I'm here. Oh, what a delicious thought—it makes me laugh. My God, I'm going crazy. Why do I have to be old? Why can't she hear me? Her preaching, her mealy-mouthed morality, those absurd ideas about the world falling apart—I hate that kind of thinking. *(pause)* I was blind. That ridiculous professor riddled with gout was my idol. I worked like a horse for him. Sonya and I worked like peasants on this estate, selling oil, peas, and cottage cheese. We hardly ate, we watched every kopeck. We sent him thousands of rubles. I was proud of him, I lived through him. Every word he spoke and wrote seemed like genius. And now, his life's work—what does it amount to? Nothing—a soap bubble. Not a single worthwhile page. I was blind... stupid, blind... I've been cheated.

(ASTROV enters wearing a jacket but no vest or tie. He's a little drunk. TELYEGIN follows him, carrying a guitar.)

ASTROV: Go ahead, play.

TELYEGIN: But people are sleeping.

ASTROV: Play! *(TELYEGIN plays softly.)* You're alone here? No women? *(Hands on hips, he sings softly.)* "Dance my cottage, dance my bed—dance, dance, dance. In the thunder, rain and wind where will your master lay his head?" The storm woke me. What a rain. What time is it?

VOINITSKY: Who the devil knows?

ASTROV: I thought I heard Yelena Andreyevna's voice.

VOINITSKY: She just went out.

ASTROV: What a magnificent woman. *(He examines the vials on the table.)* Medicines. What a collection—Kharkov, Moscow, Tula ... He's pestered every town in the country with his gout. Is he really sick, or is he pretending?

VOINITSKY: He's sick. *(pause)*

ASTROV: Why are you sad? Feeling sorry for the professor?

VOINITSKY: Leave me alone.

ASTROV: Or in love with the Madame Professor?

VOINITSKY: She's my friend.

ASTROV: Already?

VOINITSKY: What do you mean, "already?"

ASTROV: A woman only becomes a man's friend after first being his acquaintance, and then his mistress.

VOINITSKY: What a vulgar remark!

ASTROV: Yes, I'm becoming vulgar. I'm drunk. I get drunk once a month. It makes me arrogant and fearless. I conceive intricate surgery, and perform it perfectly. I'm not crazy anymore. I make sweeping plans for the future, render enormous services to humanity—enormous. I've even invented my own philosophical system, in which you, my friends, are nothing but insects and germs. *(to* TELYEGIN*)* Play, Waffles!

TELYEGIN: I'd like to please you, my angel—but there are people asleep.

ASTROV: Play. *(*TELYEGIN *plays softly.)* We'll drink. I think there's some cognac left. At dawn, we go to my house. Howzzat? My assistant never says, "How is that?"—he says "Howzzat?" He's such a little bastard. Well—howzzat? *(seeing* SONYA *enter)* Oops. Excuse me, I'm not wearing a tie. *(He runs out.* TELYEGIN *follows him.)*

SONYA: Uncle Vanya, you're drinking again. With the doctor. A fine pair you are. He's used to it—but you, at your age...

VOINITSKY: What does age have to do with it? If you don't have a life, pretending is better than nothing.

SONYA: The hay isn't in, it rains every day, the crops are rotting—and you talk about pretending. You've abandoned the estate. The estate's on my shoulders, and I'm tired. *(surprised)* Uncle Vanya, you're crying.

VOINITSKY: Crying? No. It's nothing. Just something silly. You looked so like your mother just then. Your poor mother. Little one. *(He avidly kisses her hands and face.)* My sister, my darling sister. Where is she now? If she only knew! If she only knew!

SONYA: If she only knew what, Uncle?

VOINITSKY: It's terrible. It's not right. It doesn't matter... I have to go. Later... It doesn't matter... *(He goes out.)*

SONYA: *(knocking at a door)* Mikhail Lvovich? If you're not sleeping, would you come out here a moment?

ASTROV: *(from behind the door)* Coming. *(He appears a moment later. He's put on a vest and tie.)* What can I do for you?

SONYA: It's your business if you drink, if you don't find it disgusting. But please don't encourage Uncle. It's bad for him.

ASTROV: Alright. We won't drink. *(pause)* I'm leaving. I'm nearly gone. It'll be dawn by the time the horses are ready.

SONYA: It's raining. Why don't you wait 'til later?

ASTROV: The storm's nearly over. I'll go home. Please don't call me again for your father. I say gout, he says rheumatism. I say lie down, he sits up. This time he won't even see me.

SONYA: He's spoiled. *(She searches in the cupboard.)* Do you want something to eat?

ASTROV: Yes, why not?

SONYA: I like to nibble at night. There's always something left. They say women have always liked my father. They spoiled him. Look, here's some cheese.

(They eat standing next to the buffet.)

ASTROV: I didn't eat today, I just drank. Your father's difficult. *(He takes a bottle from the cupboard.)* May I? *(He drinks a small glassful.)* We're alone, so I'll tell you—I couldn't live a month in your house. The atmosphere is stifling—your father with his gout, his books, your uncle Vanya with his regrets, your grandmother, and of course your stepmother.

SONYA: What about my stepmother?

ASTROV: Everything in a human being should be beautiful—face, habits, soul, and thoughts. There's no doubt she's beautiful, but what does she do all day? Eat, sleep, go for walks, charm us, and that's all. She has no responsibilities—others work for her. Isn't that so? Being aimless is not good. *(pause)* But maybe I'm too harsh. I'm a malcontent, like your uncle—we're a pair of complainers.

SONYA: Are you really a malcontent?

ASTROV: No, I like living well enough. But I hate our everyday Russian mediocrity. Our provincial habits are contemptible. As for my private life—there is none. When you're in the forest at night, if you see a light in the distance you forget fatigue, the darkness, the branches hitting you in the face. I work hard, harder than anyone in the district—you know that. One thing after another hits me in the face, until sometimes I feel I can't go on. But there's no light in the distance. I don't expect one. I don't even like people. I've loved no one for a long time.

SONYA: No one?

ASTROV: No one. Oh, I feel tenderness for your Nanny. She wakens memories in me. But the peasants are crude and dirty. And our friends the intellectuals wear me out with their petty thoughts and feelings. They don't see further than the tip of their noses. They're stupid. The smart ones drain their energy analyzing themselves and other people. And all of them are hysterical. They never stop whining, hating and slandering each other. They size you up—"a lunatic" or, "a big talker." And if they don't know what label to pin on you, they think—"strange, what a strange man." You love the forest—"strange." You don't eat meat—"strange." There's nothing spontaneous in them, nothing left free or pure in their feelings for nature or for people. Nothing. Nothing left. *(He wants to drink more.)*

SONYA: *(holding back his hand)* No. Please. Don't drink any more.

ASTROV: Why not?

SONYA: It's not you. You're so distinguished, you have a soft voice. You're the most beautiful person I know. Why do you want to be like people who drink and play cards? Please, don't. You say instead of creating more, people are always destroying. So why do you destroy yourself? Please, don't. You mustn't. Please.

ASTROV: *(holding out his hand to her)* I won't drink any more.

SONYA: Give me your word.

ASTROV: Word of honor.

SONYA: *(shaking his hand, sincere)* Thank you.

ASTROV: It's over. I'm not drunk anymore. I'm sober, and I'll stay sober 'til the end of my days. *(He looks at his watch.)* Anyway, as I was saying, my time is up. It's too late for me now. I've worn myself out—I'm vulgar, my feelings are numb. I can't be close to anyone, I can't love anymore. Only beauty still moves me. Beauty's the only thing to which I'm not indifferent. If Yelena Andreyevna wished, she could make me lose my head in a day. But even then it wouldn't be love—it wouldn't be a real attachment. *(He shudders, covers his eyes with his hand.)*

SONYA: What's the matter?

ASTROV: During Lent a patient died under chloroform.

SONYA: You have to let that go. *(pause)* Tell me, Mikhail Lvovich, if I had a friend, or a younger sister, and you discovered that she—well, that she... she loved you. What would you do?

ASTROV: *(shrugging)* I don't know. Nothing, probably. I'd make her understand I can't love her, that I have my own worries. Well, if I want to get home it's time to start. Goodbye, dear friend— or we'll talk all night. *(He takes her hand.)* I'll slip out if you don't mind. I'm afraid your uncle might distract me from leaving. *(He goes out.)*

SONYA: *(alone)* He didn't tell me anything. I still don't know his heart. So why am I so happy? *(She laughs with pleasure.)* I said to him you're so distinguished, you have a soft voice. I shouldn't have said that. But his voice does vibrate, caresses. I can still feel it in the air. But when I talked about my sister, he didn't understand. *(She wrings her hands.)* How horrible to be ugly. Horrible. I'm not pretty. I know it. On Sunday after church, I heard a woman talking about me: "She's so good and generous, too bad she's not pretty." Not pretty.

(YELENA ANDREYEVNA comes in.)

YELENA ANDREYEVNA: *(opening the window)* The storm has passed. Mmmm, the air is fresh. *(pause)* Where's the doctor?

SONYA: Gone. *(pause)*

YELENA ANDREYEVNA: *Sophie.*

SONYA: Yes?

YELENA ANDREYEVNA: How long are you going to sulk? I have nothing against you, you have nothing against me. Why should we be enemies? Let's stop it.

SONYA: Oh, I want to. (*She embraces her.*) No more anger.

YELENA ANDREYEVNA: Good. I'm glad. (*Both are moved.*)

SONYA: Has Papa gone to bed?

YELENA ANDREYEVNA: No, he's up—in the sitting room. We haven't spoken for weeks, God knows why. (*seeing the open cupboard*) What's that?

SONYA: Mikhail Lvovich had something to eat.

YELENA ANDREYEVNA: And here's wine. Shall we have some? We'll drink to each other, to our friendship.

SONYA: Yes, I'd like to.

YELENA ANDREYEVNA: From the same glass. (*She pours some wine.*) That's better. So, here's to friendship.

SONYA: Yes. (*They drink and kiss.*) I've been wanting to make peace with you for a long time, but I was embarrassed. (*She cries.*)

YELENA ANDREYEVNA: Why are you crying?

SONYA: It's nothing.

YELENA ANDREYEVNA: Come now, that's enough. (*She cries.*) You silly, you've made me cry too. (*pause*) You were angry because you thought I married your father for his money. I swear I didn't. It was for love. I was seduced by his knowledge and his fame. It wasn't really love, but it felt like it at the time—I thought it was. It's not my fault. But since the day we married, you've stared at me, followed me with those eyes—so penetrating, so suspicious.

SONYA: Well, it's over now. Peace. Peace. Let's forget it.

YELENA ANDREYEVNA: Never look at people that way. You have to trust people, or life becomes impossible. (*pause*)

SONYA: Tell me honestly, friend to friend—are you happy?

YELENA ANDREYEVNA: No.

SONYA: I knew it. One more question. Tell the truth—would you have preferred a younger husband?

YELENA ANDREYEVNA: You're such a baby. Of course I would. (*She laughs.*) Well, go ahead, ask another question.

SONYA: Do you like the doctor?

YELENA ANDREYEVNA: Yes, very much.

SONYA: *(laughing)* I still have a silly look on my face, don't I? Even though he's gone, I still hear his voice, and the sound of his footsteps. And when I look at the dark window, I think I see his face. I want to tell you—no, I can't say it, I'm embarrassed. Come to my room and talk. You think I'm silly, don't you? You do. Oh, talk to me about him.

YELENA ANDREYEVNA: What do you want me to say?

SONYA: He's so clever, so intelligent. He knows everything. He can do anything—heal the sick, plant forests.

YELENA ANDREYEVNA: It's not about planting forests or healing the sick. Darling, he's creative. Do you understand? Do you know what that means? He's daring, a free spirit—he has vision. When he plants a tree, he wonders what will become of it in a hundred years. He dreams of a day when humanity will be happy. Men like that are rare. We have to love them. If he drinks, if he's is a little vulgar sometimes so what? No creative man can live in Russia and be perfect. Think of the life he leads—muddy roads, the cold, the snowstorms, the distances, the miserable savage people he has to treat. And the diseases. Working under those conditions day after day—how could he possibly stay sober, proper? He's nearly forty. *(She kisses* SONYA.*)* With all my heart I wish you happiness. You deserve it. *(She gets up.)* As for me, I'm only a minor character, a boring one. I've always been a minor character—with my music, in my husband's house, in my love affairs—always. To tell the truth, Sonya, now that I think about it, I'm unhappy—very unhappy. *(Moved, she paces.)* Why are you laughing?

SONYA: *(laughing, covering her face)* I'm happy, so happy.

YELENA ANDREYEVNA: You know, I'd like to play the piano now. I would.

SONYA: Oh, do play. Play. *(She embraces her.)* I can't sleep tonight. Play something.

YELENA ANDREYEVNA: Wait. Your father's not asleep. Music irritates him when he's sick. Go ask him. If he's willing, I'll play. Go.

SONYA: I'm going. *(She goes out. We hear the night watchman's tapping.)*

YELENA ANDREYEVNA: I haven't played in a long time. I'm going to play and cry—cry and cry, like a foolish woman. *(through the window)* Is that you, Yefim?

THE WATCHMAN'S VOICE: Uhh, yes.

YELENA ANDREYEVNA: Don't tap any more. Your master's sick.

THE WATCHMAN'S VOICE: I'm going. *(He whistles for his dogs.)* Here! Here, boy! Here Zhuchka! *(pause)*

SONYA: *(coming back)* He says no.

Curtain

A sitting room in Serebryakov's house. There is a door on the left, the right, and in the middle. Afternoon. VOINITSKY *and* SONYA *are seated.*

YELENA ANDREYEVNA *paces pensively.*

VOINITSKY: The Herr Professor deigned to express a wish we be here at one o'clock. *(He looks at the time.)* Quarter to one. It seems he has an important message for the world.

YELENA ANDREYEVNA: Just some business, probably.

VOINITSKY: What business? He doesn't have a business. All he does is write trash, complain and be jealous.

SONYA: *(reproachfully)* Uncle Vanya.

VOINITSKY: I'm sorry, I'm sorry. *(pointing to* YELENA ANDREYEVNA*)* Look how she sways as she walks. She moves so easily, so lazily. How pretty, how very pretty.

YELENA ANDREYEVNA: And you—from morning 'til night all you do is complain. Don't you ever stop? *(in a weary voice)* I'm dying of boredom. I don't know what to do with myself.

SONYA: *(shrugging)* There's work if you want it.

YELENA ANDREYEVNA: What work?

SONYA: You could help with the estate, or teach, or visit the sick. Before you and Papa came, Uncle Vanya and I went to the market ourselves to sell flour.

YELENA ANDREYEVNA: I don't know how to do that, and it doesn't interest me. People in novels always teach and take care of the peasants. But you can't just jump into it.

SONYA: I don't know how anyone can resist helping them. Just wait. You'll change your mind. Even you. *(She puts her arm around* YELENA ANDREYEVNA.*)* Don't be bored, darling. *(She laughs.)* Laziness, idleness—they're contagious. Look at us. You're bored, you wander around like a lost soul. So Uncle Vanya does nothing but follow you like a shadow. And I drop everything to talk with you—I'm getting lazy. It's contagious. The doctor came here no more than once a month. Now he's here every day—his practice and forests forgotten. Maybe you're a witch.

VOINITSKY: You're wilting, my dear. Don't. *(animatedly)* You're too splendid to waste your life. You have siren's blood in your veins—so be a siren. For once in your life let yourself go. Fall head over heels with some spirit of the deep—dive in, head first. Leave the Herr Professor and the rest of us wide-eyed on the shore, amazed and awed.

YELENA ANDREYEVNA: *(angrily)* Leave me alone. You're so cruel. *(She starts to leave.)*

VOINITSKY: *(holding her back)* Come back, my treasure. I apologize. I'm sorry. *(He kisses her hand.)* Peace.

YELENA ANDREYEVNA: You'd try the patience of an angel.

VOINITSKY: I'll offer you roses as peace offering. I picked some for you this morning. Autumn roses are so lovely, so sad. *(He goes out.)*

SONYA: Autumn roses. So lovely, so sad.

(They look out the window.)

YELENA ANDREYEVNA: September already. How will we survive the winter? *(pause)* Where's the doctor?

SONYA: In Uncle Vanya's room, at his work table. I'm glad Uncle went out. I want to talk to you.

YELENA ANDREYEVNA: About what?

SONYA: About what? *(She puts her head on* YELENA ANDREYEVNA's *breast.)*

YELENA ANDREYEVNA: Come now, what is it? *(She caresses her hair.)* Well? What is it?

SONYA: I'm not pretty.

YELENA ANDREYEVNA: You have beautiful hair.

SONYA: No! *(She turns to look at herself in the mirror.)* That's what they always say to ugly people—you have beautiful hair, beautiful eyes. I've loved him for six years. I love him more than I loved my mother. Every moment I think I hear him, I think I feel his hand on mine, I look at the door thinking he's about to come in. I can't help talking to you about him all the time. He's here every day but he doesn't look at me, he doesn't see me. It hurts. I have no hope, none. *(with despair)* God, give me strength. I prayed all last night. Now I just walk up to him, look him in the eye, and start to talk. I have no pride. I can't control myself. Yesterday—I couldn't help it—I told Uncle Vanya I love him. All the servants know I love him. Love… Everyone knows.

YELENA ANDREYEVNA: Does he?

SONYA: No. He doesn't notice me.

YELENA ANDREYEVNA: *(musing)* He's a strange man. Let me talk to him. I'll be careful—only allude to it. *(pause)* It's hard not knowing. Shall I? (SONYA *nods yes.*) Good. Does he love you, yes or no? I'll find out. Don't worry, darling—I'll ask him cleverly, so he won't realize. Yes or no? That's we need to know. *(pause)* If it's no, then he can't come here anymore. You'll suffer less if you don't see him. Agreed? (SONYA *nods.*) What's the good of putting it off? He said he'd show me his drawing. Go tell him I want to see him.

SONYA: *(very moved)* You'll tell me everything?

YELENA ANDREYEVNA: Yes. Whatever the truth, it's better than not knowing. Trust me, darling.

SONYA: Yes. I'll tell him you want to see his drawing. *(She takes a few steps, stops at the door.)* No, not knowing is better. Then there's still hope.

YELENA ANDREYEVNA: What did you say?

SONYA: Nothing. *(She goes out.)*

YELENA ANDREYEVNA: *(alone)* It's awful to know someone's secret, and not be able to help. *(She thinks.)* Obviously he's not in love with her. But why not marry her? She's not pretty—but for a country doctor of his age, she's perfect. She's bright, good and pure. No, that's not it. That's not what it's about. *(pause)* I understand her, poor thing. In this endless boredom, people are like gray shadows— every day eating, drinking, sleeping, mouthing the same tired words. Then, from time to time, he appears. He's so different from them. He's handsome, interesting and passionate. He's like moonlight piercing through clouds. How could she not love a man like that? How could anyone help it? I'm a little in love with him too. When he's not here, I'm bored. When I think of him, I can't help smiling. Uncle Vanya said there's siren's blood in your veins, for once in your life let yourself go. Well, why not? Why not fly like a bird far from here, free from their sleepy faces, their insipid conversations—forget they exist. Because I'm frightened, I'm timid, and I'd have too many regrets. I know why he comes here every day. I'm ashamed. I should fall on my knees to Sonya, ask her to forgive me, beg her...

ASTROV: *(entering with a rolled-up surveyor's map)* Hello. *(He shakes her hand.)* You want to see my drawings?

YELENA ANDREYEVNA: Yes, you promised to show them to me yesterday. Do you have time now?

ASTROV: Of course. *(He spreads the map out on a table, fixes it with thumbtacks.)* Where were you born?

YELENA ANDREYEVNA: *(helping him lay out the drawings)* Petersburg.

ASTROV: Where did you study?

YELENA ANDREYEVNA: At the conservatory.

ASTROV: Then maybe this won't interest you.

YELENA ANDREYEVNA: Why not? I haven't lived much in the country, but I've read about it.

ASTROV: I have a work table in this house, in Ivan Petrovich's room. When I'm completely worn out, numb—I drop everything, run here and draw. It's my play time for an hour or two. Vanya and Sonya do their accounts. I doodle near them, quietly. It's warm and peaceful—a cricket chirps in a corner. Not that I allow myself that pleasure often—once a month maybe. *(showing the map)* Now look, please. This is our district fifty years ago. The dark and light greens are forests, covering half the map. Where the green is striped with red—elk and deer. Here, in the lakes—swan, geese, and ducks. The old people say there were vast numbers of every kind of bird, clouds of them. Here are the retreats of the Old Believers, here water mills, here cattle, horses—that's the blue. See, this corner is mostly blue—there were herds of horses, at least three to a peasant. *(pause)* Now here's the district twenty-five years ago. The forest covers only a third of the land. The deer are gone, there are still elk. The blue and green are paler. The third map— down here—is the district today. There's still some green, but only in spots. No more elk, swan or geese. There are no monasteries or mills left. This is a picture of destruction, which in ten or fifteen years will be complete. You could say the old must give way to the new. And I'd agree if forests were replaced by roads, railways, factories and schools. Then maybe people would be richer, more educated. But in this district things don't change. We have swamps, mosquitoes, typhoid, diphtheria and misery. People lose the fight for survival here. Degraded by inertia and ignorance, starving, sick and freezing—in order to save their lives and their children, they clutch at whatever feeds or warms them. They destroy without a thought for the future. Everything is destroyed. Nothing is replaced. *(coldly)* I have the impression this doesn't interest you.

YELENA ANDREYEVNA: I know so little about it.

ASTROV: It's not a question of knowing about it. It doesn't interest you, that's all.

YELENA ANDREYEVNA: To tell the truth, I was thinking about something else. Forgive me, but I must subject you to a little cross-examination. I don't know where to begin.

ASTROV: A cross-examination?

YELENA ANDREYEVNA: Yes, a cross-examination. A harmless one. Let's sit. *(They sit.)* It's to do with a certain young person. We'll talk as friends, openly—and later we'll forget what was said. Agreed?

ASTROV: Agreed.

YELENA ANDREYEVNA: It's about my stepdaughter, Sonya. Do you like her?

ASTROV: Yes, I admire her.

YELENA ANDREYEVNA: Do you like her as a woman?

ASTROV: *(after a little silence)* No.

YELENA ANDREYEVNA: Just one or two more questions, and that's all. You've noticed nothing?

ASTROV: Nothing.

YELENA ANDREYEVNA: *(taking his hand)* I can read it in your eyes—you don't love her. She's in pain. Please understand—you have to stop coming here.

ASTROV: My time for all that is past. I-I'm too busy. I-I can't— *(shrugging)* I-I don't have time. *(He is obviously embarrassed.)*

YELENA ANDREYEVNA: Ouf! What an unpleasant conversation. I'm as worn out as if I'd been carrying stones. Well, it's over, thank God. We'll forget it. Nothing was said. But you'll have to go. You do understand? You're a sensitive man. *(pause)* My face is burning. I must be turning red.

ASTROV: If you had said all that a month ago, I would have considered not coming anymore, but now— *(He shrugs.)* Though, if she's in pain—But I'm confused. What was your cross-examination really about? *(He looks her straight in the eye, shakes his finger at her.)* Sly, aren't you?

YELENA ANDREYEVNA: What do you mean?

ASTROV: *(laughing)* Sly. Sonya may be in pain, but how does your cross-examination help her? *(stopping her from speaking, agitatedly)* Now it's my turn to speak. Don't look so surprised. You know why I come here every day—and for whom. Don't look so surprised. My lovely beast of prey, I've been around.

YELENA ANDREYEVNA: *(stupefied)* Beast of prey? I don't understand.

ASTROV: A pretty minx with soft pretty fur needs victims. For a month now I've done nothing, dropped everything, thought only of you, hungered for you—and you're delighted. Is that why the cross-examination? Well, here I am—vanquished. *(He folds his arms on his chest, bows his head.)* I give up. Go ahead, devour me.

YELENA ANDREYEVNA: You're completely crazy.

ASTROV: *(laughing bitterly)* You're shy…

YELENA ANDREYEVNA: I'm not who you think I am. I'm not that low. I swear I'm not. *(She wants to go.)*

ASTROV: *(blocking her way)* I'll go, I won't come back, but— *(He takes her hand, looks around quickly.)* Where shall we meet? Tell me. Hurry, someone might come. *(with passion)* How splendid you are, how marvelous… Just one kiss… If I could just once kiss your perfumed hair…

YELENA ANDREYEVNA: I swear to you—

ASTROV: *(stopping her from speaking)* Why swear? No words. So beautiful. Such beautiful hands. *(He kisses her hands.)*

YELENA ANDREYEVNA: No. Please go. *(She pulls her hands back.)* You're mad, you're forgetting—

ASTROV: Tell me where we meet tomorrow. *(He takes her by the waist.)* You know we will. We will meet.
(He kisses her. At that moment VOINITSKY appears with a bouquet of roses. He stops at the door.)

YELENA ANDREYEVNA: *(not seeing VOINITSKY)* Don't. Please. Leave me alone. *(She leans her head on ASTROV's chest.)* No. *(She wants to go.)*

ASTROV: *(holding her by the waist)* Meet me tomorrow—the tree nursery. At two? Yes? You'll come?

YELENA ANDREYEVNA: *(noticing* VOINITSKY*)* Leave me alone. *(She goes toward the window, extremely agitated.)* This is horrible.

*(*VOINITSKY*, deeply disturbed, puts the bouquet on a chair. He nervously wipes his face and neck with a handkerchief.)*

VOINITSKY: It's nothing. It's alright. It's alright.

ASTROV: *(assuming a casual air)* Ah, Vanya, esteemed Ivan Petrovich—nice weather we're having. It was gray this morning. I was sure it would rain, but the sun finally came out. It's a beautiful fall, and the hay's doing well. *(He rolls up his map.)* Of course, the days are getting shorter. *(He goes out.)*

YELENA ANDREYEVNA: *(agitated, going to* VANYA*)* Please make the arrangements. My husband and I leave today—today. Do you hear me?

VOINITSKY: *(wiping his face)* What? Yes. Yes. *Helene*, I saw everything.

YELENA ANDREYEVNA: *(nervous)* Do you hear me? I must leave today.

*(*SEREBRYAKOV, SONYA, TELYEGIN *and* NANNY *enter.)*

TELYEGIN: I don't feel well myself, Excellency. I haven't eaten for two days. It's my head, mostly.

SEREBRYAKOV: Where is everyone? This house is a maze. I don't like it. Twenty-six huge rooms, everyone always off in different directions. You can never find anyone. *(He rings.)* Ask Maria Vasilyevna and my wife to come here.

YELENA ANDREYEVNA: I'm here.

SEREBRYAKOV: Then sit down, ladies and gentlemen.

SONYA: *(going to* YELENA ANDREYEVNA, *asking impatiently)* What did he say?

YELENA ANDREYEVNA: Later.

SONYA: You're trembling. You're upset. *(She studies* YELENA ANDREYEVNA*'s face.)* He said he wouldn't come back, didn't he? *(pause)* Answer me. That's it, isn't it?

*(*YELENA ANDREYEVNA *nods.)*

SEREBRYAKOV: *(to* TELYEGIN*)* I can live with illness. What I can't bear is living in the country. I feel I'm on another planet. Please sit down, all of you. Sonya. *(*SONYA *doesn't hear him. She remains standing, sad, her head hanging.)* Sonya! *(pause)* She doesn't hear me. *(to* MARYINA*)* You too, Nanny—sit down. *(She sits, knits a sock.)* Well, ladies and gentlemen, may I have your ears, please? So to speak. *(He laughs.)*

VOINITSKY: *(nervous)* I'm not needed here. May I go?

SEREBRYAKOV: No, on the contrary—I need you especially.

VOINITSKY: What do you want?

SEREBRYAKOV: Why are you angry? *(pause)* If you feel I've wronged you in any way, please forgive me.

VOINITSKY: Don't take that tone with me. Just state your business. What do you want?

(MARIA VASILYEVNA enters.)

SEREBRYAKOV: Ah, here's *Maman*! Ladies and gentlemen, I begin. *(pause)* I've invited you here, my friends, to tell you the Inspector General is coming. No. No jokes. I need your advice and help, all of you. I know I can count on your cooperation, as always. I'm merely a scholar, just a bookworm. I know nothing of practical matters. So I turn to you, Ivan Petrovich, to you, Ilya Ilyich, and to you, *Maman. Manet omnes una nox*—a single night awaits us all. We are here for a short while only, and by the grace of God. I'm old and sick. It's time to put my affairs in order. My life is finished, of course, so it's not a question of me. But I have a young wife, and a daughter to marry. *(pause)* To continue living here is not possible. We're not country people. On the other hand, we can't live in the city on the income from this property. If we were to sell the forest, we could do it only once. What we need is a plan for a guaranteed income. Well, I've made such a plan. In broad outline, ladies and gentlemen, as the estate brings in only two per cent in revenue, I propose we sell it. If we convert the money from the sale into bonds, we realize four to five percent, maybe more—which would permit us to buy a small country house in Finland.

VOINITSKY: Excuse me. I don't think I heard you correctly. Would you repeat what you just said?

SEREBRYAKOV: Convert the money into interest-bearing bonds, and, if there's a surplus, buy a small country house in Finland.

VOINITSKY: No, not the Finland part—something you said just before that.

SEREBRYAKOV: I propose we sell this estate.

VOINITSKY: I see. You want to sell the estate. Fine. A wonderful idea. And what becomes of us—of me, my old mother and Sonya?

SEREBRYAKOV: We'll consider that in due course. We can't decide everything at once.

VOINITSKY: I must be very stupid. Until now I thought this estate belonged to Sonya. My father bought it as a dowry for my sister. And, naively, I was under the impression that we live under Russian law, not Turkish. I believed that since my sister died, this estate belongs to Sonya.

SEREBRYAKOV: Yes. So, the estate is Sonya's. Who denies that? I won't sell it without her consent. And it's for her own good.

VOINITSKY: I can't believe this. It's unbelievable. Either I'm going crazy, or—

MARIA VASILYEVNA: *Jean*, don't contradict *Alexandre*. He knows better than you what to do.

VOINITSKY: Give me some water. *(He drinks some water.)* Go ahead. Say whatever you want, whatever you want.

SEREBRYAKOV: I don't understand why you're in such a state. I don't say my solution is ideal. If everyone dislikes it, I won't insist. *(pause)*

TELYEGIN: *(confused)* I not only greatly respect scholarship, your Excellency, but I'm related to it. My brother Grigori Ilyich's wife's brother, Mr. Konstantin Trofimovich Lakedemonov, who you may know, holds a degree of Master of Arts—

VOINITSKY: Not now, Waffles. This is business. *(to SEREBRYAKOV)* As a matter of fact, his uncle sold us the estate. Ask him.

SEREBRYAKOV: Ask him what?

VOINITSKY: We bought it for ninety-five thousand rubles. Father had only seventy thousand, so we were twenty-five thousand in debt. Now listen carefully. This estate could never have been bought at all if I hadn't given up my inheritance in favor of my sister, whom I dearly loved. And then it took me ten years of working like an ox to pay off the debt.

SEREBRYAKOV: I'm sorry I brought it up.

VOINITSKY: If the estate is here, and free from debt—it's because of me. And now I'm old, and you want to throw me out.

SEREBRYAKOV: What are you trying to say?

VOINITSKY: For twenty-five years I ran this estate for you. I worked hard. I sent you money, like a good steward. And did you once thank me? For that whole time, from my youth 'til now, I received from you five hundred rubles a year, my wages—nothing! Did you once think to raise that amount by a single ruble?

SEREBRYAKOV: How was I to know? I'm not a practical man, I don't know about all that. You could have raised your salary yourself—whatever you needed.

VOINITSKY: Yes, of course, why not steal? Have contempt for me—I didn't steal. I should have. I wouldn't be a beggar today.

MARIA VASILYEVNA: *(severely)* Jean!

TELYEGIN: Vanya, please, I'm trembling. We're all friends here. Stop it. *(He kisses him.)* Stop it, please.

VOINITSKY: Twenty-five years I lived like a mole within these walls, with my mother. All our feelings, all our thoughts, were for you. We talked of nothing but you and your writing. We were proud of you, we spoke your name with reverence. How many nights wasted reading and rereading your articles and books, for which today I have nothing but contempt?

TELYEGIN: Please, Vanya, I can't bear any more.

SEREBRYAKOV: *(angrily)* What do you want from me? I don't understand.

VOINITSKY: You were a superior being to us. We knew every word you wrote by heart. But not now—my eyes are open now. You write about art, but understand nothing. Nothing. Your articles are worth nothing. You tricked us.

SEREBRYAKOV: If you don't calm him down, ladies and gentlemen, I'm leaving.

YELENA ANDREYEVNA: Ivan Petrovich, be quiet. I order you to be quiet. Do you hear me?

VOINITSKY: I will not be quiet. *(barring* SEREBRYAKOV's *way)* Wait, I haven't finished. You've ruined my life. I haven't lived. My best years were wasted, destroyed—by you. You're my enemy.

TELYEGIN: I can't bear any more... I can't... I'm going... *(Deeply disturbed, he leaves.)*

SEREBRYAKOV: What do you want? What gives you the right to talk to me like this? If the estate is yours, keep it. I don't need it.

YELENA ANDREYEVNA: I'm in hell. I'm leaving, now. *(She shouts.)* I can't bear it.

VOINITSKY: I've wasted my life! I'm intelligent, talented, daring—I could have been Schopenhauer, Dostoyevsky! What am I saying? I'm going crazy. Mother, I'm in despair! Mother!

MARIA VASILYEVNA: *(severely)* Listen to *Alexandre*.

SONYA: *(kneeling in front of* MARYINA, *hugging her close)* Nanny! Nanny!

VOINITSKY: *Maman!* What shall I do? No, don't tell me. I know what to do. *(to* SEREBRYAKOV) You won't forget me! *(He goes out by the middle door.* MARIA VASILYEVNA *follows him.)*

SEREBRYAKOV: Keep him away from me. He's crazy. And to think he lives in that room. *(indicating the middle door)* The room next to mine. Make him move to the village, or one of the cottages. We can't live in the same house. Either he goes, or I go.

YELENA ANDREYEVNA: *(to her husband)* We leave today. Give the orders— now.

SEREBRYAKOV: Who is he, anyway? He's a nobody.

*(*SONYA, *on her knees, speaks nervously to her father. There are tears in her voice.)*

SONYA: Please understand, Papa. Try to understand us. Uncle Vanya and I are so unhappy. *(controlling herself)* Be kind. Remember when Uncle Vanya and Grandmother translated books for you every night, and copied your papers? Everything Uncle Vanya and I have ever done was for you. We worked for you all the time. We never spent an extra kopeck. We worked for our living. No, I'm not saying it right. But please understand us, Papa. Be kind. You must be kind.

YELENA ANDREYEVNA: *(very moved, to her husband)* For God's sake, Alexander, make up with him, please.

SEREBRYAKOV: Yes, yes, alright. I'll talk to him. I'm not accusing him. I'm not angry. But you must admit his conduct is strange, to say the least. Alright, I'll go find him. *(He goes out the middle door.)*

YELENA ANDREYEVNA: Try to calm him. Be gentle. *(She follows him.)*

SONYA: *(hugging* MARYINA) Nanny. Little nanny.

MARYINA: Don't worry, little one. It's nothing. They honk like geese. They'll calm down.

SONYA: Little nanny.

MARYINA: *(caressing her hair)* You're shivering, my little orphan, as if you were cold. Calm down. God is good. You'll have some linden blossom tea, or raspberry leaf. It'll be over soon, my little orphan. Calm down. *(She looks at the middle door and speaks with anger.)* Bah!

Gaggle of geese. Crazy geese. *(From offstage, a gunshot. A cry from* YELENA ANDREYEVNA. SONYA *shudders.)* Ach, you—

SEREBRYAKOV: *(running in, staggering and swaying with fright)* Hold him back! Stop him, he's crazy.

YELENA ANDREYEVNA: *(trying to keep* VOINITSKY *at the door and to get the gun away from him)* Give me that. Give it to me.

VOINITSKY: *Helene,* leave me alone. Leave me alone! *(He pushes her away, runs into the room looking for* SEREBRYAKOV.*)* Where—there he is! *(He fires.)* Bang! *(pause)* I missed him? Again? *(with anger)* Oh, hell! Hell!

(He throws the gun away violently, falls into a chair, exhausted. The professor is overwhelmed. YELENA ANDREYEVNA *leans against a wall, feeling ill.)*

YELENA ANDREYEVNA: Take me away. Take me away from here, kill me. I can't stay here.

VOINITSKY: *(in despair)* What am I doing? What am I doing?

SONYA: *(softly)* Nanny, Nanny.

Curtain

A large room which serves both as Ivan Petrovich's bedroom and an office. Near the window, on a big table, are ledgers and papers. There's a chest of drawers, an armoire and a scale. To the side is a little table for Astrov with drawing supplies and paints. A portfolio is next to it. There's a starling in a cage. On the wall is a map of Africa, seemingly of no use. There is a large couch upholstered in oilcloth. To the left a door leads to other bedrooms. To the right another door leads to the hallway, a doormat in front of it so the peasants won't dirty the floor. It is evening. Fall. It is quiet. TELYEGIN *and* MARYINA, *seated across from each other, are winding wool.*

TELYEGIN: Hurry, Maryina Timofeyevna. We'll miss the goodbyes. They've ordered the carriage.

MARYINA: *(trying to hurry)* Almost finished.

TELYEGIN: They're going to live in Kharkov.

MARYINA: A good thing too.

TELYEGIN: They were frightened. Yelena Andreyevna said, "I can't stay here one more day. We go to Kharkov now, we send for our things later." They're going without their baggage. It's Fate, Nanny. They can't live here. Fate's against it.

MARYINA: It's better this way. Such a commotion. Shooting—shameful.

TELYEGIN: It's true. It was a scene from an Aivazovsky painting.

MARYINA: Shameful. I never thought I'd live to see the day... *(pause)* We'll go back to breakfast at eight, lunch at one, and a proper sit-down supper at night—just like everyone else, the way it's supposed to be, like good Christians. *(a sigh)* It's been a long time since I ate noodles, poor sinner that I am.

TELYEGIN: It's true. We haven't had noodles in a long time. *(pause)* A long time... This morning when I passed the grocer in the village, he shouted, "Hey, Sponger, how are you?" That made me feel sad.

MARYINA: Pay no mind, *Batyushka*. We all sponge off God. And we all work here—you, Sonya, and Ivan Petrovich—we work, all of us... Where is Sonya?

TELYEGIN: In the garden with the Doctor, looking for Ivan Petrovich. They're afraid he might hurt himself.

MARYINA: Where's his gun?

TELYEGIN: *(lowering his voice)* I hid it, in the cellar.

MARYINA: *(with a smile)* Hmm—did you now?

(VOINITSKY and ASTROV enter from outside.)

VOINITSKY: Leave me alone. *(to MARYINA and TELYEGIN)* Get out of here. Can't you leave me alone for five minutes? I can't bear being spied on all the time.

TELYEGIN: Right away, Vanya. *(He goes out on tiptoes.)*

MARYINA: Geese. Gaggle, gaggle, gaggle. *(She picks up her wool, goes out.)*

VOINITSKY: Leave me alone.

ASTROV: With pleasure, with the greatest of pleasure. But not until you give me back what you took. Do I have to ask you again?

VOINITSKY: I didn't take anything.

ASTROV: I mean it. Don't keep me waiting any more. I should have been gone a long time ago.

VOINITSKY: I didn't take anything.

(They sit.)

ASTROV: Alright, I'll wait. But if you don't give it to me soon, we'll have to use force. We'll tie you up and search you. I'm serious. I mean it.

VOINITSKY: Go ahead. *(pause)* To fire twice, and to miss—twice. Idiot. I'll never forgive myself.

ASTROV: If you want to play with a gun, why not put a bullet through your own head?

VOINITSKY: *(shrugging)* Isn't it odd? I try to murder someone, but I'm not arrested. No one's called the police. Apparently you all think I'm crazy. *(He laughs bitterly.)* I'm crazy—but he, of course, is not crazy to hide mediocrity and meanness under the mask of scholarship and academic rank. And she's not crazy to marry an old man, and then to deceive him in front of everyone. I saw you kiss her. Don't think I didn't.

ASTROV: Yes, so I kissed her. So what? Here's to you. *(He makes an insulting gesture, and—his hand to his mouth—a razzing sound.)*

VOINITSKY: *(looking at the door)* The earth is crazy to allow you all to live on it.

ASTROV: Don't talk nonsense.

VOINITSKY: Why not? I'm crazy. I can talk nonsense.

ASTROV: You're not crazy. You're a crank and a fool. Once I thought cranks were rare, abnormal. Now I think everyone's a crank. You're just like everyone else.

VOINITSKY: *(hiding his face in his hands)* I'm ashamed. I'm so ashamed. It hurts. I'm in pain. *(in despair)* I can't bear it. *(leaning on the table)* What should I do? What should I do?

ASTROV: Nothing.

VOINITSKY: Give me something to make me forget. Oh, God—I'm forty-seven. What if I live to be sixty? That's thirteen years. What will I do for thirteen years? Do you understand? *(He convulsively squeezes* ASTROV's *hand.)* If I could only spend the rest of my life in a new way—wake up some clear morning knowing that I can start again, that the past has vanished like smoke. *(He cries.)* Tell me how to find a new life. How to find one... How?

ASTROV: *(annoyed)* A new life? What are you talking about? Leave me alone. Our situation is hopeless.

VOINITSKY: Is it?

ASTROV: Yes. Hopeless. Absolutely hopeless. I know it.

VOINITSKY: Give me something. *(He indicates his heart.)* For here. It hurts.

ASTROV: *(shouting, furious)* That's enough! *(softening)* People in a century or two will sneer at us for stupidly wasting our lives. Perhaps they'll have the secret of happiness. But our only hope is that we'll dream in our coffins—maybe good dreams. Who knows? *(He sighs.)* Listen, friend, ten years ago there were two intelligent honest men in this district—you and me. In ten years this rotten, narrow little life we lead has poisoned us, made us crude and stupid like everyone else. *(animatedly)* But don't try to distract me. Give back what you took.

VOINITSKY: I didn't take anything.

ASTROV: You took a vial of morphine from my bag. *(pause)* Listen—if you really want to kill yourself, go into the forest and blow your brains out. But give me back the morphine. You know how people are. People will say I gave it to you. Bad enough to have to perform your autopsy. Imagine the fun that'll be.

(SONYA *comes in.*)

VOINITSKY: Leave me alone.

ASTROV: *(to* SONYA*)* Your uncle stole a vial of morphine from my bag. He won't give it back. Tell him that's not very smart. I don't have any more time to waste. I have to go.

SONYA: Uncle Vanya, did you take the morphine? *(pause)*

ASTROV: He took it. I know it.

SONYA: Give it back. Why frighten us? *(affectionately)* Give it back, Uncle Vanya. I'm as miserable as you, but I don't give in. I'll endure 'til I die a natural death. You must endure too. Be patient. *(pause)* Give back the morphine. *(She kisses his hands.)* Dear, sweet Uncle Vanya, give it back. *(She cries.)* You're good. Be kind to us. Be patient, Uncle Vanya, be patient.

VOINITSKY: *(taking a vial from the table drawer, giving it to* ASTROV*)* Alright. Here. *(to* SONYA*)* But we must start to work now, or I can't, I won't be able to—

SONYA: Yes. We must work. As soon as they're gone—back to work. *(She leafs nervously through the papers on the table.)* We're so behind.

(ASTROV *puts the vial in the bag, tightens the straps.*)

ASTROV: I'm off.

YELENA ANDREYEVNA: *(entering, to* VANYA*)* Here you are. We're leaving now... Go find Alexander. He wants to talk to you.

SONYA: Yes, Uncle Vanya. *(She takes* VOINITSKY's *arm.)* Come with me. You and Papa must make peace. (SONYA *and* VOINITSKY *go out.*)

YELENA ANDREYEVNA: I'm leaving. *(She extends her hand to* ASTROV.*)* Goodbye.

ASTROV: Already?

YELENA ANDREYEVNA: Yes, the carriage is waiting.

ASTROV: Well then, goodbye.

YELENA ANDREYEVNA: You promised you'd leave today.

ASTROV: I haven't forgotten. I'm leaving. *(pause)* You were frightened. *(takes her hand)* Was it that frightening?

YELENA ANDREYEVNA: Yes.

ASTROV: And what if you stayed, hmmm? Tomorrow—the tree nursery?

YELENA ANDREYEVNA: No. It's decided—which is why I can look you in the eye. But one thing—think better of me. I'd like you to respect me.

ASTROV: Bah. *(He makes an impatient gesture.)* Why don't you stay? Please. You have nothing to do, no goals. Sooner or later you'll give in to your feelings—it's inevitable. Wouldn't it be better here than in Kharkov or Kursk? In nature, at least it's poetic. Autumn is beautiful. There's the tree nursery, and abandoned old estates—just like in Turgenev.

YELENA ANDREYEVNA: You're funny. I'm angry with you, but I'll remember you with pleasure. You're interesting—unique. We'll never see each other again, so why hide it? I was in love with you. Well, let's shake hands. Don't think badly of me.

ASTROV: *(shaking her hand)* Well then, go. *(thinking)* You seem good, kind—but there's something strange about you. Since you came, we've all dropped our work to worry about your husband's gout—and you. You've infected us with idleness, both of you. I've fallen in love with you, and done nothing in a month. People are sick, and peasants allow their cattle to eat the saplings in my forests. You and your husband bring destruction. That's a joke, of course. Still, its strange—I'm sure if you stayed, it would end in disaster. I wouldn't come out alive, and neither might you. Well then, go. *Finita la commedia!*

YELENA ANDREYEVNA: *(taking a pencil from his table and quickly hiding it)* I'm taking this pencil, as a memento.

ASTROV: Strange. We meet, and suddenly we're apart. That's how it is in this world. But since we're alone, and as Uncle Vanya is not about to arrive with roses for you—may I give you a farewell kiss? May I? *(He kisses her on the cheek.)* There. Good.

YELENA ANDREYEVNA: I wish you luck. *(She looks around.)* Oh, well. For once in my life. *(She throws herself into his arms. They separate quickly.)* I have to go.

ASTROV: Well then, go. The carriage is waiting. Go.

YELENA ANDREYEVNA: Someone's coming.

(They listen.)

ASTROV: *Finita.*

(SEREBRYAKOV, VOINITSKY, MARIA VASILYEVNA *with a book,* TELYEGIN *and* SONYA *enter.*)

SEREBRYAKOV: *(to* VOINITSKY*)* Well, "no regrets," as they say. I've been through so much in these last hours, I believe I'll write a book about it—on how to live. I accept your apologies, and I offer you mine. Farewell. *(He exchanges a ceremonial three kisses with* VOINITSKY*.)*

VOINITSKY: You'll receive the same amount you received before—regularly. The same.

(YELENA ANDREYEVNA *kisses* SONYA*.)*

SEREBRYAKOV: *(kissing* MARIA VASILYEVNA*'s hand)* Maman.

MARIA VASILYEVNA: *(kissing him) Alexandre*, have a new picture taken of yourself, and send it. You know how dear you are to me.

TELYEGIN: Goodbye, Excellency. Don't forget us.

SEREBRYAKOV: *(kissing his daughter)* Farewell, everyone. Goodbye. *(shaking* ASTROV*'s hand)* I respect your ideas, your enthusiasm and good intentions. But allow an old man to give you some advice—you must work. That's the key word, my friend—work. *(He bows to everyone.)* Good luck. *(He goes out accompanied by* MARIA VASILYEVNA *and* SONYA*.)*

VOINITSKY: *(passionately kissing* YELENA ANDREYEVNA*'s hand)* Goodbye. We'll never see each other again. Goodbye. Forgive me.

YELENA ANDREYEVNA: *(moved)* Dear friend. Goodbye. *(She kisses his hair, goes out.)*

ASTROV: Waffles, will you ask them to bring my carriage around too?

TELYEGIN: Of course. At your service.

(He goes out. VOINITSKY *and* ASTROV *remain alone.* ASTROV *gathers his drawings spread out on the table, puts them into his suitcase.)*

ASTROV: And you—you won't wave goodbye?

VOINITSKY: I can't. Let them leave. I don't feel well. I have to work. Work. *(He rummages among the papers on the table. A pause. We hear the sound of harness bells.)*

ASTROV: There they go. Imagine how happy the professor is. A thousand horses couldn't drag him back.

MARYINA: *(entering)* They're gone. *(She sits, starts to knit a sock.)*

SONYA: *(entering)* They're gone. *(She wipes her eyes)* God protect them. *(to her uncle)* And now, Uncle Vanya—to work.

VOINITSKY: Work. Yes. Work.

SONYA: It's been a long time since we sat at this table together. *(She lights a lamp on the table.)* There's no ink. *(She takes the inkwell, goes to the armoire to fill the inkwell with ink.)* It's sad to see them go.

MARIA VASILYEVNA: *(entering slowly)* Gone. *(She sits, immediately immersing herself in a book.* SONYA *sits at the table, leafs through a ledger.)*

SONYA: We must make out the bills first, Uncle Vanya. We're so behind. Someone came by today asking for one. You take these, I'll do these.

VOINITSKY: *(writing)* To Mr...

(They both write in silence.)

MARYINA: *(yawning)* I'm so sleepy. Sleepytime.

ASTROV: It's quiet here, warm and cozy—pens scratching, crickets chirping. I don't want to leave. *(We hear the sound of harness bells.)* My horses. Time to say goodbye to my little table. I'm off. *(He puts his charts into his portfolio.)*

MARYINA: What's the hurry? Stay a little.

ASTROV: I can't.

VOINITSKY: *(writing)* So there's a balance of two seventy-five.

(A WORKER *enters.)*

WORKER: The horses are waiting.

ASTROV: I know. *(He hands the* WORKER *his doctor's bag, suitcase and portfolio.)* Here, take these. Be careful. Don't crush the drawings.

WORKER: Yes, *Batyushka*, I'll be careful. *(He goes out.)*

ASTROV: Well. *(He is preparing to say his goodbyes.)*

SONYA: When will we see you again?

ASTROV: I don't think before summer—it won't be possible in winter. Of course, if anything happens, let me know—I'll come right away. *(He shakes hands with* VOINITSKY *and* SONYA.*)* Thank you for your hospitality, kindness—everything. *(He goes to* MARYINA, *kisses her hair.)* Goodbye, old one.

MARYINA: You won't go without tea?

ASTROV: I don't want any tea, Nanny.

MARYINA: Vodka? You don't want any vodka?

ASTROV: *(hesitating)* Well—maybe a little. *(MARYINA goes out. A pause.)* My lead horse started to limp. I wonder why. I noticed it yesterday as Petrushka led him to water.

VOINITSKY: He needs reshoeing.

ASTROV: I'll stop at the blacksmith's. *(He goes to the map of Africa, looks at it.)* It must be blazing hot in Africa right now.

VOINITSKY: Probably.

(MARYINA returns carrying a tray with a little glass of vodka and a piece of bread.)

MARYINA: Help yourself. *(ASTROV empties the little glass.)* To your health, Batyushka. *(She bows deeply to him.)* And the bread? You don't want the bread?

ASTROV: No, thanks. That's enough. And now, I wish you the best—all of you. *(to MARYINA)* Don't walk me to the door, Nanny, don't. *(He goes out. SONYA follows him, a candle in her hand. NANNY settles into her armchair.)*

VOINITSKY: *(writing)* February second, twenty pounds of oil delivered. February sixteenth—twenty more pounds. Buckwheat.

(A pause. We hear the sound of harness bells.)

MARYINA: He's gone.

SONYA: *(coming back, placing the candle on the table)* He's gone. *(pause)*

VOINITSKY: *(doing the accounts with the help of an abacus, writing)* That's fifteen, and twenty-five...

MARYINA: *(yawning)* Poor sinners that we are.

(TELYEGIN comes in on tiptoe, sits near the door, and softly tunes his guitar.)

VOINITSKY: *(to SONYA, caressing her hair)* Sweet little Sonyechka—if you only knew how unhappy I am.

SONYA: What can we do, Uncle? We're alive. *(pause)* We'll live a long chain of days and endless nights. We'll bear patiently whatever happens. We'll work for others with no rest until we die. And when our hour comes, we'll go without a murmur. But in the next world, Uncle, we'll say we suffered, that we were miserable—and God will take pity on us. Then, dear Uncle, a new life will start—radiant and beautiful. We'll rejoice, and remember these sufferings with a smile. We'll rest. I believe that, Uncle, with all my heart. *(She kneels in front of* VOINITSKY, *puts her hand on his hands, and speaks in a tired voice.)* We'll rest. *(*TELYEGIN *plays the guitar quietly.)* Yes, rest. We'll hear angels sing, see the sky filled with diamonds. Our trouble and pain will melt into compassion. Our lives will be calm, gentle—sweet as a caress. I believe that, Uncle. I believe it. *(She wipes away her uncle's tears with her handkerchief.)* Dear, poor Uncle Vanya—you're crying. *(through her own tears)* You've had no joy in your life. But wait, Uncle. Just wait. We'll rest. *(She embraces him.)* We'll rest. *(We hear the tapping of the night watchman.* TELYEGIN *plays softly.* MARIA VASILYEVNA *writes in the margins of her pamphlet.* MARYINA *darns a sock.)* We'll rest.

The curtain falls slowly

THREE
SISTERS
A DRAMA IN FOUR ACTS

Jean-Claude van Itallie's version in English of Anton Chekhov's *Three Sisters* was first produced in July, 1979 at Rokeby Estate in Rhinebeck, New York, directed by Lawrence Sacharow.

It was presented on WBAI radio in New York City in October, 1979. The cast included Seth Allen, Shami Chaikin, Wendy Gimbel, Sandy Kadet, Linda Hunt, Karen Ludwig, Rosemary Quinn, Jean-Claude van Itallie, David Willinger and David Wolpe.

It was produced in December, 1982 at the Manhattan Theatre Club in New York City, directed by Lynne Meadow. The cast included Sam Waterston as Vershinin, Jeff Daniels as Andrei, and Dianne Wiest as Masha.

It was produced in December, 1982 at the American Repertory Theatre (Robert Brustein, artistic director) in Cambridge, Massachusetts directed by Andrei Serban, with Alvin Epstein as Vershinin.

CAST OF CHARACTERS

PROZOROV, ANDREI SERGEYVICH

NATALYA IVANOVNA, his fiancee, later his wife

His sisters: **OLGA**

        MASHA

        IRINA

KULYGIN, FYODOR ILYICH, a high school teacher, Masha's husband

VERSHININ, ALEXANDER IGNATYEVICH, Lieutenant Colonel, Battery Commander

TUZENBACH, NICOLAI LVOVICH, Baron, army lieutenant

SOLYONY, VASILY VASILYEVICH, army captain

CHEBUTYKIN, IVAN ROMANYICH, army doctor

FEDOTIK, ALEXEI PETROVICH, army lieutenant

RODE, VLADIMIR KARLOVICH, army lieutenant

FERAPONT, caretaker at the County Council, old

ANFISA, the nanny, in her eighties

The play takes place in a provincial Russian town.

The Prozorovs' house. A sitting room with colonnades, behind which we see a larger room, the main hall. It's noon. Outside it's bright, sunny. In the main hall the table is being set for lunch. OLGA, *in the dark blue uniform of a teacher at the girls' high school, correcting students' notebooks, sits, gets up, walks about.* MASHA, *in black, sits reading a thin book, her hat on her knees.* IRINA, *in white, stands daydreaming.*

OLGA: The fifth of May, Irina—your name day. Papa died just a year ago. It was so cold then, and snowing. I didn't think I'd survive. You fainted, and lay like a corpse. Just a year ago, and look—we can talk about it, the pain's not unbearable. You're wearing white, and your face is beaming. *(The clock strikes twelve.)* Just like it struck a year ago. *(pause)* I can still see them carrying him. I can hear the music, and the guns saluting at the cemetery. There weren't many people there for a general, commander of brigade. Of course, it was raining—snowing and heavy rain.

IRINA: Why think about it?

(Behind the columns in the main hall BARON TUZENBACH, CHEBUTYKIN, *and* SOLYONY *can be seen by the table.)*

OLGA: It's warm. We can open the windows wide today. The birches here don't have leaves yet at this season. Eleven years since we left Moscow, when Father was given command of the brigade—eleven years, and it's still crystal clear in my mind. In early May it's warm in Moscow. Flowers bloom, the city's flooded with sunlight. I feel as if I had been there yesterday. My God, this morning I awoke, saw the light, the spring—I was full of joy, and wanting so to go home.

CHEBUTYKIN: To hell with that.

TUZENBACH: It's nonsense, of course.

*(*MASHA, *who's been sitting dreamily over her book, begins quietly whistling a song.)*

OLGA: Don't whistle, Masha. How can you? *(pause)* Since I started working at the high school, and tutoring every afternoon—I have a constant headache. I think like an old woman. I'm becoming an old woman. For four years I've felt my energy, my youth, drain from me drop by drop, day by day. I dream only of one thing...

IRINA: To go to Moscow—to sell this house, everything—to go to Moscow...

OLGA: Yes! To go to Moscow soon.

(CHEBUTYKIN *and* TUZENBACH *laugh.*)

IRINA: Our dear brother will probably be a professor. Anyway he won't want to stay here. The only problem is our poor Masha.

OLGA: Masha will come to Moscow for the summer, every year.

(MASHA *whistles quietly.*)

IRINA: God willing, it will all happen. (*She looks out the window.*) So beautiful today. Why do I feel so happy? This morning when I remembered it was my name-day, I felt joy suddenly—just like when I was a child and Mama was alive. Suddenly what wonderful feelings, what feelings!

OLGA: You look radiant today—beautiful. So does Masha. Andrei would look good too, only he's getting fat—it doesn't suit him. And I've aged. I'm too thin. It's from getting angry at the high school girls. But today I'm free—I can stay home, I have no headache, and I feel younger than yesterday. I'm only twenty-eight... It's all for the best. It's all God's will. Still, it might have been better if I'd married and stayed home. (*pause*) I would have loved my husband.

TUZENBACH: (*to* SOLYONY) You're too full of rumors. I can't listen anymore. (*He comes into the sitting room.*) I forgot to tell you—today you'll have a visit from our new battery commander, Vershinin. (*He sits at the piano.*)

OLGA: Good. That's fine.

IRINA: Is he old?

TUZENBACH: Not that old. Forty, forty-five. (*He plays softly.*) He seems very nice. Definitely not stupid. But he likes to talk.

IRINA: Is he interesting?

TUZENBACH: Yes, I suppose so. But he has a wife, a mother-in-law, and two little girls. He always talks about his wife and little girls. It's his second marriage. The wife is a sort of half-wit. She wears braids like a child, talks furiously about intellectual things, and occasionally attempts suicide—probably just to annoy him. I would have left her long ago. But he's patient—he just complains.

SOLYONY: *(entering from the main hall with* CHEBUTYKIN*)* I can lift thirty kilos with one hand. With two I can lift eighty or eighty-five. I conclude—two men are more than twice as strong as one, maybe three times as strong, maybe more...

CHEBUTYKIN: *(reading from the newspaper as he walks)* For baldness—ten grams of napthaline to a half liter of alcohol. Dissolve, and apply daily. *(He makes notes in his notebook.)* We'll make a note of that. *(to* SOLYONY*)* So, you push a cork pierced by a small glass tube into a bottle. Then take a pinch of alum, the most ordinary substance in the world...

IRINA: Ivan Romanyich, my dear Ivan Romanyich!

CHEBUTYKIN: What? What, my little angel, my delight?

IRINA: Why do I feel so happy today. I feel I have sails, and above me an endless wide blue sky with great white birds gliding. Why do I feel like that? Why?

CHEBUTYKIN: *(tenderly kissing both her hands)* My white bird...

IRINA: This morning when I got up and bathed, suddenly everything seemed clear to me. I know how to live now, dear Ivan Romanyich. I know. Each of us must work by the sweat of his brow. Work is the meaning of life—its goal, happiness, and joy. The worker getting up at dawn to break stones on the road is happy. So is the shepherd, and the teacher of little children, and the engineer on the railway... God, it's easy for a man. But better to be an ox, a horse—anything—than a young woman who wakes up at noon, has coffee in bed, and spends two hours dressing. That's dreadful. I need to work, just as I need to drink water on a hot day. And if I don't start getting up early, if I continue doing nothing, you must stop being my friend, Ivan Romanyich.

CHEBUTYKIN: *(tenderly)* Alright. I promise.

OLGA: Papa taught us to get up at seven. Irina wakes at seven but stays in bed 'til nine, dreaming—serious dreams. *(She laughs.)*

IRINA: I'm still little to you. You're always surprised when I'm serious. I'm twenty.

TUZENBACH: The longing for work—God, how I understand it. I've never worked, never. I was born in Petersburg—a cold city where people do nothing. My family never knew work nor care. When I'd come home from the Cadet Corps, a footman removed my boots.

I was frivolous, said and did whatever I wanted. My admiring mother was amazed the whole world wasn't as charmed by me as she was. I was sheltered. Will that world last? I doubt it. Its hour has struck. Something vast is coming toward us, a powerful storm is brewing—a good one. It's coming soon. In its wake laziness, snobbery, prejudice against work, our whole morbid boring society will be swept away. I'll work, and in twenty-five or thirty years everyone will work—everyone.

CHEBUTYKIN: Not me.

TUZENBACH: You don't count.

SOLYONY: Thank God, in twenty-five years there's a good chance you'll be dead. You'll have apoplexy soon or I'll lose patience with you, my angel, and lodge a bullet in your forehead. (*He takes a vial of perfume from his pocket, puts some on his chest and hands.*)

CHEBUTYKIN: (*laughing*) It's true, I've never done a damn thing. Since I left university, I haven't lifted a finger. I don't even read books. Only newspapers. (*He takes a newspaper from his pocket.*) Here—I read there was once a writer named Dobrolyubov. But what did he write? I have no idea. God knows. (*A knocking is heard from the floor below.*) They're calling me from downstairs. Someone needs me. I'll be right back. (*He hurries out, combing his beard.*)

IRINA: He has something up his sleeve again.

TUZENBACH: Yes, he had his poker-faced solemn look. It's probably a present for you.

IRINA: No. That's so embarrassing!

OLGA: It's awful. He's so extravagant.

MASHA: "By the curved seashore, an oak tree greening. Wound 'round that oak, a golden chain..." (*She gets up, singing softly.*)

OLGA: You're not very cheerful today, Masha. (MASHA *puts on her hat, still singing softly.*) Where are you going?

MASHA: Home.

IRINA: That's strange...

TUZENBACH: You're leaving on a name day?

MASHA: I don't care. I'll be back tonight. Goodbye, my sweet. (*She kisses* IRINA.) Again—health and happiness. In Papa's time, thirty, forty officers came here on name days—it was exciting. Now there's only a person and a half. It's too quiet. It's like a desert. I'm leaving. I'm not feeling cheerful. Don't mind me. *(She smiles through her tears.)* We'll talk later. Goodbye, my darling. I'm off—I don't know where.

IRINA: *(displeased)* You're so —

OLGA: *(through tears)* I understand you, Masha.

SOLYONY: When a man philosophizes, the result is sophistication or sophistry. When a woman philosophizes, or two do, the result is—nothing.

MASHA: What do you mean, you dreadful man?

SOLYONY: Nothing. "Lying under a tree, he thought he had time to spare. He looked up too late to see the oncoming bear." *(pause)*

MASHA: *(to OLGA, angrily)* And stop crying.

(ANFISA and FERAPONT enter. FERAPONT carries a cake.)

ANFISA: Come in, little daddy. Come in. Your feet are clean. *(to IRINA)* It's from the County Council, from Protopopov, Mikhail Ivanovich—a cake.

IRINA: Thank you. Tell him thank you. *(She takes the cake.)*

FERAPONT: What?

IRINA: *(louder)* Tell him thank you.

OLGA: Nanny dear, give him some cake. Go, Ferapont. Have some cake.

FERAPONT: What?

ANFISA: Come, little daddy. Come, Ferapont. Come with me.

(ANFISA and FERAPONT leave.)

MASHA: I don't like that Protopopov, Mikhail Ivanovich or Mikhail Potapovich—whatever his name is. You shouldn't have invited him.

IRINA: I didn't.

MASHA: You were right.

(CHEBUTYKIN enters followed by a SOLDIER carrying a silver samovar. There is a murmur of astonishment and disapproval.)

OLGA: *(covering her face with her hands)* A samovar! How awful. *(She goes into the hall.)*

IRINA: Ivan Romanyich, my dear—what have you done?

TUZENBACH: *(laughing)* What did I tell you?

MASHA: Ivan Romanyich, you should be ashamed.

CHEBUTYKIN: My darlings, my sweet little angels—I have no one but you. You're my dearest in the world. I'm nearly sixty—old, alone, and insignificant... My love for you is the only good thing I have. Without it I would have left this world long ago... *(to* IRINA*)* My darling, I've known you since you were born... I carried you in my arms... I loved your poor mama...

IRINA: But why such expensive presents?

CHEBUTYKIN: *(half-moved, half-angry)* Such expensive presents?... Leave me alone. *(to the* SOLDIER*)* Put the samovar out there. *(mimicking* IRINA*'s tone)* Such expensive presents.

(The SOLDIER *puts the samovar in the main hall.)*

ANFISA: *(coming across the room)* My darlings, a colonel is here. He's not someone we know. He's taking off his coat now. He's coming, my darlings. Be nice to him, Irinushka... Be polite. *(as she leaves)* And it's lunch time... Oh, Lord.

TUZENBACH: It must be Vershinin. *(*VERSHININ *enters.* TUZENBACH *announces him.)* Lieutenant Colonel Vershinin.

VERSHININ: *(to* MASHA *and* IRINA*)* May I present myself? Vershinin. I'm happy to be here at last. My, how you've grown. My.

IRINA: Won't you sit down? We're pleased to meet —

VERSHININ: *(cheerfully)* I'm happy to be here, very happy. There are three of you, aren't there—three sisters? I remember three little girls. I don't remember your faces, but I know your father, Colonel Prozorov, had three little girls. I saw them. How time flies. My, how it flies.

TUZENBACH: Alexander Ignatyevich is from Moscow.

IRINA: From Moscow? You come from Moscow?

VERSHININ: Yes, of course. When your father was a battery commander, I was an officer in the same brigade. *(to* MASHA*)* Hmm, it seems to me I recognize you, a little.

MASHA: I don't recognize you at all.

IRINA: Olya, Olya! Olya, come quickly! *(*OLGA *comes from the hall.)* Colonel Vershinin is from Moscow!

VERSHININ: So you're Olga Sergeyvna, the eldest. And you, Maria... And you, Irina—the youngest...

OLGA: And you are from Moscow?

VERSHININ: Yes. I studied in Moscow, and did my military service in Moscow. I lived there a long time—until I was appointed battery commander here. And here I am, as you can see. To tell the truth, I don't remember you well. I just remember three sisters. But I have a clear memory of your father. If I close my eyes I see his face. I was often at your house in Moscow...

OLGA: I thought I remembered everyone, and now suddenly...

VERSHININ: My name is Alexander Ignatyevich.

IRINA: Alexander Ignatyevich. From Moscow... What a surprise!

OLGA: You know, we're going back.

IRINA: We're hoping to be there by fall. It's our home—we were born there... On Old Basmanny Street...

(OLGA *and* IRINA *laugh with pleasure.*)

MASHA: What a surprise to meet a fellow Muscovite. *(excitedly)* Yes—now, wait a minute. I have it! You remember, Olya—we called him the lovesick major. You were a lieutenant, and in love. So to tease you, we called you a major, God knows why...

VERSHININ: *(laughing)* That's right, that's right—the lovesick major. It's true...

MASHA: You had only a moustache then. Oh, how you've aged. *(through tears)* How you've aged...

VERSHININ: Yes, the lovesick major was young and in love. It's not the same now.

OLGA: But you don't have a single gray hair. You've aged, but you don't look old.

VERSHININ: Yes, well, I'm forty-two now. I'm in my forty-third year. How long ago did you leave Moscow?

IRINA: Eleven years. Why are you crying, Masha, you silly? *(through tears)* Now I'm starting.

MASHA: It's nothing. Where did you live?

VERSHININ: Old Basmanny Street.

OLGA: So did we!

VERSHININ: Later I lived on German Street. From German Street I walked to the Red Barracks. I had to pass over a gloomy bridge. Alone, crossing that bridge—just to hear the water made me sad. *(pause)* But here there's a big and vigorous river! A marvelous river!

OLGA: Yes, but it's cold here, too cold and full of mosquitoes.

VERSHININ: Come, it's a healthy climate—a good, Slavic climate. There's the forest, the river... And the birches—the sweet, gentle birches, my favorite trees. Living is good here. It is strange, of course, that the station is twelve miles from town... And no one knows why.

SOLYONY: I do. (*They all look at him.*) If the station were closer—it wouldn't be farther. And since it's farther—it's not closer. (*an embarrassed silence*)

TUZENBACH: Vasily Vasilyevich, what a joker.

OLGA: Now I recognize you. I remember you.

VERSHININ: I knew your mother.

CHEBUTYKIN: She was so good, God rest her soul.

IRINA: Mama's buried in Moscow.

OLGA: At the new cemetery of the Blessed Virgin.

MASHA: You know, I'm already beginning to forget her face. No one will remember us either. We'll all be forgotten.

VERSHININ: Yes, forgotten. That's our fate. There's nothing we can do about it. A day will come when everything which seems important to us today will be forgotten, or irrelevant. (*pause*) It's strange. We can't know now what will seem important to the future, and what will seem ridiculous. The discoveries of Copernicus or Columbus seemed useless and laughable then, while nonsense written by an idiot seemed true. What we think is true may one day seem strange, stupid, dishonest, or even shameful...

TUZENBACH: Who knows? Maybe they'll say this was a great time. Maybe they'll speak of us with respect. After all, there's no more torturing, executions, or invasions—'though there's enough suffering.

SOLYONY: (*in falsetto, as if calling little birds to feed*) Here, tsik tsik, tsik. Here, tsik, tsik, tsik. But no grain for the Baron—just let him philosophize.

TUZENBACH: Vasily Vasilyevich, will you please leave me alone... (*He changes seats.*) You're starting to annoy me.

SOLYONY: (*falsetto*) Here, tsik, tsik, tsik. Here, tsik, tsik, tsik.

TUZENBACH: (*to* VERSHININ) God knows we have suffering, but maybe the *kind* of suffering we have shows we've already reached a certain moral level...

VERSHININ: Yes, yes, of course.

CHEBUTYKIN: Baron, you just said our time may be great—but our people are small... *(He gets up.)* Look how small I am, for instance. You're just saying our time is great to console me. *(A violin is heard playing offstage.)*

MASHA: That's Andrei, our brother, playing.

IRINA: Andrei is our intellectual. He'll be a professor probably. Papa was military, but his son chose the university.

MASHA: Just as Papa wished.

OLGA: We've teased him today. I think he's a little in love.

IRINA: She's from here. We'll probably have the pleasure of her company today.

MASHA: How she dresses! My God, her clothes aren't just ugly or unfashionable—they're pathetic. A gaudy bright yellow skirt with a weird fringe and a red blouse! And her cheeks shiny with rouge. Andrei can't be in love with her, it's impossible. He has taste, after all. He's just teasing us. Yesterday I heard she might marry Protopopov, president of the County Council. So that's good... *(She turns toward the door and calls.)* Andrei! Come! Come here, darling, just for a moment.

(ANDREI enters.)

OLGA: Here's my brother, Andrei Sergeyvich.

VERSHININ: Vershinin.

ANDREI: Prozorov. *(He wipes the sweat from his face.)* You're the new battery commander?

OLGA: Can you believe it? Alexander Ignatyevich is from Moscow.

ANDREI: Really? Then I congratulate you. Now my sisters will allow you no peace.

VERSHININ: It's I who have already succeeded in boring them.

IRINA: Look at the little frame Andrei gave me today. *(She shows him the frame.)* He made it himself.

VERSHININ: *(looking at the frame, not knowing what to say)* Yes. It's—a frame.

IRINA: And the one there on the piano. He made that too. *(ANDREI waves his hand modestly, moving off.)* He's a scholar, plays the violin, and makes all sorts of little things out of wood. He can do anything. Andrei, don't go away. You're always leaving. Come here.

(MASHA *and* IRINA, *laughing, take him by the arm, bring him back.*)

MASHA: Come here, come on.

ANDREI: Will you leave me alone, please.

MASHA: How funny he is! When we called Alexander Ignatyevich "the lovesick major," he was never angry.

VERSHININ: Never.

MASHA: I'm going to call you the lovesick violinist!

IRINA: Or the lovesick professor…

OLGA: He's in love! Andryusha's in love!

IRINA: *(applauding)* Bravo! Bravo! Again! Andryusha's in love!

CHEBUTYKIN: *(coming up behind* ANDREI, *putting both arms around his waist)* Love—we are made only for love. *(He bursts out laughing. He is still holding his newspaper.)*

ANDREI: Come on, come on now, that's enough. *(He wipes his face.)* I couldn't sleep. I really don't feel well. I read 'til four, and when I finally turned off the light, I couldn't sleep. I was thinking of too many things. And dawn is early now. I was invaded by sunlight. During the summer, since I'm staying here, I intend to translate a book from the English.

VERSHININ: You know English?

ANDREI: Yes. My father, God rest his soul, made us learn many things. It's funny, and maybe stupid, but I confess that since he died, I've started getting fat—as if my body had been released from a corset. Thanks to Papa, my sisters and I know French, German, and English. Irina even knows Italian. But what work to learn all that.

MASHA: In a town like this knowing three languages is a luxury—maybe not a luxury but an absurd extra growth, a sixth finger. We know many useless things.

VERSHININ: What a funny idea. *(He laughs.)* We know many useless things! An intelligent educated person is never superfluous—even in a sad gloomy town like this. If there were only three of you among the hundred thousand in this vulgar backwater, and even if you couldn't conquer the shadows, the ignorance around you, even if little by little you yielded, became lost in the crowd, and life suffocated you—still, you wouldn't disappear without traces. After you, six people like you would spring up, then twelve, and so on, until people like you become the majority. In two or three centuries life on earth will be indescribably beautiful, astonishing. And that's what we must work toward—it's what Humanity needs. We must sense it coming, expect it, dream about it—prepare it. So you see it's important to know more than our ancestors. *(He laughs.)* And you complain about knowing too much.

MASHA: *(taking off her hat)* I'm staying for lunch.

IRINA: *(with a sigh)* Really, you should write that down.

(ANDREI has discreetly left.)

TUZENBACH: You say it will be many years before life is wonderful and beautiful. Alright. But we can take part in it even now, from far off—we can prepare ourselves for it, we can work...

VERSHININ: *(getting up)* Yes. Well. So many flowers. *(glancing around)* What beautiful rooms! I envy you! I've dragged around my whole life in little rooms with a couple of chairs, a couch, and smokey chimneys. Flowers like these are what I've missed... *(He rubs his hands together.)* Ah, well.

TUZENBACH: We must work. You're probably thinking what a sentimental German he is. But I'm Russian, word of honor—I don't even speak German. My father is Orthodox. *(pause)*

VERSHININ: *(pacing)* I often say to myself—what if we could start again, this time with awareness. What if this life were, so to speak, only a first draft, and another a final copy. I think we'd try not to repeat ourselves, or at least to create a different ambiance—rooms like yours, for instance, full of light and flowers. I have a wife and two little girls. My wife is not in good health and so on and so on. Well, if I had it to do again, I wouldn't marry—I wouldn't.

(KULYGIN enters in the uniform and coat of a high school teacher.)

KULYGIN: *(coming up to IRINA)* My dear sister, allow me to congratulate you and present my sincere wishes for your good health and anything else a girl of your age might wish. And to offer you this little book— *(He holds out a book to her.)* —the fifty-year history of our high school—an unimportant book I wrote in my spare time. But—read it anyway. Hello everyone. *(to VERSHININ)* Kulygin, high school professor. *(to IRINA)* You will find in it a list of all who have completed their studies in our high school for the past fifty years. *Feci, quod potui, faciant meliora potentes. (He kisses* MASHA.)

IRINA: But you gave it to me already, for Easter.

KULYGIN: *(laughing)* Really? Then, give it back, or no, better yet, give it to the Colonel. Here, Colonel. Read it when you have nothing else to do.

VERSHININ: Thank you. *(He prepares to leave.)* I am so happy to have met you.

OLGA: You're leaving? Oh, no. No.

IRINA: You'll stay to lunch. Please. Stay.

OLGA: Please do stay.

VERSHININ: *(bowing)* It seems I dropped in on a name day. Forgive me. I didn't know. I haven't congratulated you. *(He follows* OLGA *into the hall.)*

KULYGIN: Today, my friends, is Sunday—day of rest. Therefore let us rest, and amuse ourselves—each according to his age and station. In summer, it is appropriate to take up the rugs, to store them in mothballs until winter. The Romans enjoyed good health because they knew how to work, and how to rest. *Mens sana in corpore sano.* Roman life followed a fixed form. Our high school principal says form is essential to life—that which loses its form is doomed. That's true in our lives too. *(Laughing, he puts his arm around* MASHA's *waist.)* Masha loves me. My wife loves me. And the curtains leave with the rugs. Today, I'm cheerful, in a wonderful mood. Masha dear, at four we go to the principal's house. There's a nature walk for teachers and their families.

MASHA: I'm not going.

KULYGIN: *(vexed)* Masha, why not?

MASHA: We'll talk about it later. *(with anger)* Oh, alright, I'll go. Just leave me alone now, please. *(She moves off.)*

KULYGIN: We'll spend the evening with the principal. Despite ill health, our principal makes being social his first duty—an excellent man, a luminous personality. Yesterday, after a meeting, he said to me, "I'm tired, Fyodor Ilyich, I'm tired." *(He looks at the clock, then consults his watch.)* Your clock is seven minutes fast. He said to me, "I'm tired."

(A violin is heard playing offstage.)

OLGA: My friends, come eat now, please. Lunch is ready. We're having pirog!

KULYGIN: Dear, dear Olga—yesterday I worked from morning 'til almost midnight. I was exhausted. But today, dear Olga, I'm happy.

(He goes into the main hall. CHEBUTYKIN *puts his newspaper into his pocket, combs his beard.)*

CHEBUTYKIN: We're having pirog? Perfect.

MASHA: *(to* CHEBUTYKIN, *severely)* But be careful— there's to be no drinking today. Do you understand? It does you no good.

CHEBUTYKIN: Oh, come, come. That's all over. It's two years since I've been drunk. *(impatiently)* And besides, dear little girl, what difference does it make?

MASHA: I don't care. I forbid you to drink—I forbid it. *(With anger, but lowering her voice so her husband doesn't hear.)* Another evening at the principal's! The hell with it.

TUZENBACH: If I were you, I wouldn't go. I just wouldn't go.

CHEBUTYKIN: That's right, my sweet—don't go.

MASHA: Oh, of course—don't go... What a damned, unbearable life...

(She goes into the main hall.)

CHEBUTYKIN: *(following her)* Come, come.

SOLYONY: *(going into the main hall)* Here, tsik, tsik, tsik.

TUZENBACH: Enough, Vasily Vasilyevich. Stop it, now!

SOLYONY: Here, tsik, tsik, tsik.

KULYGIN: *(cheerfully)* To your health, Colonel. I'm a professor, and in this house I'm at home. I'm Masha's husband. Masha's a kind woman, very kind...

VERSHININ: I'd like to taste that dark vodka. *(He drinks.)* To your health. *(to* OLGA*)* I feel so at home here, so well.

(In the sitting room, IRINA *and* TUZENBACH *are alone.)*

IRINA: What a mood Masha's in. She married him at eighteen, thinking he was the cleverest man. She doesn't think so now. He's kind, but as for being clever...

OLGA: *(impatiently)* Andrei, will you come now?

ANDREI: *(from offstage)* I'm coming. *(He comes in, goes toward the table.)*

TUZENBACH: What are you thinking about?

IRINA: Nothing much. I don't like your Solyony. He frightens me. He only talks nonsense.

TUZENBACH: He's strange, pitiful and irritating—mostly pitiful. Maybe he's shy. When we're alone, he can be intelligent, even pleasant. But when we're with other people he becomes rude and aggressive. Stay here while they seat themselves. Let me be near you. What are you thinking about? *(pause)* You're twenty. I'm not even thirty. We have years ahead of us, a long line of days—each filled with my love for you.

IRINA: Don't talk to me about love, Nicolai Lvovich.

TUZENBACH: *(not listening to her)* I'm so thirsty for life—for the struggle, the work. That thirst is like my love for you, Irina. You're so beautiful. Life seems so beautiful. What are you thinking about?

IRINA: Is life beautiful? Maybe. But maybe you're wrong. For us three sisters—life hasn't been beautiful yet. It's stifled us like a weed. You see—tears. No need for that... *(She quickly wipes her eyes, smiling.)* We must work. We must work. If we're sad and see life darkly, it's because we don't work. We're born of people who had only contempt for work. *(NATASHA enters. She wears a pink dress with a green belt.)*

NATASHA: They're sitting down already... I'm late... *(She glances furtively in the mirror, fixes her hair.)* My hair's not too bad... *(seeing IRINA)* Dear Irina Sergeyvna—all my congratulations. *(She kisses her effusively again and again.)* You have so many guests. I'm embarrassed... Hello, Baron.

(OLGA comes back into the sitting room.)

OLGA: Ah, here's Natalya Ivanovna. Hello, dear.

(They kiss.)

NATASHA: Congratulations. You have so many guests—it makes me feel shy.

OLGA: Come, come, they're only friends. *(lowering her voice, alarmed)* But, my dear, that green belt—it's not right.

NATASHA: Is it bad luck?

OLGA: No, but it doesn't go with... It looks odd...

NATASHA: *(in a teary voice)* Oh, it's not really that green. It's really a dull green.

(She follows OLGA *into the main hall. Everyone sits at table. No one is left in the sitting room.)*

KULYGIN: Irina dear, I hope you'll find a good fiance soon. It's time you were married.

CHEBUTYKIN: And you too, Natalya Ivanovna. I wish you a good little fiance.

KULYGIN: Natalya Ivanovna already has a good little fiance.

MASHA: *(hitting a plate with a fork)* Well, let's drink. Life is beautiful. To hell with tomorrow.

KULYGIN: C minus for manners.

VERSHININ: This is excellent. What did you put in it?

SOLYONY: Cockroaches.

IRINA: *(tearfully)* Ugh, that's disgusting.

OLGA: Tonight we're having roast turkey and apple tart. I'm home all day today, thank God, and tonight. Come back tonight, my friends.

VERSHININ: And—may I come back too?

IRINA: Please.

NATASHA: They don't stand on ceremony here.

CHEBUTYKIN: Love—we are made only for love. *(He laughs.)*

ANDREI: *(angry)* Stop. Gentlemen, aren't you tired of that yet?

(FEDOTIK and RODE *enter carrying a large basket of flowers.)*

FEDOTIK: Oh, they're already having lunch.

RODE: *(in a loud voice, mispronouncing his r's)* They're having lunch. Yes, so they are.

FEDOTIK: Just a moment. *(He takes a photograph.)* That's one. Good. One more. *(He takes another photograph.)* That's two. Good. That's it. *(They take the basket into the main hall where they are greeted loudly.)*

RODE: *(in a loud voice)* Congratulations—all the best. It's delicious out today, marvelous. I walked all morning with my students, teaching them gymnastics.

FEDOTIK: You can move, Irina Sergeyvna—it's alright. *(He takes a photograph.)* You look very pretty today. *(He takes a spinning top out of his pocket.)* This top, by the way, makes a remarkable sound.

IRINA: Oh, how pretty!

MASHA: "By the curved seashore, an oak tree greening. Wound 'round that oak, a golden chain..." *(plaintively)* Why do I keep saying that? It's been going through my mind since morning...

KULYGIN: We're thirteen at table!

RODE: *(loudly)* Might you be given to superstition, ladies and gentlemen? *(laughter)*

KULYGIN: If we are thirteen at table, it's because we have lovers among us. Are you one of them, Ivan Romanyich? *(laughter)*

CHEBUTYKIN: Me—I'm an old sinner. But why does Natalya Ivanovna look disturbed? Is there something I don't know? *(General laughter.* NATASHA *leaves the table, runs into the sitting room.* ANDREI *follows her.)*

ANDREI: Come, don't pay any attention. Wait. Stop, please.

NATASHA: I'm ashamed. I don't know what's the matter with me. They're laughing at me. I know I shouldn't leave the table like that, but I don't know... I can't... I can't... *(She covers her face with her hands.)*

ANDREI: My darling, please calm down. They're only joking. I promise you, they have only the best of intentions. My dear, my sweet, they're good people. They have kind hearts, they love us very much. Come over by the window where they can't see us... *(He looks around him.)*

NATASHA: I'm not accustomed to going out into society!

ANDREI: Oh youth, wonderful youth! My little one, my baby, my sweet baby—calm down. Trust me. I feel so happy, full of love, full of— No, no one can see us, no one. How have I come to love you so much—since when? Oh, I don't know anything. My darling, you're so pure, good. I love you. Be my wife. I love you, I love you as I've never...never...

(They kiss. Two OFFICERS *enter. Seeing the couple they stop, stupefied.)*

Curtain

ACT II

Same setting. Eight o'clock at night. We faintly hear sounds of an accordion coming from the street. No light. NATALYA IVANOVNA *enters in a dressing gown, holding a candle. She stops by the door of Andrei's room.*

NATASHA: What are you doing, Andryusha? Reading? No, it's nothing— I don't want to bother you. *(She opens another door. She looks inside. She closes it again.)* No—no light.

(ANDREI enters, a book in hand.)

ANDREI: What is it, Natasha?

NATASHA: I'm checking to see no candles are left burning. Servants forget everything at carnival time. We have to watch them—make sure nothing happens. At midnight yesterday I went by the dining room, and saw a candle burning. I asked who'd left it. Of course no one would say. *(She puts the candle on the table.)* What time is it?

(ANDREI looks at his watch.)

ANDREI: Eight fifteen.

NATASHA: Olga and Irina aren't back. They work so hard, poor lambs— Olga at the teacher's council, Irina at the telegraph office. *(She sighs.)* This morning I said to Irina—Sweetheart, you must take care of yourself. Of course she doesn't listen to me. Eight fifteen, you say? I'm afraid our little Bobik isn't feeling so well. He's so cold. Yesterday he had a fever, and today he's an icicle. I'm frightened for him.

ANDREI: Now, Natasha, there's nothing wrong with the baby.

NATASHA: Still, it would help to put him on a diet. Really, I am frightened. And I was told the carnival maskers are coming at nine. Do they have to come, Andryusha? Darling, it would be much better if they didn't.

ANDREI: I don't know. It's not up to me. They were invited.

NATASHA: This morning when our little one woke up, he looked at me and smiled—he recognized me. Hello, Bobik, hello, my little darling, I said. And you should have heard him laugh. Children understand everything, absolutely everything. Andryusha, I'll tell the servants we won't receive the carnival maskers, alright?

ANDREI: *(hesitating)* But—that's up to my sisters. They're in charge here.

NATASHA: I'll tell them too. They're so understanding. *(She starts to leave.)* We'll have yogurt for dinner. Doctor says if you want to lose weight, eat only yogurt. *(She stops.)* Bobik is so cold. His room is too chilly. Can't we put him in another one—at least until warm weather? Irina's room, for instance, is not humid. It's sunny. It's perfect. I'll tell Irina she can share Olga's room for a while. She's never home during the day anyway. She only sleeps there... *(pause)* Andryusha dear? Say something.

ANDREI: I was thinking about something else... Anyway, I have nothing to say.

NATASHA: There was something I wanted to say. Oh, yes. Ferapont is here from the County Council. He wants to see you.

ANDREI: *(yawning)* Tell him to come in. (NATASHA *goes out.* ANDREI *reads by the light of the candle which* NATASHA *has forgotten.* FERAPONT *comes in wearing an old overcoat with the collar turned up, and a headband around his ears.)* Hello, my friend. What's new?

FERAPONT: The president has sent you a book, and some papers. Here. *(He holds out a book and papers to* ANDREI.*)*

ANDREI: Thank you. Good. But why are you here so late? It's past eight.

FERAPONT: What?

ANDREI: *(raising his voice)* I said, you're here late. It's past eight.

FERAPONT: That's true. But when I came to the house, it was still light. They wouldn't let me up. They said the master's busy. Well, if he's busy, he's busy. I'm in no hurry. *(thinking* ANDREI *asked him something)* What?

ANDREI: No, nothing. *(He looks at the book.)* Tomorrow's Friday. The council doesn't meet. I'll come by anyway. It'll keep me busy. It's too boring at home, too boring... *(pause)* Well, little grandfather, how life changes and plays tricks on us. Today when I was bored, I picked up this old notebook—my university courses. What a laugh. My God, I'm secretary to the County Council, of which Protopopov is president. I'm secretary, and the best I can hope for is to become a member, a member of the County Council—I who dream every night I'm a university professor in Moscow, a famous scholar, the pride of Russia.

FERAPONT: Probably... I can't hear very well...

ANDREI: If you heard better, I wouldn't talk to you. I have to talk to someone. My wife doesn't understand me. And I'm afraid of my sisters,
afraid they'll laugh at me, make me feel ashamed. I don't usually
drink or go to cafes, but, my friend, what I wouldn't give to spend
just one hour at Testov's, or at the Great Muscovite in Moscow.

FERAPONT: I hear—some contractor told the council—in Moscow the
merchants eat pancakes. One merchant ate forty pancakes. He
died. Maybe forty, maybe fifty. I don't remember.

ANDREI: In Moscow you sit in a huge restaurant where no one knows
you, and you don't know anyone—but you don't feel alone. Here
you know everyone, everyone knows you—but you feel as lonely as
a stranger, as lonely as a stranger...

FERAPONT: What? *(pause)* That same contractor said—only maybe he
was lying—they stretched a cable across the whole of Moscow.

ANDREI: What for?

FERAPONT: I don't know. The contractor said it.

ANDREI: Nonsense. *(He leafs through the book.)* Have you ever been to
Moscow?

FERAPONT: *(after a silence)* No. Never. It's not God's will. *(pause)* Can I
go now?

ANDREI: Yes. Take care. (FERAPONT *goes out.*) Take care now. *(He reads.)*
Come back in the morning for these papers... You may go... *(pause)*
Well. He's gone. *(The doorbell rings.)* So. That's how it is.
*(He stretches, goes unhurriedly into his room. Offstage a nurse sings a
lullabye to put the child to sleep.* MASHA *and* VERSHININ *enter. As they
speak, a maid lights a lamp and some candles.)*

MASHA: I don't know. *(pause)* I don't know. Yes, it may, in part, be habit.
After Papa died, for example, it took a while to get used to having
no orderlies in the house. But apart from that, however it may be
anywhere else, it's obvious to me that in this town at least, the
noblest, the finest, and most educated people are the military officers.

VERSHININ: I'm thirsty. I'd like some tea.

MASHA: *(glancing at her watch)* They'll bring it soon. I was married at
eighteen, in awe of my husband. He was a teacher, and I'd just finished school, so to me he seemed terribly important and smart.
Now, unfortunately, I don't feel that way.

VERSHININ: Yes. Of course.

MASHA: But I'm used to him—I don't mean him. Most civilians here are coarse, dry, and uneducated. Coarseness sickens me—I feel assaulted by it. I suffer when I feel a lack of refinement, tenderness, or kindness around me. When I'm unlucky enough to have to be around teachers, my husband's colleagues, I'm miserable.

VERSHININ: Yes...But civilian or military, they're all the same in this town, all the same. Just listen to the educated people here. Everything exasperates them—their wives, homes, land, horses—everything. The Russian worships philosophical thinking and ideals. But why does he live in such a mediocre way? Why, hmmm?

MASHA: Why?

VERSHININ: Why can't he bear being around his wife or children? Why can't his wife or children bear being around him?

MASHA: You're feeling low today.

VERSHININ: That's possible. I've eaten nothing since this morning. One of my daughters is sick. When my little ones are sick I become anxious. I feel remorse for having given them such a mother. If you could only have heard her this morning. She has no common sense. We started fighting at seven. I left at nine, slamming the door. (pause) I never talk about it. It's strange—I complain only to you. (He kisses her hand.) Don't be angry at me. I have only you, only you in the world... (pause)

MASHA: That noise in the stove... Just before Papa's death the stove made the same noise—the same noise.

VERSHININ: Are you superstitious?

MASHA: Yes.

VERSHININ: That's strange. (He kisses her hand.) You're a wonderful woman, magnificent—just wonderful, magnificent! It's dark in here, but I can see your eyes shining.

MASHA: (changing seats) There's more light over here.

VERSHININ: I love, I love, I love—I love your eyes, your way of moving. I dream about you. You're wonderful, magnificent!

MASHA: (laughing softly) When you talk like that, it makes me want to laugh—and it frightens me. Stop, please stop. (in a low voice) No, say it. I don't care. (She covers her face with her hands.) I don't care. Someone's coming. Talk about something else.

(IRINA *and* TUZENBACH *enter from the hall.*)

TUZENBACH: I have a triple name. I'm Baron Tuzenbach Krone-Alt-schauer. But I'm Russian and Orthodox—just like you. There's nothing German about me, except maybe my patience, and my stubbornness in insisting on annoying you by walking you home every night.

IRINA: I'm so tired.

TUZENBACH: I'll meet you at the telegraph office and walk you home every night for ten years, twenty years—unless you chase me away. (*seeing* MASHA *and* VERSHININ, *joyously*) It's you. Good evening.

IRINA: Home at last. (*to* MASHA) A woman came to send a telegram to her brother in Saratov—to tell him her son died today. She couldn't remember his address. She said just send it to Saratov. She made me send it there with no street address. And I was rude to her, for no reason. I said, you're wasting my time. She cried. I was so stupid. Are the carnival maskers coming tonight?

MASHA: Yes.

IRINA: (*falls into an armchair*) I have to rest. I'm tired.

TUZENBACH: (*smiling*) When you come home from work you look like a little unhappy child. (*pause*)

IRINA: I'm tired. I don't like the telegraph office. I don't, no.

MASHA: You've lost weight... (*She gives a little whistle.*) It makes you look younger, like a street urchin.

TUZENBACH: It's her hair.

IRINA: I have to find other work. This work is not good for me. It lacks everything I've ever wanted. It's work without poetry, without spirit... (*Someone knocks on the floor.*) It's the doctor. (*to* TUZENBACH) Knock back for me, please... I can't move anymore... I'm too tired... (TUZENBACH *knocks on the floor.*) He's coming up. We must do something. Yesterday the doctor and Andrei played again, and they lost. Andrei lost two hundred rubles.

MASHA: (*indifferently*) So, what can we do about it?

IRINA: He lost two weeks ago, and he lost in December. If only he'd lose everything fast then we could leave. My God, I dream of Moscow every night. I'm going crazy. (*She laughs.*) We're leaving in June. There's still February, March, April, and May—almost half a year!

MASHA: Let's hope Natasha doesn't find out he lost.

IRINA: I don't think she cares.

> (CHEBUTYKIN *enters. He just woke up from his after-dinner nap. He combs his beard, sits at the table in the main hall, pulls a newspaper from his pocket.*)

MASHA: There he is. Has he paid his rent?

IRINA: (*laughing*) No, not a kopeck for eight months. He's probably forgotten.

MASHA: (*laughing*) He looks so important!

> (*General laughter. A pause.*)

IRINA: Why don't you say something, Alexander Ignatyevich?

VERSHININ: I don't know. I'd like some tea. I'd give my life for a glass of tea. I've had nothing since this morning...

CHEBUTYKIN: Irina Sergeyvna!

IRINA: What?

CHEBUTYKIN: Come here. *Venez ici!* (IRINA *goes to him, sits at the table.*) I can't do anything without you.

> (IRINA *lays out the cards for a game of patience.*)

VERSHININ: Well, if there's no tea, at least let's talk.

TUZENBACH: Let's talk. About what?

VERSHININ: About what? For instance, let's imagine life in two or three hundred years.

TUZENBACH: Well, maybe we'll fly in balloons, the cut of jackets will be different, we'll have discovered a sixth sense, maybe even developed it—I don't know. But life will be the same—difficult, full of unknowns, and happy. In a thousand years, just like today, people will sigh and say, oh, how hard it is to be alive. They'll still be scared of death, and won't want to die.

VERSHININ: (*after a moment of thought*) How to explain? It seems to me everything does change, little by little. It's changing in front of our eyes. In a century or two, or in a millennium, people will live in a new way, a happier way. We won't be there to see it—but it's why we live, why we work. It's why we suffer. We're creating it. That's the purpose of our existence. The only happiness we can know is to work toward that goal.

> (MASHA *laughs softly.*)

TUZENBACH: Why are you laughing?

MASHA: I don't know. I've been laughing since this morning.

VERSHININ: I studied the same subjects you did. I didn't just go to military school. I read. Of course, maybe I didn't choose the right books, maybe I should have read something else. The more I live, the more I want to know. My hair's turning white, soon I'll be old—and yet I know so little, so little. But I believe I know the essential, and I know it without doubt. How to explain? There isn't, there can't be happiness for us. We'll never know happiness. For us there's only work, only work. Happiness is for our distant descendants. *(pause)* Not for me but for my children's children, or for their children.

(FEDOTIK and RODE appear in the main hall. They sit, start to sing softly, accompanying themselves on the guitar.)

TUZENBACH: So, according to you, I can't even dream of happiness? But what if I am happy?

VERSHININ: You aren't.

TUZENBACH: *(throwing up his hands, laughing)* Well, clearly, we don't agree. How can I convince you? *(MASHA laughs softly. He points at her.)* Well, laugh if you want. *(to VERSHININ)* Life will be the same not only in two hundred years, but in a million years. Life doesn't change. It remains the same. It conforms to its own laws, and those laws don't concern us. We can't know them anyway. Migrant birds, cranes for instance, must fly. Whatever sublime or insignificant thoughts cranes may have—they fly, they fly on, migrate. Cranes don't know why or where they're flying. They fly, and they will fly. If there are philosopher cranes, they can philosophize—as long as they fly.

MASHA: So, what does that mean?

TUZENBACH: Mean? Look, it's snowing. What does that mean? *(pause)*

MASHA: It seems to me a person must have a purpose, or be looking for one. Otherwise life is empty—empty... We can live not knowing why cranes fly, why children are born, or why there are stars in the sky— but we have to know why we live. Otherwise life is meaningless, silly. *(pause)*

VERSHININ: Yes—and sad when youth is over.

MASHA: As Gogol says, "Ladies and gentlemen, to live in this world is boring."

TUZENBACH: And as I say, ladies and gentlemen—to win an argument with you is impossible. That's enough. I give up.

CHEBUTYKIN: *(reading a newspaper)* Balzac was married in Berdichev. *(IRINA hums softly.)* We'll make a note of that. *(He makes a note in his notebook.)* Balzac was married in Berdichev. *(He goes back to his reading.)*

IRINA: *(completing a game of patience, dreamily)* Balzac was married in Berdichev.

TUZENBACH: The die is cast. Do you know, Maria Sergeyvna, that I've handed in my resignation?

MASHA: I've heard. I'm not cheering. I don't like civilians.

TUZENBACH: Too bad. *(He gets up.)* I don't look like a soldier anyway, do I? I'm not handsome. Well, so what? I'll work. For the first time in my life, I'll work 'til I drop. And when I get home, I'll sleep like a log. *(He goes toward the main hall.)* Workers must sleep very well.

FEDOTIK: *(to IRINA)* I bought you some colored pencils at Pyzhikov's on Moscow Street. And this little knife...

IRINA: You still treat me like a child. I'm grown up. *(She takes the pencils and the knife, joyously.)* Oh, how pretty!

FEDOTIK: This knife I bought for myself. Look—one blade, two, this for cleaning your ears, little scissors, and a nail file...

RODE: *(in a loud voice)* Doctor, how old are you?

CHEBUTYKIN: Me? Thirty-two.

(laughter)

FEDOTIK: I'll teach you a different solitaire.

(He spreads out the cards. They bring in the samovar. ANFISA settles herself next to it. NATASHA arrives, fusses around the table. SOLYONY enters. After greeting everyone, he sits at the table.)

VERSHININ: There's a wind today.

MASHA: I'm tired of winter. I've forgotten what summer's like.

IRINA: It's going to work out. I can see it— We're going to Moscow!

FEDOTIK: No, you're not. See—the eight's covering the two of spades. *(He laughs.)* It won't work out. I don't think you'll go to Moscow.

CHEBUTYKIN: *(reading)* Several cases of smallpox in Tsitsikar.

ANFISA: *(approaching MASHA)* Come have some tea, Masha my little one.

(to VERSHININ*)* You too, your honor... Forgive me, I've forgotten your name.

MASHA: Bring the tea here, Nanny dear. I don't want to go over there.

IRINA: Nanny dear.

ANFISA: Coming.

NATASHA: *(to* SOLYONY*)* Babies understand everything perfectly. Hello, I said to my little Bobik. Hel-lo, darling, I said. And he gave me a look. He did. I suppose you think that's just a mother talking. But I tell you he's exceptional. He is.

SOLYONY: If that child were mine—I'd roast him and eat him. *(He goes into the sitting room, his glass of tea in his hand. He sits in a corner.)*

NATASHA: *(covering her face with her hands)* Oh, how crude!

MASHA: If I lived in Moscow, I wouldn't care about the weather. When you're happy, you don't care about the weather.

VERSHININ: I just read the journals of a French minister sentenced for the Panama Affair. He writes with ecstasy and passion about the birds he sees outside the window of his prison cell. Before, he'd never noticed birds. Now he's free, probably back to his old ways—and to hell with birds. You'll be like him. When you're living in Moscow, you probably won't even notice it. There's no happiness for us. Happiness doesn't exist. We can only want it.

TUZENBACH: *(picking up a box from the table)* Where are the bon-bons?

IRINA: Solyony ate them.

TUZENBACH: All of them?

ANFISA: *(bringing the tea)* A letter for you, your honor, dear.

VERSHININ: For me? *(He takes the letter.)* It's from my daughter. *(He reads.)* Of course. Again. Excuse me, Maria Sergeyvna I'll just slip out. I won't have tea. *(He gets up, disturbed.)* Same old story.

MASHA: What is it? If I'm not being too —

VERSHININ: *(lowering his voice)* My wife has swallowed poison again. I have to go. I'll just slip out. How painful it all is. *(He kisses* MASHA*'s hand.)* My dear Masha—so sweet and good. I'll just slip out. *(He goes out.)*

ANFISA: Where? Where's he going now? His tea is here. Where's he going, I—

MASHA: *(angrily)* Stop nagging. Leave me alone. *(She goes with her cup of tea toward the big table.)* Tiresome old woman.

ANFISA: Why are you angry, my darling?

ANDREI'S VOICE: Anfisa!

ANFISA: *(imitating him)* Anfisa! He never lifts a finger, that one.

MASHA: *(in the main hall, angrily)* Will you make room here, please? *(She disturbs the cards on the table.)* You're always playing cards. Why don't you have tea?

IRINA: You're being mean, Mashka.

MASHA: Then don't talk to me. Just leave me alone.

CHEBUTYKIN: *(laughing)* Just leave her alone. Just leave her alone.

MASHA: And you—at sixty you're like a child always talking nonsense about God knows what.

NATASHA: *(sighing)* Masha, the way you talk! With your looks, my dear, you'd go far in Society—but, I can tell you, not with that way of talking. *Pardonnez-moi, Marie, je vous en prie, mais vous avez des manieres un peu grossieres.*

TUZENBACH: *(stifling a laugh)* I'd like some... um, I think, some cognac. I'd like some...

NATASHA: *Il parait que mon Bobik ne dort deja pas.* He's awake. My little Bobik isn't feeling well today. I am going to see him now. Excuse me. *(She goes out.)*

IRINA: And Alexander Ignatyevich? Where's he gone?

MASHA: Home. His wife is acting up again.

    (TUZENBACH goes to join SOLYONY, a small decanter of cognac in his hand.)

TUZENBACH: Here you are. Always alone in your corner, ruminating on God knows what. Shall we make peace? Let's have some cognac. *(They drink.)* I suppose I'll be at the piano all night, playing whatever they want. God knows that's fine with me.

SOLYONY: Why make peace? Are we having a fight?

TUZENBACH: It seems to me there's something going on between us. Or you have a strange personality.

SOLYONY: *(he recites)* "I am a strange one, who is not? Do not be angry at me, Aleko."

TUZENBACH: Who's Aleko? What does he have to do with it?

SOLYONY: Alone with someone, I'm just like everyone else. In a group I feel isolated and tongue-tied, so I say whatever comes to mind. But I'm a man of honor, and ready to prove it.

TUZENBACH: Well, I'm angry with you. When we're with people, you're always pestering me. But I like you, God knows why. I want to get drunk today. And so what? Drink up!

SOLYONY: Drink up! *(They drink.)* I have nothing against you personally, Baron. But I've been told I have the character of Lermontov. *(lowering his voice)* I've been told I even look like Lermontov. *(He takes a perfume vial from his pocket, sprinkles some perfume on his hands.)*

TUZENBACH: I handed in my resignation. Basta! It's done. I hesitated five years, and now it's done. I'll work.

SOLYONY: *(reciting)* "Do not be angry with me, Aleko. Forget, oh forget your dreams..."
(During their conversation ANDREI *enters noiselessly, carrying a book. He sits near a candle.)*

TUZENBACH: I'll work.

CHEBUTYKIN: *(coming into the sitting room with* IRINA) Then they treated us to a real Caucasian banquet—onion soup and chekhartma roast.

SOLYONY: Cheremsha isn't meat. It's a plant, of the same genus as the onion.

CHEBUTYKIN: No, no, my angel. Chekhartma isn't onion—it's roast lamb.

SOLYONY: I say cheremsha is onion.

CHEBUTYKIN: And I repeat—chekhartma is roast lamb.

SOLYONY: Cheremsha is onion.

CHEBUTYKIN: Why argue with you? You've never even been to the Caucasus. You've never eaten chekhartma.

SOLYONY: No, I hate it! Cheremsha stinks of garlic.

ANDREI: *(pleading)* Enough, friends! Please!

TUZENBACH: When are the carnival maskers coming?

IRINA: They said nine. It must be time.

TUZENBACH: *(putting an arm around* ANDREI, *singing)* "My little porch, my little porch, my own little porch of mine."

ANDREI: *(dancing and singing)* "My little porch, made of wood, made of wood."

CHEBUTYKIN: "My little porch, all shingled with maple wood."
(*laughter*)

TUZENBACH: (*kissing* ANDREI) What the hell, drink up. Andryusha, we'll drink to you, my darling. I'll follow you to Moscow, Andryusha—to the university.

SOLYONY: Which one? There are two universities in Moscow.

ANDREI: No, only one.

SOLYONY: I say there are two.

ANDREI: Well, three if you like. The more, the merrier.

SOLYONY: There are two universities in Moscow. (*murmuring, hissing*) Two—the old one and the new one. But if you refuse to listen to me, if I irritate you—I'll shut up. I'll go—to the next room. (*He goes out by one of the doors.*)

TUZENBACH: Bravo, bravo! (*He laughs.*) Start, my friends. I'm at the piano. Funny fellow, that Solyony. (*He plays a waltz.*)

MASHA: (*waltzing alone*) The Baron is drunk, the Baron is drunk, the Baron is drunk!

(NATASHA *enters.*)

NATASHA: (*to* CHEBUTYKIN) Ivan Romanyich!

(*She talks into his ear, then goes out noiselessly.* CHEBUTYKIN *touches* TUZENBACH's *shoulder, whispers to him.*)

IRINA: What is it?

CHEBUTYKIN: It seems it's time for us to leave. Take care of yourselves.

TUZENBACH: Good night. It's time to go.

IRINA: What happened? What about the carnival maskers?

ANDREI: (*embarrassed*) There won't be any carnival maskers. You see, my dear, Natasha says Bobik isn't feeling well, so... Anyway, I don't know anything about it. It doesn't matter to me.

IRINA: (*shrugging*) Well, if Bobik isn't well...

MASHA: Too bad for us. We're driven out, we leave. (*to* IRINA) Bobik's not sick, she is. See? (*She taps her forehead with her finger, indicating* NATASHA *is deranged.*) Little petty bourgeois bitch!

(ANDREI *goes into his room.* CHEBUTYKIN *follows him. The others say goodbye in the main hall.*)

FEDOTIK: That's too bad. I'd been looking forward to spending the evening here, but, of course, if the child is sick—I'll bring him a toy tomorrow...

RODE: *(in a loud voice)* I took a nap after dinner, on purpose. I thought we'd dance all night. It's only nine!

MASHA: Come out into the street. We'll talk there, decide what to do.

(From offstage we hear "goodbye," and "take care of yourself," and TUZENBACH's *gay laugh. All are gone.* ANFISA *and the maid clear the table, put out the lights. We hear the wet nurse singing.* ANDREI *enters quietly, dressed to go out.* CHEBUTYKIN *is talking to him.)*

CHEBUTYKIN: I had no time to marry. Life went by too fast—in a flash. Of course I loved your mother madly, but she was married...

ANDREI: One shouldn't get married. It's boring.

CHEBUTYKIN: Maybe, but loneliness—no matter how you look at it—is horrible, my dove. Although, in the end... of course, it's all the same.

ANDREI: Let's go out quickly.

CHEBUTYKIN: Why hurry? There's time.

ANDREI: I'm afraid my wife will stop me.

CHEBUTYKIN: Ah! I see.

ANDREI: I won't gamble tonight. I'll just look. I don't feel well. What should I take for shortness of breath, Ivan Romanyich?

CHEBUTYKIN: Why ask me? How should I know? I don't remember, my darling.

ANDREI: We'll go out through the kitchen.

(They go out. The bell rings once, then again. Voices, laughter.)

IRINA: *(entering)* What is it?

ANFISA: *(whispering)* The carnival maskers.

(The bell rings again.)

IRINA: Nanny dear, tell them we're out. All of us. Ask them to forgive us.

(ANFISA goes out. IRINA *paces, thinking. agitated.* SOLYONY *enters.)*

SOLYONY: *(surprised)* No one? Where did they go?

IRINA: Home.

SOLYONY: That's strange. Are you alone?

IRINA: Alone. *(pause)* Goodbye.

SOLYONY: I behaved badly. I behaved without tact. But you're not like the others. You're pure. You see the truth. You understand me—only you. I love you—profoundly, infinitely.

IRINA: Goodbye! Go.

SOLYONY: I can't live without you. (*He follows her.*) Oh, my happiness! (*through tears*) Those incredible eyes. How marvelous they are, astonishing—I've never seen anything like them.

IRINA: (*coldly*) That's enough, Vasily Vasilyevich!

SOLYONY: I'm speaking of my love to you for the first time! I'm not on earth anymore. I'm on a different planet. (*He rubs his forehead.*) Well, never mind. One can't force a person to love. But I will not allow any rival to win you—never! I swear by all that's holy—I'll kill any rival... Oh, my beautiful one.

(NATASHA *crosses the stage carrying a candle. She half opens and looks through a door, then another. She passes in front of her husband's room.*)

NATASHA: Andrei's in his room. We'll let him read. Excuse me, Vasily Vasilyevich, I didn't know you were here. I'm in my nightgown...

SOLYONY: So what? Goodbye. (*He goes out.*)

NATASHA: Poor little Irina, you look so tired. (*She kisses* IRINA.) You should go to bed earlier.

IRINA: Is Bobik asleep?

NATASHA: Yes, but he's not well. By the way, dear, there's something I've been wanting to talk to you about, but either you're not home, or I'm busy. Bobik's room is too cold, too damp. Yours would be better for him. And, darling, you can stay with Olya-dear.

IRINA: (*who doesn't understand*) Where?

(*The little bells of a troika are heard stopping in front of the house.*)

NATASHA: You'll share Olya's room, and Bobik will have yours. He's so adorable. Today I said to him, you're mine, Bobik, you're mine. And he looked at me with those pretty little eyes. (*The bell rings.*) It's probably Olga. She comes in so late. (*The* MAID *approaches* NATASHA, *speaks into her ear.*) Protopopov? What a funny fellow! It's Protopopov. He's come to invite me for a troika ride. (*She laughs.*) Men are so funny. (*The bell rings.*) Is someone here? Shall I go? Just for a fifteen minute ride? (*to the* MAID) Tell him I'm coming. (*The bell rings.*) That must be Olga.

(*She goes out. The maid goes out too, running.* IRINA, *in an armchair, thinks.* OLGA, KULYGIN, *and* VERSHININ *enter.*)

KULYGIN: What's happening? I heard there was a party here.

VERSHININ: How strange. When I left half an hour ago, carnival maskers were expected...

IRINA: Everyone left.

KULYGIN: Masha too? Where is she? And Protopopov—why is he waiting downstairs with a troika? Who's he waiting for?

IRINA: Don't ask so many questions... I'm tired.

KULYGIN: My, aren't we nervous...

OLGA: The meeting just now finished. I'm half dead. The head-mistress is sick, and I'm taking her place. My head—my head hurts, my poor head. *(She sits.)* Yesterday Andrei lost two hundred rubles gambling. The whole town is talking about it.

KULYGIN: Me too. The meeting tired me too. *(He sits down.)*

VERSHININ: My wife just wanted to scare me. She almost poisoned herself, but it's alright now. I'm happy, I'm released. So, we have to go? Too bad. I wish you sweet dreams. Fyodor Ilyich, let's go somewhere—the two of us. I can't stay at home, it's not possible. Come.

KULYGIN: I'm too tired, I can't go anywhere. *(He gets up.)* Tired. Has my wife gone home?

IRINA: Probably.

KULYGIN: *(kissing* IRINA*'s hand)* Goodbye. Tomorrow and the day after, I can rest all day. Good night. *(He gets ready to leave.)* I would like to have tea! I counted on an evening in good company. *Fallacem hominum spem*—accusative case with exclamation points.

VERSHININ: So, I'll go alone. *(He goes out with* KULYGIN, *whistling.)*

OLGA: My head hurts—hurts, hurts. Andrei lost... Everyone's talking about it... I'm going to bed. Tomorrow I'm free. Oh God, what happiness. Free tomorrow, free the day after. My head, my poor head. *(She goes out.)*

IRINA: *(alone)* All gone. No one left.

(An accordion is heard playing from the street. The wet nurse sings. NATASHA, *in fur coat and hat, crosses the hall, followed by the maid.)*

NATASHA: I'll be back in half an hour. I'm just going for a little ride. *(She goes out.)*

IRINA: *(alone, suddenly very sad)* To Moscow, to Moscow! To Moscow!

Curtain

Olga and Irina's room, with beds behind screens on the left and right. It is two or three in the morning. Evidently no one has yet gone to bed. We hear the alarm sounding for a fire in town which has been burning for some time. MASHA, wearing black as usual, is lying on the couch. OLGA and ANFISA enter.

ANFISA: They're sitting by the stairs. I said to them, please come upstairs—don't just sit there. But they just sit, and they cry, "Where's Papa? He might have burned up, God help him." What a thing to think! And there are people in the courtyard too—half naked.

OLGA: *(taking clothes out of the closet)* Take this gray one, this one too, this blouse, and the skirt, Nanny dear. My God, how dreadful—all Little Kirsanov Street burned down. Here, take this one too. *(She throws another dress into her arms.)* Those poor Vershinins, so frightened—their house nearly burned. They must stay here. We can't let them leave. Poor Fedotik. He's lost everything—he has nothing left now...

ANFISA: Please call Ferapont, Olyushka. I can't carry all this.

OLGA: *(ringing)* No one's answering tonight... *(She calls from the door.)* Come here. Anyone. Come! *(Through the open door we see the red glow of the fire. We hear the firemen's wagon passing the house.)* It's dreadful, it's making me sick! *(FERAPONT enters.)* Here, take all this down. By the stairs you'll see the two Miss Kolotilins. Give them this, and this...

FERAPONT: Yes, Miss. Moscow burned too—in 1812. And, by God, weren't the French surprised?

OLGA: Go now—go.

FERAPONT: Yes, Miss. *(He goes out.)*

OLGA: Give them everything, Nanny dear. What do we need? Give them everything. I'm so tired, I can hardly stand up. Don't let the Vershinins leave. The girls can sleep in the sitting room, and Alexander Ignatyevich downstairs with the Baron. Fedotik too. Or he can stay in the main hall. Of course, as if he'd planned it, the doctor's drunk—totally drunk. So we can't put anyone in with him. And Vershinin's wife—can sleep in the sitting room!

ANFISA: *(wearily)* Olyushka, dear, don't send me away. Please—don't send me away!

OLGA: What are you talking about, Nanny? No one is sending you away.

ANFISA: *(resting her head on* OLGA's *breast)* My treasure, my sweet Olga, I work hard—I work hard, I do. And now when I'm getting feeble—go away, they say. Where do you want me to go? Where can I go? I'm past eighty. I'm almost eighty-two.

OLGA: Sit down, little Nanny. Poor thing, you're tired. *(She makes her sit down.)* Rest, rest, my darling. There. You're so pale!

(NATASHA enters.)

NATASHA: They've asked us to form a Committee to Assist the Homeless. I think it's a good idea. It's the duty of the rich to help the poor. Bobik and little Sophie are asleep, little angels, without a care in the world. There are so many people in the house—everywhere people, in every corner. The house is full of people, and there's flu going around. I'm scared for the children.

OLGA: *(not listening to her)* It's quiet in this room. You can't see the fire.

NATASHA: Yes. My hair must look terrible. *(in front of the mirror)* They say I'm getting fat... It's not true, it's not true! Masha's sleeping. She's tired, poor thing. *(to* ANFISA, *coldly)* I forbid you to sit in my presence! Get up! Get out of here. *(ANFISA goes out. A pause.)* Why do you keep that old woman? I don't understand you.

OLGA: *(stupefied)* Excuse me, but I don't understand you.

NATASHA: She's not needed. She's a peasant—she can go live in the country... She's a luxury. I like order—no unnecessary servants in my house. *(She caresses* OLGA's *cheek.)* My poor lamb, you're tired. Our headmistress is tired. When my Sophie's a big girl, and goes to high school—I'll be frightened of you.

OLGA: I won't be headmistress.

NATASHA: You'll be elected, Olechka. It's been decided.

OLGA: I won't accept. I can't—it's beyond my strength. *(She drinks some water.)* You're so rude to Nanny. Forgive me, but I can't bear it. I can hardly see straight.

NATASHA: *(moved)* Forgive me, Olya, forgive me. I don't mean to hurt you.

(MASHA gets up, takes her pillow, goes out. She looks angry.)

OLGA: My dear, try to understand us. Maybe we had an unusual upbringing, but I can't bear that sort of thing. To treat servants like that makes me ill... I lose heart. It kills me.

NATASHA: Forgive me, forgive me... *(She kisses her.)*

OLGA: Each rudeness, however slight—each harsh word, wounds me.

NATASHA: It's true I often don't think before I speak. But, my dear, you do agree—she could perfectly well live in the country.

OLGA: She's been with us for thirty years.

NATASHA: But she can't work anymore! Either I don't understand you, or you refuse to understand me. She can't work anymore. She just sleeps and rests.

OLGA: So, let her rest.

NATASHA: *(surprised)* What do you mean, let her rest? She's a servant! *(through tears)* I don't understand you, Olya. I have a nursemaid and a wet nurse. We have a housemaid and a cook. What good does that old woman do us? What good does she do us? *(We hear the alarm.)*

OLGA: I've aged ten years tonight.

NATASHA: We must understand each other, Olya. You're at the high school, and I'm at home—you worry about teaching, and I'll take care of the house. When I talk about servants, I know what I'm talking about. I know what I'm talking about! She goes tomorrow, that old thief, that old hag! *(She stamps her feet.)* That witch! No one here has the right to contradict me! No one here has the right to contradict me! *(gaining control of herself)* Listen, if you don't move downstairs, we'll never stop quarreling. It's terrible.

(KULYGIN enters.)

KULYGIN: Where's Masha? It's time to go home. The fire's almost out. *(He stretches.)* Only one neighborhood burned. With this wind, the whole town could've been in flames. *(He sits.)* I'm exhausted. Olechka, my dear, I often say to myself—if there'd been no Masha, I would have married you. You're so good, Olechka. I'm tired. *(He listens.)*

OLGA: What is it?

KULYGIN: As if he'd planned it—the doctor's having an alcoholic fit. He's dead drunk. *(He gets up.)* I think he's coming this way. Do you hear him? He's coming. *(He laughs.)* What a character. I'm hiding. *(He goes toward the armoire, hides in the corner.)* What a devil he is.

OLGA: He didn't drink for two years. Now suddenly he's started again.

(She goes with NATASHA *toward the back of the room.* CHEBUTYKIN *enters. He walks as if he weren't drunk. He crosses the room, stops, looks in front of him, then goes toward the sink, washes his hands.)*

CHEBUTYKIN: *(mournfully)* To hell... To hell with them all... They think I'm a doctor, that I can cure everything. But I remember nothing. I've forgotten everything. I remember nothing, absolutely nothing. *(*OLGA *and* NATASHA *go out without his noticing them.)* To hell with them all. Last Wednesday I treat a woman in Zasypi—and she dies, yes. It's my fault. I knew something, a little something, twenty-five years ago. But now I know nothing, absolutely nothing. Maybe I'm not human. Maybe I just dream I have arms and legs and a head. Maybe I don't exist. Maybe I just dream I walk, eat, and sleep. *(He cries.)* Oh, if only I didn't exist. *(He stops crying. He speaks mournfully.)* To hell with them all. At the club last week someone mentions Shakespeare and Voltaire. I haven't read them, but I pretend I have. And so do the others. Oh, misery—hell. When I think about that woman who died Wednesday because of me, and about everything else—it's too terrible to bear. I'm disgusting. And I drink... drink. I'm disgusting.

*(*IRINA, VERSHININ, *and* TUZENBACH *enter.* TUZENBACH *wears new and elegant civilian clothing.)*

IRINA: Let's stay here. No one will bother us.

VERSHININ: The whole town would have burned without the soldiers. They're good soldiers— *(He rubs his hands together with enthusiasm.)* good people, and good soldiers.

KULYGIN: *(coming from behind the armoire, approaching them)* Excuse me. Gentlemen, can you tell me the time?

TUZENBACH: Nearly four. It's dawn.

IRINA: They're all in the main hall. No one's even thinking of leaving. Your Solyony's there too. *(to* CHEBUTYKIN*)* You should go to bed.

CHEBUTYKIN: It doesn't matter. But thank you. *(He combs his beard.)*

KULYGIN: Drunk as a lord, our Ivan Romanyich. *(He pats him on the shoulder.)* Bravo. As the ancients said, *in vino veritas.*

TUZENBACH: They want me to organize a benefit concert for the homeless.

IRINA: We couldn't do it—who would play?

TUZENBACH: We can do it if we want. In my opinion, Masha plays the
piano beautifully.

KULYGIN: She plays the piano beautifully!

IRINA: But she's forgotten. She hasn't played in three... or four years.

TUZENBACH: Only I understand music in this town. I understand music,
and I swear to you Masha plays well. She has talent.

KULYGIN: You're right, Baron. You're right, of course. I love her very
much, Masha. She's a fine woman.

TUZENBACH: To play like an angel, and to feel that no one, no one understands you...

KULYGIN: *(with a sigh)* Yes. But would it be proper for her to play in a
concert? *(pause)* I don't know, my friends—I don't know. Maybe it
would. But, to be perfectly frank, our principal is a fine person,
very fine, extremely intelligent—but his ideas are a little... Well,
it's not his decision, of course, but, if you like, I'll ask him what he
thinks.

(CHEBUTYKIN *picks up a little porcelain clock, examines it.*)

VERSHININ: I'm so dirty from the fire, I hardly look human. *(pause)* Oh—
I heard yesterday they may transfer the brigade, to Poland, or
Tchita.

TUZENBACH: I heard that too. Well—the town will be deserted.

IRINA: And we'll be leaving too.

CHEBUTYKIN: *(letting the ceramic clock fall and break)* Smithereens. *(A
pause. All seem sad and confused.)*

KULYGIN: *(picking up the debris)* Breaking such a valuable object, Ivan
Romanyich—you deserve less than zero in conduct!

IRINA: Poor Mama's clock.

CHEBUTYKIN: Maybe. Maybe Mama's. Maybe I didn't break it. Maybe it's
all a dream anyway. Maybe we only dream we exist, but we don't.
I don't know. Nobody knows. *(He goes toward the door.)* Why are
you looking at me, all of you? Natasha's having an affair with
Protopopov. You sit there, and don't see that, do you? Natasha's

having an affair with Protopopov. *(He sings.)* "Allow me to offer you this fig …"

VERSHININ: Yes. *(He laughs.)* How strange it all is. *(pause)* The fire starts. I run home. The house is out of danger, but my two little girls stand at the door, half dressed, their mother not there. Near them busy people, horses, barking dogs, and on their little faces—alarm, horror, helplessness, and God knows what else. I see those faces, and my heart stops. My God, I think, what else will they have to bear in their lifetimes, these little ones? I take them and run, thinking— what else will they have to bear in this world? *(We hear the alarm. A pause.)* We arrive here to find their mother screaming and angry. (MASHA *comes in carrying her pillow. She sits on the couch.*) My girls by the front door in their nightgowns, the street glowing red from the fire, and the terrible noises... It makes me think such things happened in the past too—the enemy arrives suddenly, pillaging, burning. But how different, then and now. And soon, in two or three hundred years, they'll view us with the same horror and amazement. What we have will seem to them awkward, heavy, uncomfortable, and strange. What a life they'll have—what a life! *(He laughs.)* Forgive me—there I go again, philosophizing. But indulge me, my friends. I feel very much like philosophizing tonight. *(pause)* It's as if in the midst of sleep for the moment there are only three of you awake in this town. But in the future there'll be more. With you as examples, more and more people will change, become more like you. Finally even you will be surpassed. Others will spring up even better than you. *(He laughs.)* I'm in an extraordinary mood. I feel very much like living. *(He sings.)* "Love, queen of the ages, how sweet her ecstasies..."

MASHA: Tram-tam-tam.

VERSHININ: Tam-tam...

MASHA: Tra-ra-ra.

VERSHININ: Tra-ta-ta...

(He laughs. FEDOTIK *enters.)*

FEDOTIK: *(dancing)* Burned, burned, all burned down! Everything gone! *(laughter)*

IRINA: What's so funny about everything being burned?

FEDOTIK: *(laughing)* Everything, everything burned. Nothing left. My guitar burned, all my photos burned, my letters burned, and the notebook I bought for you—burned.

(SOLYONY enters.)

IRINA: No, Vasily Vasilyevich. Please, go. You can't come in here.

SOLYONY: Why is the Baron allowed in, and I am not?

VERSHININ: Quite right—it's time for all of us to go. How's the fire?

SOLYONY: Seems to be dying down. It's very peculiar the Baron is allowed in here, and I am not.

(He takes a vial of perfume from his pocket, puts some on himself.)

VERSHININ: Tram-tam-tam?

MASHA: Tram-tam.

VERSHININ: *(laughing, to SOLYONY)* Let's go to the main hall.

SOLYONY: We'll remember this. We could press it further now, but "'twould annoy the geese, I fear." *(He looks at TUZENBACH.)* Here, tsik, tsik, tsik...

(SOLYONY, VERSHININ and FEDOTIK go out.)

IRINA: Solyony stinks of tobacco smoke. *(She looks at TUZENBACH with surprise.)* The Baron's sleeping! Baron! Baron!

TUZENBACH: *(waking up)* So tired. The brickyard. No, I'm not delirious. I'm talking about the brickyard. I'm going to work there. I've asked them. *(To IRINA, tenderly.)* You're so pale and beautiful. Enchanting. Your pale face lights up the night. You're sad, unhappy with living. Come with me. Come with me—we'll work together!

MASHA: Nicolai Lvovich, go.

TUZENBACH: *(laughing)* Are you there? I didn't see you. *(He kisses IRINA's hand.)* Goodbye. I'm going. Looking at you, I remember how you were on your name day—it seems so long ago. You were cheerful, happy, talked about the joys of work. And I dreamed of such a happy life. What happened to it? *(He kisses her hand.)* You have tears in your eyes. You should sleep. It's dawn, daybreak. If only I could give my life for you.

MASHA: Go, Nicolai Lvovich. Really. Go! Please...

TUZENBACH: I'm going. *(He goes out.)*

MASHA: *(lying down)* Are you asleep, Fyodor?

KULYGIN: Hunh?

MASHA: Go home.

KULYGIN: My sweet, my precious Masha.

IRINA: She's tired. Let her rest, Fedya.

KULYGIN: I'm going. Now. My wonderful wife, my sweet, my only—I love you.

MASHA: *(with some anger)* Amo, amas, amat, amamus, amatis, amant.

KULYGIN: *(laughing)* She's amazing. Really. I'm her husband seven years, and yet I feel as if we were married yesterday. Really, you're amazing. I'm so happy, I'm so happy, I'm so happy.

MASHA: I'm so bored, I'm so bored, I'm so bored. *(She sits up.)* I can't not think about it. The thought keeps hammering at me. It's revolting. I can't not talk about it. It's Andrei. He's mortgaged the house, and his wife has pocketed the money. But the house belongs to us, all four of us—not just to him. He has to acknowledge that, if he's honest.

KULYGIN: Why talk about it, Masha? It can't help. Andrei's riddled with debts. Leave him alone.

MASHA: Anyway, it's disgusting. *(She lies back down.)*

KULYGIN: We're not poor. I work at the high school, and I tutor. I'm an honest man, simple. *Omnia mea mecum porto.*

MASHA: It's not that I want anything. It's the unfairness that disgusts me. *(pause)* Go, Fyodor.

KULYGIN: *(kissing her)* You're tired. Take a nap for half an hour. I'll be downstairs waiting for you. *(He goes toward the door.)* I'm so happy, I'm so happy, I'm so happy. *(He goes out.)*

IRINA: It's true. Our Andrei has become petty and insignificant. He's aged so with that woman. He wanted to be a university professor. Now he's proud to be a member of the County Council—of which Protopopov is president. The whole town talks about it, laughs. He's the only one who doesn't know. And when everyone runs to the fire, he sits in his room not caring, playing the violin. *(nervously)* Oh it's hideous—hideous, hideous! *(She cries.)* I can't bear any more. I can't. I can't! (OLGA *comes in, starts tidying her dressing table.* IRINA *cries loudly.)* Kill me, I can't bear any more! Kill me!

OLGA: *(frightened)* What is it? Darling!

IRINA: *(sobbing)* Where? Where's it all gone? Oh, God, my God, I've forgotten everything! I can't think straight. I don't even know how to say "window" or "ceiling" in Italian anymore. I'm forgetting more every day. And life is passing—it'll never come back. We'll never, never go to Moscow... I know it—we're never going to leave...

OLGA: My darling... Darling...

IRINA: *(controlling herself)* I'm miserable. I can't work anymore, I don't want to work anymore. I've had enough, enough! First it was the telegraph office, now it's the County Council. I hate and have contempt for everything they make me do there. I'm almost twenty-four. I've worked a long time. My brain is drying out. I'm thinner, uglier, and older—and nothing, nothing, no happiness. Time is passing—and I'm farther and farther from what's real, what's beautiful. I'm approaching a cliff. I'm desperate. I don't know why I'm alive, I don't know why I haven't killed myself.

OLGA: Don't cry, sweetheart, don't cry. It hurts me.

IRINA: I'm not crying. That's enough. You see, I'm not crying. It's over.

OLGA: Darling, listen to me. I'm telling you as your sister and your friend—marry the Baron. (IRINA *cries softly.*) You respect him, and appreciate him. No, he's not handsome, but he's good and pure. One doesn't marry for love. One marries because one must. That's how I feel about it. I would have married any man who asked me, even an old man—as long as he was a good person.

IRINA: I was waiting. I thought when we go to Moscow, I'll meet the one I'm destined to meet. I've dreamed of him, I love him. But that's silly, just silly.

OLGA: *(embracing her sister)* My darling little sister, I understand—I do. When the Baron resigned from the army and came here in civilian clothes—he seemed so unattractive I cried. He asked, "Why are you crying? What could I say? But if God wants you to marry him, I'll be happy. That would be different, very different.
(NATASHA, a candle in her hand, crosses the stage from right to left in silence.)

MASHA: *(sitting up)* Look at that. From the way she walks—you'd think she lit the fire.

OLGA: Don't be stupid. You're stupid, Masha. You're the most stupid person in the family, if I may say so. *(pause)*

MASHA: My sweet sisters, there's something I must confess. I can't keep it in anymore. I'll confess to you, but not to anyone else. I want to tell you. *(lowering her voice)* It's my secret, but I want to tell you. I can't keep it in anymore. *(pause)* I love—I love—that man. The man who was just here. Why hide it? I love Vershinin.

OLGA: *(behind the screen)* Stop it. I can't hear you anyway.

MASHA: What to do? *(She holds her head.)* First I thought he was strange. Then I felt sorry for him. Then I started to love him —his voice, how he speaks, his troubles, his little girls.

OLGA: *(behind the screen)* I can't hear you. Whatever nonsense you're saying, I can't hear you.

MASHA: It's you who's stupid, Olya. I love him. That's my destiny, my fate. And he loves me. I'm frightened. It's not supposed to be this way, is it? *(She takes* IRINA'S *hand, pulls it toward her.)* Oh, darling, how are we going to live? What will happen to us? In a novel it's simple, it all works out. But when you're in love yourself, you realize no one knows anything. We each have to decide for ourselves. My darlings, sweet sisters, I've confessed. Now I won't say any more. I'll be like the madman in Gogol—silent, silent.

(ANDREI enters, followed by FERAPONT.*)*

ANDREI: *(irritated)* What do you want? I don't know what you want.

FERAPONT: *(stopping at the door, impatiently)* I've told you ten times, Andrei Sergeyvich.

ANDREI: First of all, don't call me Andrei Sergeyvich. Call me your honor.

FERAPONT: It's the firemen, your honor. They want to go through your garden to the river. Otherwise they have to go around.

ANDREI: Alright. Tell them it's alright. *(FERAPONT goes out.)* So irritating, all of them. Where's Olga? *(OLGA comes out from behind the screen.)* I was looking for you. Give me the key to the cupboard. I've lost mine. Your little key. *(OLGA hands him the key in silence.* IRINA *goes behind her screen. A pause.)* It was a big fire. It's dying down now. Oh, the hell with it—Ferapont annoyed me, so I said something stupid. Your honor. *(pause)* Why don't you say something, Olya? *(pause)* Isn't it time to drop this nonsense? Stop sulking for no rhyme or reason. You're here, and Masha and Irina too. Fine. Let's have it out now, once and for all. What do you have against me? What? I'd like to know.

OLGA: Let's not talk now, Andryusha. We'll see tomorrow. *(upset)* What a horrible night.

ANDREI: *(very embarrassed)* Don't worry, Olga, I'm not—I'm completely calm. What do you have against me? Tell me.

VERSHININ'S VOICE: *(from offstage)* Tram-tam-tam!

MASHA: *(standing, raising her voice)* Tram-tam! *(to* OLGA*)* Goodbye, Olga. God keep you. *(She goes behind the screen, kisses* IRINA*.)* Sleep well. Goodbye, Andrei. Leave them alone. They're tired. Talk tomorrow. *(She goes out.)*

OLGA: Yes, Andryusha. We'll talk tomorrow. *(She goes behind the screen.)* Time to sleep now.

ANDREI: I'll say it, and then I'll go. In the first place, you seem to have something against my wife, ever since I married her. I believe Natasha's a good person. She's honest, straightforward, and honorable. I love her—I respect her, you understand. I want others to respect her too. I tell you again—she's honest and honorable. And your disagreements with her, forgive me, are just whims. *(pause)* Secondly, I suppose you're angry because I'm not a professor devoting myself to higher learning. But I'm a member of the County Council, and that work is just as sacred and important. I'm a member of the County Council and proud of it, if you want to know. *(pause)* Thirdly—one more thing. I've mortgaged the house without asking your permission. I admit that, and ask your forgiveness. It's my debts—thirty-five thousand. I don't gamble anymore, I gave up gambling. My only excuse is that you, the girls, have a pension, and I have no income, so to speak.

KULYGIN: *(from the door)* Masha's not here? *(anxious)* That's odd. Where is she? *(He goes out.)*

ANDREI: You're not listening to me. Natasha is an excellent woman, she's honest, she's honorable. *(He paces, then stops.)* When I married her, I thought we'd all be happy. But, oh my God… *(He cries.)* My darling precious sisters—don't believe me, don't believe a word I say. *(He goes out.)*

KULYGIN: *(at the door, anxious)* Where's Masha? She's not here? That's very odd. *(He goes out. We hear the alarm. The stage is empty.)*

IRINA: *(behind the screen)* Olya, who's knocking on the floor?

OLGA: The doctor. He's drunk.

IRINA: This night is an agony! *(pause)* Olya! *(Her head appears from behind* *the screen.)* Did you hear what he said? They're going to transfer the brigade—send it away.

OLGA: It's just a rumor.

IRINA: Then we'll be alone here. Olya?

OLGA: Yes?

IRINA: Olga, I respect and appreciate the Baron. He's an excellent man—I'm willing to marry him. I agree. Only—let's go to Moscow. Please, let's go! Moscow is what's best in the world! Let's go, Olya. Let's go!

Curtain

ACT IV

The formerly private garden of the Prozorovs, now sometimes crossed by passersby to reach the river through a long avenue of pines.

To the right the terrace of the house. A bottle and glasses are on a table—champagne has just been drunk. It's noon. On the other shore of the river a forest can be seen. Five soldiers pass through rapidly.

CHEBUTYKIN, *in a placid mood he maintains throughout the act, sits in an armchair in the garden, waiting to be called. He wears an officer's hat and holds a cane.* IRINA, KULYGIN, *and* TUZENBACH *say goodbye to* FEDOTIK *and* RODE *in dress uniform on the terrace steps.* KULYGIN *has a medal around his neck, his moustache is shaved off.*

TUZENBACH: *(kissing* FEDOTIK*)* You're a good man. We've been friends. *(He kisses* RODE*.)* Again. Goodbye, dear friend.

IRINA: Goodbye.

FEDOTIK: Not goodbye. Farewell. We'll never see each other again.

KULYGIN: Who knows? *(He wipes his eyes, smiling.)* Now me too—I'm crying.

IRINA: Maybe we'll meet again, some day.

FEDOTIK: Maybe, in ten or fifteen years. We'll hardly recognize each other. We'll say hello politely. *(He takes a photograph.)* Don't move. The last one.

RODE: *(embracing* TUZENBACH*)* We won't see each other again. *(He kisses* IRINA's *hand.)* Thank you for everything—everything!

FEDOTIK: *(emotionally)* Please don't move!

TUZENBACH: We'll meet again, God willing. Write us. Be sure to write.

RODE: *(glancing lovingly at the garden)* Goodbye, trees. *(He shouts.)* Hop-hop! *(pause)* Goodbye, echo!

KULYGIN: Who knows, maybe you'll marry in Poland. Your Polish wife will kiss you and call you "*kochane.*" *(He laughs.)*

FEDOTIK: *(looking at his watch)* We have less than an hour. From our battery, only Solyony rides in the barge. We march with the troops. Today three batteries, in formation—the other three tomorrow. Then you'll have peace and quiet.

TUZENBACH: And deadly boredom.

RODE: Where's Maria Sergeyvna?

KULYGIN: Masha's in the garden.

FEDOTIK: We want to say goodbye to her.

RODE: Goodbye. I have to go, or I'll cry... *(He quickly embraces* TUZEN-BACH *and* KULYGIN, *kisses* IRINA's *hand.)* Such happy times here.

FEDOTIK: *(to* IRINA*)* Here's a memento—a notebook and pencil... We'll go that way, toward the river... *(They move off, both looking back.)*

RODE: *(shouting)* Hop-hop!

KULYGIN: *(shouting)* Goodbye!

(At the back of the stage FEDOTIK *and* RODE *meet* MASHA. *She goes out with them as they make their goodbyes to her.)*

IRINA: Gone... *(She sits on the bottom step of the terrace.)*

CHEBUTYKIN: They forgot to say goodbye to me.

IRINA: And you, why didn't you say goodbye to them?

CHEBUTYKIN: Yes, I forgot too. I don't know why. Anyway, I'll see them soon—I'm leaving tomorrow. Yes... Just one more little day. Then, in a year, I get my pension, and I'm back—to finish my days with you. Only one little year 'til I get my pension. *(He stuffs a newspaper into his pocket, pulls out another.)* And when I'm back—total reformation. I'll be good—very good, completely respectable.

IRINA: It's true, dear old friend, you have to change your ways. You have to.

CHEBUTYKIN: I know. I know. *(He sings quietly.)* Ta-ra-ra boom dia, just one more little day

KULYGIN: Incorrigible, our Ivan Romanyich—incorrigible.

CHEBUTYKIN: If I were your student, I'd get an A.

IRINA: Fyodor's shaved off his moustache. I can't bear to look at him.

KULYGIN: Why?

CHEBUTYKIN: I could tell you what you look like, but I won't.

KULYGIN: Too bad! It's the fashion, the *modus vivendi*. The principal shaved off his moustache. I've shaved off mine. I've been made school inspector. No one likes the way I look, but that doesn't bother me. I'm happy, with or without a moustache. *(He sits. At the back of the garden,* ANDREI *pushes his child in a baby carriage.)*

IRINA: Ivan Romanyich, you're my friend. Tell me. I'm worried. You were on the boulevard last night. Tell me what happened there.

CHEBUTYKIN: What happened? Nothing. Nothing happened. *(He reads his newspaper.)* Just nonsense.

KULYGIN: People say Solyony and the Baron had an argument on the boulevard near the theatre —

TUZENBACH: Please, let's not talk about it. Stop it. Really. *(He gestures, goes into the house.)*

KULYGIN: Near the theatre Solyony picked on the Baron. The Baron wouldn't put up with it, and insulted Solyony...

CHEBUTYKIN: I know nothing about it. Just nonsense.

KULYGIN: At a seminary once, a teacher wrote the word "nonsense" on a student paper. The student thought he'd written "notable," in Latin. *(He laughs.)* Incredibly funny. They say Solyony's in love with Irina, so he hates the Baron. It's natural. Irina is a charming young girl—just like Masha, always lost in thought. But you have a softer character, Irina. Of course, Masha has a good character too. I love my Masha. *(From the end of the garden we hear "Yoo-hoo," and, "hop-hop.")*

IRINA: *(shuddering)* Everything frightens me today. *(pause)* I'm all packed. I send off my things after dinner. Tomorrow I marry the Baron, and we leave for the brickworks. The next day I teach school—with God's help begin a new life. When I passed my teaching exam, I cried—I was so happy, so grateful. *(pause)* A cart will come for my things later.

KULYGIN: That's very nice, although I daresay not very sensible. High-minded ideals, but not very sensible. But that doesn't stop me from wishing you the best of—

CHEBUTYKIN: *(moved)* My angel, my dove, my little golden girl. You've gone so far, all of you. I can't catch up. I've stayed behind like an old migrant bird who can't fly anymore. Fly, fly away, my dears, and may God keep you well. *(pause)* Fyodor Ilych, you shouldn't have shaved off your moustache.

KULYGIN: Oh, leave me alone. *(He sighs.)* The army leaves today. Everything will be the way it was. I don't care what anyone says, Masha is an honorable woman and a good one. I love her, and I thank God for my luck. We're not all lucky. A worker in the tax office was in class with me in high school. He was left back in tenth grade because he couldn't understand *ut consecutivum*. Now he's poor as a churchmouse, and sick too. When I meet him on the street, I say, hello, *ut consecutivum!* He says, "Yes, *consecutivum*, that's right," and he coughs. But I'm lucky. Look how happy I am. They even gave me the Stanislaus medal, second degree. And I teach others that famous *ut consecutivum*. Of course, it's true I'm brighter than most people, but happiness doesn't lie there. I know that.

(In the house someone plays "The Maiden's Prayer" on the piano.)

IRINA: As of tomorrow night I'll never have to hear "The Maiden's Prayer" again, and I won't have to see Protopopov. *(pause)* Protopopov is there again, in the sitting room...

KULYGIN: The headmistress isn't here yet?

IRINA: No. She's been sent for. It's been so painful living here without Olya. She's headmistress, living at the high school, busy all day. And I'm alone, bored. I have nothing to do. I hate my room. But if it's my fate I can't go to Moscow, then I can't—that's that. I yield. It's my fate. There's nothing I can do about it. We all depend on the will of God. The Baron proposed. I thought about it, and said yes. He's an excellent man. It's amazing how good he is. And suddenly, now, it's as if I had wings. I'm happier, I feel lighter, and I want to work again—work. But something happened yesterday, something mysterious. I feel something's hanging over me, and I don't know what it is.

CHEBUTYKIN: Nonsense—"notable" nonsense.

NATASHA: *(at the window)* Here comes the headmistress!

KULYGIN: The headmistress is here. Let's go. *(He goes into the house with IRINA.)*

CHEBUTYKIN: *(reading his newspaper, singing softly)* Ta-ra-ra boom dia, just one more little day.

(MASHA approaches. Toward the back ANDREI pushes the baby carriage.)

MASHA: There he is, the picture of peace and tranquility—all innocence.

CHEBUTYKIN: So?

MASHA: *(sitting)* So nothing. *(pause)* Did you love my mother?

CHEBUTYKIN: Very much.

MASHA: Did she love you?

CHEBUTYKIN: *(after a silence)* That I don't remember.

MASHA: Is Mine here? In the old days our cook, Marfa, called her police-man that. Mine. Is Mine here?

CHEBUTYKIN: Not yet.

MASHA: When you grab at bits of happiness, crumbs—and even that's taken away, you become vulgar, mean. *(She points to her chest.)* I'm boiling, in here. *(She looks at her brother* ANDREI *pushing the carriage.)* There's brother Andrei, our lost hope. It takes a hundred people to hoist a bell—so much labor and money to cast and hoist a bell. Then suddenly it falls and breaks into a thousand pieces—just like that, for no reason. That's Andrei.

ANDREI: When will it be quiet in that house? What a racket!

CHEBUTYKIN: Soon. *(He looks at his watch.)* This is an old watch. It rings. *(He winds the watch. It rings.)* The first, second, and fifth battery leave precisely at one. *(pause)* And I leave tomorrow.

ANDREI: Forever?

CHEBUTYKIN: I don't know. Maybe I'll be back in a year. Although—who knows? What difference does it make?

(We hear from far off the sounds of a violin and harp.)

ANDREI: The town'll be empty—as if we were being put under glass. *(pause)* Something happened yesterday by the theatre. Everyone's talking about it. I don't know what it was.

CHEBUTYKIN: Nothing. Some nonsense. Solyony tried to provoke the Baron who got carried away and insulted him. Things turned sour. Solyony challenged him to a duel. *(He looks at his watch.)* I think it's time. Twelve thirty in the state forest, there, on the other side of the river pif-paf! *(He laughs.)* Solyony thinks he's Lermontov. He actually writes poetry. It's gone beyond a joke—it's his third duel.

MASHA: Whose?

CHEBUTYKIN: Solyony's.

MASHA: And the Baron's?

CHEBUTYKIN: The Baron's what? *(pause)*

MASHA: I'm not thinking straight. Should we let them do this? He might wound the Baron. He might even kill him.

CHEBUTYKIN: The Baron's a good man. But one baron more or less—what difference does it make? Too bad. I don't care. *(From beyond the garden someone shouts, "Yoo-hoo, hop-hop.")* Wait a minute. That must be the second—Skvortsov, out there in a boat, waiting. *(pause)*

ANDREI: Duels are immoral. It's immoral to help them happen—even as a doctor.

CHEBUTYKIN: That's just an idea. We're not even alive. The world is a dream. We don't exist, we only think we do. So what difference does it make?

MASHA: Talk, talk, talk the livelong day... *(She takes a few steps.)* God, to have to live in this climate. It might actually snow today. *And* to have to hear this endless talking... *(She stops.)* I refuse to go into that house. I can't. As soon as Vershinin comes, let me know... *(She walks toward the pines.)* The birds are leaving already... *(She looks up.)* Swans, or ducks—my darlings, my happy ones... *(She goes out.)*

ANDREI: The house will be empty now. The officers are leaving, you're leaving, my sister's getting married, and I'll be alone.

CHEBUTYKIN: What about your wife?

(FERAPONT enters, bringing papers.)

ANDREI: A wife is a wife. She's honest and honorable, sometimes even a good person. But there's something animal in her—blind and stingy, hard to the touch. She's not quite human. I say this only to you. I can only talk to you. I love her, but sometimes she seems vulgar. Then I'm confused. I don't know why I love her so, or even why I ever loved her.

CHEBUTYKIN: *(getting up)* I'm leaving tomorrow, my friend. We may never see each other again. So listen to me. Pick up your hat and cane—and go... Go. Don't look back. The farther you go, the better.
(SOLYONY and two officers appear at the back. SOLYONY approaches CHEBUTYKIN. The officers go out.)

SOLYONY: Doctor, it's time—almost twelve thirty. *(He bows to ANDREI.)*

CHEBUTYKIN: I'm coming, I'm coming. You're so boring, all of you. You make me sick. *(to ANDREI)* If anyone asks, Andryushka, I'll be back soon. *(sighing a great sigh)* Arghhhhh.

SOLYONY: "Lying under a tree, he thought he had time to spare. He looked up too late to see the oncoming bear." *(He goes with him.)* What are you groaning about, old man?

CHEBUTYKIN: Leave me alone.

SOLYONY: How do you feel?

CHEBUTYKIN: *(angrily)* Fine, just fine. Just leave me alone.

SOLYONY: No reason for an old doctor to worry. I won't indulge myself.

I'll just wing him—like a bird. *(He takes a vial of perfume from his pocket, puts some on his hands.)* I've emptied a whole bottle of perfume on them today. *(looking at his hands)* But they still smell. They smell of corpse. *(pause)* There. Do you know this? "Restless, he seeks the storm, as if the storm would bring him peace."

CHEBUTYKIN: Yes. "Lying under a tree, he thought he had time to spare. He looked up too late to see the oncoming bear."

(SOLYONY and CHEBUTYKIN go out. We hear shouts of "hop-hop," and "yoo-hoo." ANDREI and FERAPONT enter.)

FERAPONT: It's papers to sign.

ANDREI: *(nervous)* Leave me alone. Leave me alone, please. *(He leaves, pushing a baby carriage.)*

FERAPONT: But the papers. That's what papers are for—to sign.

(He goes toward the back of the stage. IRINA comes in with TUZENBACH who is wearing a boater. KULYGIN crosses the stage, shouting, "Yoo-hoo, MASHA, yoo-hoo!")

TUZENBACH: There goes the only person in town delighted to see the army leave.

IRINA: It's understandable. *(pause)* The town will be deserted.

TUZENBACH: *(looking at his watch)* Darling, I'll be back in a little while.

IRINA: Where are you going?

TUZENBACH: To town... To see some friends off.

IRINA: That's not true... Nicolai, why are you so distracted today? *(pause)* Is it what happened last night in front of the theatre?

TUZENBACH: *(with an impatient gesture)* I'll be back in an hour. I'll see you then. *(He kisses her hands.)* Oh, my joy. *(He looks at her closely.)* I've loved you for five years, and you still seem more beautiful every day. Your hair—so marvelous. Those eyes. Tomorrow, I take you away, and we'll work. We'll be rich. My dreams will come true— you'll be happy. There's just one thing missing, one—you don't love me.

IRINA: That's not in my power. I'll be your wife, your faithful, obedient wife. But it's true, I'm not in love with you. What can I do about it? *(She cries.)* I've never known love. I've dreamed about it. But my heart is locked, like the keyboard of a precious piano—and the key is lost. *(pause)* You look worried.

TUZENBACH: I didn't sleep last night. But I'm not worried—there's nothing in my life to frighten me. I'm just tortured by that lost key. I lose sleep over it. Say something to me. *(pause)* Say something.

IRINA: What? What can I say?

TUZENBACH: Something.

IRINA: I can't. That's enough. *(pause)*

TUZENBACH: I know it's silly. It's funny how in life sometimes a detail can take on such importance for no reason. You can laugh at it, but you can't stop thinking about it. Let's forget it now. I'm happy. It's as if I'm seeing these pines for the first time—these maples, these birches. And they're looking at me too, with curiosity. They're waiting. How beautiful trees are. Life should be beautiful around them. *(We hear cries, "Yoo-hoo! Hop-hop!")* I have to go. It's time. Look at that tree. It's dead, but it's swaying in the wind with the others. I think when I die, I too will still be alive in some way. Darling, goodbye… *(He kisses her hands.)* Your papers, the ones you gave me, are on my table, under the calendar.

IRINA: I'm going with you.

TUZENBACH: *(worried)* No! No! *(He leaves rapidly, but stops in the pines.)* Irina?

IRINA: What?

TUZENBACH: *(not knowing what to say)* I—had no coffee this morning. Will you ask them to make me some?

(IRINA remains standing, thoughtful, then goes toward the back, sits on the swing. ANDREI enters, pushing the baby carriage. FERAPONT follows him.)

FERAPONT: Andrei Sergeyvich, these are not my papers. They are the administration's. I didn't invent them.

ANDREI: What happened? What happened to the way I was? Young, joyous, smart—I had dreams, marvelous ideas. I was full of hope for the future. Why, when we grow up, must we become boring, dull, insignificant, lazy, callous, useless, and miserable? This town is here two hundred years, has a hundred thousand inhabitants, and each is identical to the next. There's not one hero, leader, scholar, or artist, no one remarkable, no one to envy or make you want to walk in their footsteps. No one here does anything but eat, drink, sleep and then die. When others are born—they too just eat, drink, and sleep. Afraid of dying of boredom, they entertain themselves with malicious gossip, vodka, card games, and intrigue. Wives deceive husbands. Husbands lie, pretend to see nothing, hear nothing. And the children are lost, sucked in by the irresistible pull of vulgarity which finally snuffs out their divine spark. They too become the living dead, each identical to the next, as pitiful as their parents. *(to* FERAPONT, *angrily)* What do you want?

FERAPONT: What do I want? I want you to sign these.

ANDREI: You're so irritating.

FERAPONT: *(handing him the papers)* The janitor at the tax office said in Petersburg last winter it was two hundred degrees below.

ANDREI: Everything disgusts me, except the future. Thinking about the future, I feel lighter and more spacious. I see the light of freedom shining in the distance, my children and I freed from laziness, drink, goose and cabbage supper, the after-dinner nap—freed from the slothful life of parasites.

FERAPONT: Two thousand people died of the cold, he said. Everybody's scared in Petersburg. Maybe it was Moscow. I don't remember.

ANDREI: *(suddenly moved)* My sisters. My darling, wonderful sisters! *(through tears)* Masha, my sister!

NATASHA: *(through the window)* Who's talking so loud out there? Is that you, Andryusha? You'll wake Sofochka. *Il ne faut pas faire du bruit, la Sophie est dormee deja. Vous etes un ours. (getting angry)* If you're going to talk, give the baby to someone else. Ferapont, take the carriage from your master.

FERAPONT: Yes, ma'am. *(He pushes the carriage.)*

ANDREI: *(confused)* I was being quiet.

NATASHA: *(behind the window, caressing her child)* Bobik, little rascal—Bobik, naughty little Bobik! Bobik!

ANDREI: *(examining the papers)* Alright, alright. I'll look through these, sign what needs to be signed. Then you can take them back to the Council...

(He goes toward the house reading the papers. FERAPONT *pushes the baby carriage toward the end of the garden.)*

NATASHA: *(at the window, caressing her child)* Bobik, what's your mama's name? Little sweetheart, who's there? It's Auntie Olya. Say hello to Auntie—hello, Olya.

(Wandering musicians, a man and a young woman, play the violin and the harp. VERSHININ, OLGA *and* ANFISA *come out of the house to listen to them quietly.* IRINA *joins them.)*

OLGA: Our garden has become a public way. People cross it on foot and on horse. Give them something, Nanny.

ANFISA: *(giving coins to the musicians)* Here you are, dear hearts. God bless you. *(The musicians bow and leave.)* Poor things. A full stomach makes no music. *(to* IRINA*)* Hello, Arisha. *(She kisses her.)* Well, little one, aren't I the lucky one? Here I am living at the high school with Olyushka, in an official apartment. God is good to me in my old age, poor sinner that I am. I never before had such a life. The apartment is big—my own little room, my own little bed. I have all that. I wake up in the night and think, "Dear Mother of God, no one in the world is luckier than I am."

VERSHININ: *(looking at his watch)* We're leaving right away, Olga Sergeyvna. It's time to— *(pause)* With all my heart I wish you— Where is Maria Sergeyvna?

IRINA: Somewhere in the garden. I'll find her.

VERSHININ: If you'd be so kind. I must hurry.

ANFISA: Me too. I'll go find her. *(She shouts.)* Mashenka! Yoo-hoo! *(She goes with* IRINA *toward the back of the garden.)* Yoo-hoo! Yoo-hoo!

VERSHININ: Everything ends. Now we must be apart. *(He looks at his watch.)* The town gave us a luncheon today with champagne. The mayor made a speech. I ate and listened, but my heart was here with you. *(looking at the garden)* I've become accustomed to you.

OLGA: Will we ever see each other again?

VERSHININ: I don't think so. *(pause)* My wife and little girls will still be here for two more months. If anything happens—if they need—please...

OLGA: Of course. Don't worry. *(pause)* Tomorrow there won't be a single soldier left. It'll all be memory. And I suppose we'll start a new life. *(pause)* Nothing ever happens the way we want it. I didn't want to be headmistress, but I am. And it seems we're not to go to Moscow.

VERSHININ: Well, thank you again. Forgive me if for any reason... I talked too much. Forgive me for that too. Remember me well.

OLGA: *(wiping her eyes)* Where's Masha? Why doesn't she come?

VERSHININ: What can I tell you before leaving? What shall I philosophize about one last time? *(He laughs.)* Life is hard. To many it seems flat and hopeless. But still, little by little things get better. There's more clarity in the world. The time is probably not far off when life will be luminous. *(He looks at his watch.)* I have to leave. So far

Humanity's been occupied with war—campaigns, invasions, and victories. But we're past that now. There remains a great void demanding to be filled. But how? The world is looking desperately for a solution. We'll find something—eventually. Hopefully soon. *(pause)* If only we could combine the love of work with learning, and learn to love work— *(He looks at his watch.)* It's time.

OLGA: Here she is.

(MASHA enters.)

VERSHININ: I've come to say goodbye...

(OLGA moves off a little so as not to disturb them.)

MASHA: *(looking him in the eyes)* Goodbye... *(a long kiss)*

OLGA: That's enough, enough.

(MASHA sobs.)

VERSHININ: Write to me. Don't forget me. You must let me go—it's time. Hold her, Olga Sergeyvna. I have to—it's time. I'm late... *(Deeply moved, he kisses OLGA's hands, embraces MASHA again, goes out rapidly.)*

OLGA: Enough, Masha. Enough, my darling.

(KULYGIN enters.)

KULYGIN: *(troubled)* It's alright, let her cry. Leave her alone. My good little Masha, my gentle Masha—you're my wife, and I'm glad of it in spite of everything. I'm not complaining, I don't reproach you—Olya is my witness. We'll be just as we were—never a single word, not the slightest mention...

MASHA: *(trying to hold back her sobs)* "By the curved seashore, an oak tree greening. Wound 'round that oak, a golden chain... Wound 'round that oak, a golden chain, a golden chain..." I'm going crazy. "By the curved seashore, an oak tree greening."

OLGA: Calm down, Masha, calm down. Give her some water.

MASHA: I'm not crying anymore.

KULYGIN: She's not crying anymore. She's being good.

(A shot reverberates dully in the distance.)

MASHA: "By the curved seashore, an oak tree greening. Wound 'round that oak, a golden chain." A green cat? "An oak tree greening." I can't think straight. *(She drinks some water.)* My life is a failure. I don't need anything now. I'll calm down. Nothing matters anymore. What does that mean—"by the curved seashore?" Why are those words in my head? I can't think straight.

(IRINA *enters.*)

OLGA: Calm down, Masha. That's right. Be reasonable. Let's go in.

MASHA: *(with anger)* I will not go into that house. *(She starts to cry, but controls herself.)* I will not go in there. I won't go in.

IRINA: Let's sit here, the three of us. We don't have to say anything. You know I'm leaving tomorrow… *(pause)*

KULYGIN: Look what I confiscated in the fifth grade yesterday. *(He puts on a false beard and moustache.)* I look like the German professor, don't I? *(He laughs.)* Don't I? Children are funny.

MASHA: Yes, you look German.

OLGA: *(laughing)* It's true, you do.

(MASHA *cries.*)

IRINA: Enough, Masha.

KULYGIN: I look like the German professor, don't I?

(NATASHA *enters.*)

NATASHA: *(to the* MAID*)* What? Mr. Protopopov will take care of Sofochka. Give Bobik to Andrei Sergeyvich in the garden. Children are such a nuisance. *(to* IRINA*)* You're leaving tomorrow, Irina? That's too bad. Why don't you stay with us a little longer, at least another week? *(She gives a little cry, seeing* KULYGIN *who, laughing, takes off his false beard and moustache.)* Lord, you scared me! *(to* IRINA*)* Don't think your leaving will be easy for me—I'm used to you. I'll put Andrei into your room with his violin. He can scratch away there all he wants. His room will be for my little Sofochka—darling child, so adorable. Today she looked at me with her pretty little eyes, and said, "Mama."

KULYGIN: She's a beautiful child.

NATASHA: Well, tomorrow I'll be all alone here. *(sighing)* The first thing I'll do is have this avenue of trees cut down, and that maple. It's so ugly at night. *(to* IRINA*)* My dear, that belt doesn't suit you at all. It's tasteless. You need something brighter. And I'll have little flowers planted everywhere. It'll smell so nice. *(sternly)* What is this fork doing on this bench? *(She goes into the house, speaking to the maid.)* What is this fork doing on this bench? I'm speaking to you! *(She shouts.)* Be quiet!

KULYGIN: She's off again.

(*From offstage we hear the military band playing a march. All listen.*)

OLGA: They're leaving.

(CHEBUTYKIN *enters.*)

MASHA: Our soldiers are leaving. Well, have a good trip, everyone! (*to her husband*) We have to go home. Where's my hat? My cape?

KULYGIN: I put them inside. I'll get them. (*He goes into the house.*)

OLGA: Yes. Time to go home.

CHEBUTYKIN: Olga Sergeyvna!

OLGA: Yes? (*pause*) What?

CHEBUTYKIN: Nothing. I don't know how to tell you. (*He speaks into her ear.*)

OLGA: (*frightened*) Oh, no! It's not possible.

CHEBUTYKIN: Yes. What a business. I'm tired, worn out. I don't want to talk about it. (*vexed*) Anyway, it doesn't matter.

MASHA: What is it?

OLGA: (*embracing* IRINA) Oh, what a hateful day. My darling, I don't know how to tell you.

IRINA: What? Say it fast! What is it? Oh, for God's sake. (*She cries.*)

CHEBUTYKIN: The Baron was just killed in a duel.

IRINA: (*crying softly*) I knew it, I knew it.

(CHEBUTYKIN *goes to the back, sits on a bench.*)

CHEBUTYKIN: I'm worn out. (*He takes a newspaper out of his pocket.*) Let them cry. (*He sings.*) Ta-ra-ra boom dia, just one more little day. In the end, it's all the same, isn't it?

(*The three sisters remain standing, close against each other.*)

MASHA: The music... How happy it sounds! Listen. They're leaving us. One has already gone forever. We've been left alone to start our lives over again. We have to go on living—somehow, start again. We have to go on living...

IRINA: (*leaning her head on* OLGA's *breast*) Some day they'll know—it'll be clear, no more secrets. But not now. Now we must work, go on living. Tomorrow, I'll leave alone. I'll work. I'll teach at the school. I'll give my life to whoever needs it. It's autumn, almost winter. Soon the snow will cover everything, but I'll be working—I'll work.

OLGA: (*her arms around her sisters*) Such happy music, so bold. It makes you want to live. Oh, God, time will pass, and we'll be gone forever. We'll be forgotten—our faces and voices forgotten. No one will remember who or how many we were. But our suffering will make a difference, create joy for those who come after us. There'll be happiness and peace on earth, and they'll say good things of those who live now—they'll bless us. Oh, my sisters, my dears, our lives aren't over yet. We have to live. Such happy music, so joyous! Just a little longer, and we'll know why this life, this suffering. If only we knew, if only we knew…

(Little by little the music is further off. KULYGIN, *cheerful and smiling, brings the hat and cape.* ANDREI *pushes the baby carriage in which Bobik sits.)*

CHEBUTYKIN: *(singing softly)* Ta-ra-ra boom dia, just one more little day. *(reading his newspaper)* It's all the same. Doesn't matter to me—it's all the same.

OLGA: If only we knew, if only we knew…

Curtain

THE
CHERRY
ORCHARD

A COMEDY IN FOUR ACTS

An earlier version in English by Jean-Claude van Itallie of Chekhov's *The Cherry Orchard* was commissioned by the New York Shakespeare Festival (Joseph Papp, artistic director). It opened at the Vivian Beaumont Theatre at Lincoln Center, New York City on February 17th, 1977. It was directed by Andrei Serban, scenery and costumes by Santo Loquasto, lighting by Jennifer Tipton, incidental music by Elizabeth Swados, dances by Kathryn Posin. The cast included Raul Julia as Lopakhin, Meryl Streep as Dunyasha, Max Wright as Yepikhodov, Marybeth Hurt as Anya, Irene Worth as Lyubov Andreyevna, Priscilla Smith as Varya, George Voskovec as Gayev, Cathryn Damon as Charlotta, C.K. Alexander as Yasha, Michael Cristofer as Trofimov, Jon De Vries as a vagrant, and William Duff-Griffin as the station master.

CAST OF CHARACTERS

RANEVSKAYA, LYUBOV ANDREYEVNA, landowner

ANYA, her daughter, age seventeen

VARYA, her adopted daughter, age twenty-four

GAYEV, LEONID ANDREYEVICH, brother of Ranevskaya

LOPAKHIN, YERMOLAY ALEXYEVICH, a merchant

TROFIMOV, PYOTR SERGEYVICH, a student

SIMEONOV-PISHCHIK, BORIS BORISOVICH, a landowner

CHARLOTTA IVANOVNA, the governess

YEPIKHODOV, SEMYON PANTELYEVICH, the clerk

DUNYASHA, the maid

FIRS, a valet, age eighty-seven

YASHA, a valet, young

VAGRANT

STATION MASTER, POSTMASTER, GUESTS, SERVANTS

The play takes place on the estate of Lyubov Andreyevna.

In the New York production there were short intermissions after Acts I and II. Act IV followed Act III without intermission.

The children's nursery, now no longer in use. One of the doors leads to Anya's room. Daybreak—just before sunrise. It is May. The cherry trees are blooming but it is still cold—there is frost on the blossoms. The windows are closed.

DUNYASHA *enters carrying a candle, followed by* LOPAKHIN *with a book in his hand.*

LOPAKHIN: The train's arrived. What time is it?

DUNYASHA: Almost two. *(She blows out the candle.)* It's getting light out.

LOPAKHIN: That train is two hours late. *(He yawns and stretches.)* I'm an idiot. I come here to go meet them at the station, and I fall asleep. I fall asleep sitting up. It's irritating. Why didn't you wake me?

DUNYASHA: I thought you'd already gone. *(She listens.)* Listen, I think I hear them.

LOPAKHIN: *(listening)* No, they still have to get the bags—all that. *(pause)* Five years Lyubov Andreyevna has been living abroad. I wonder what she's like now. She was certainly something then—kind and unpretentious, simple. I remember—I must have been fifteen—my father, God rest his soul, was a grocer in the village. He was drunk. He punched me, and my nose was bleeding. We came here to the house for something. Lyubov Andreyevna—so thin, so young— brought me inside to wash my face—to this room, the nursery. "Don't cry, little peasant," she said. "You won't die. We'll still dance at your wedding." *(pause)* "Little peasant…" It's true. My father and family were peasants since always. Now here I am in white vest and leather boots—a bull in a china shop. Yes, I'm rich—but that's the only thing that's changed. I have money—but if you look closely I'm still a peasant, nothing more. *(He rifles the pages of the book in his hand.)* Here I am reading this book, and I don't remember a word of it. I read and I fall asleep. *(pause)*

DUNYASHA: The dogs have been barking all night. They know the mistress is coming.

LOPAKHIN: What's happening to you, Dunyasha? You look so…

DUNYASHA: My hands are trembling, they're shaking. I think I'm going to faint.

LOPAKHIN: You're too delicate, Dunyasha. Look at your clothes, your hair. You're trying to look like a young lady. It's not right. Everyone has his place.

(YEPIKHODOV *enters carrying a bunch of flowers. He wears a jacket and brightly polished high boots that squeak with every step. As he enters, he drops the flowers.*)

YEPIKHODOV: (picking them up) Here. From the gardener. He said to put it in the dining room. (*He hands* DUNYASHA *the flowers.*)

LOPAKHIN: And bring me some kvass.

DUNYASHA: Yes, sir. (*She goes out.*)

YEPIKHODOV: It's freezing out. Three degrees above zero. (*He sighs.*) And the cherry trees are in bloom. I can't get used to our climate, I really can't. It's simply not a favorable climate. On top of that, the day before yesterday I buy myself a pair of boots. Now I find they squeak—squeak, begging your pardon, which is intolerable. It makes me crazy. What am I supposed to grease them with?

LOPAKHIN: Go away. You bother me.

YEPIKHODOV: Each day I'm visited by new misfortunes. But I'm used to it. I don't complain. They merely bring a small smile to my lips. (DUNYASHA *enters, serves* LOPAKHIN *the kvass.*) I'm going. (*He bumps into a chair which falls over.*) There. (triumphantly) You see? Excuse me for mentioning it, but that sort of thing happens to me all the time. It's extraordinary—just extraordinary. (*He goes out.*)

DUNYASHA: I must confess to you, Yermolay Alexyevich, that Yepikhodov has asked for my hand in marriage.

LOPAKHIN: Humph.

DUNYASHA: I don't know what to say. He has lovely manners. But sometimes when he speaks I don't know what he's talking about. He's nice and sweet and everything—but what is he talking about? I sort of like him. Of course, he loves me madly. But he's unlucky. Every day something happens to him. Every day. People tease him, call him twenty-two misfortunes.

LOPAKHIN: (listening) I think they're here.

DUNYASHA: They're here! What's happening to me? I'm trembling all over.

LOPAKHIN: (getting up) Come. I wonder if she'll recognize me. It's been five years.

DUNYASHA: *(excitedly)* Oh, I'm going to faint, I'm going to faint.

(We hear two carriages drive up to the house. LOPAKHIN and DUNYASHA hurry out. The stage is empty. We hear noises from adjoining rooms. FIRS, who had gone to the station to meet Lyubov Andreyevna, rapidly crosses the stage using a cane. He wears livery in the old style, and a top hat. He is talking to himself but we don't understand what he's saying. From offstage the arrival sounds grow louder: "This way! Let's go in this way!" LYUBOV ANDREYEVNA, ANYA, and CHARLOTTA enter. They are wearing traveling clothes. CHARLOTTA has a dog on a leash. VARYA, who has entered with them, wears a coat and a kerchief. They are followed by GAYEV, SIMEONOV-PISHCHIK, LOPAKHIN, DUNYASHA with a bundle and an umbrella, and SERVANTS with baggage. All pass through the room.)

ANYA: Come in. This way. Do you remember, Mama? This room?

LYUBOV ANDREYEVNA: *(joyously through tears)* The nursery!

VARYA: It's so cold. My hands are stiff. *(to LYUBOV ANDREYEVNA)* Mama, your rooms are just the way you left them, the white one and the lavender one.

LYUBOV ANDREYEVNA: The nursery, my darling precious room! I slept here when I was a child. *(She cries.)* And I am still a child... *(She kisses her brother, then VARYA, then her brother again.)* And Varya is just the same—she looks like a nun. And Dunyasha. I recognized her, didn't I? *(She kisses DUNYASHA.)*

GAYEV: The train was two hours late. Two hours! What a way to run a railroad.

CHARLOTTA: *(to PISHCHIK)* And my dog even eats nuts.

SIMEONOV-PISHCHIK: *(amazed)* Incredible.

(They all go out except ANYA and DUNYASHA.)

DUNYASHA: *(helping ANYA with her coat and hat)* It feels like you've been away for so long.

ANYA: I couldn't sleep for four nights on that train, and now I'm freezing.

DUNYASHA: You left just before Easter—it was snowing and cold. And now look. You're here! *(She laughs and kisses her.)* I've been waiting for you. My joy, I have something to tell you. I can't hold it in another minute.

ANYA: *(wearily)* What is it this time?

DUNYASHA: Our clerk Yepikhodov proposed to me right after Holy Week!

ANYA: You told me that. You always tell me the same things. (*She rearranges her hair.*) I've lost every one of my hairpins. (*She's exhausted, can hardly stand.*)

DUNYASHA: I don't know what to decide. He loves me, you know. He loves me madly.

(ANYA *looks into her own room, speaks tenderly.*)

ANYA: My room, my windows—as if I'd never left. I'm home. Tomorrow I'll get up, run in the garden. Oh, just to sleep! I couldn't sleep the whole trip. I was too anxious.

DUNYASHA: Pyotr Sergeyevich arrived the day before yesterday.

ANYA: (*joyfully*) Petya!

DUNYASHA: He's sleeping in the bathhouse. He wants to. "I won't be a bother," he said. (*She glances at a watch which she pulls out of her pocket.*) I would have woken him, but Varvara Mikhailovna said no. "Don't wake him," she said.

(VARYA *enters, a ring of keys hanging from her belt.*)

VARYA: Dunyasha, make coffee quick. Mama wants coffee.

DUNYASHA: Right away. (*She goes out.*)

VARYA: You're home, thank God. My darling is home. My little angel is back. (*She holds* ANYA.)

ANYA: You don't know what I had to go through.

VARYA: I do. I can imagine.

ANYA: Easter week was so cold. And Charlotta never stopped talking. During the whole trip she was always performing tricks. Why did I have to have Charlotta?

VARYA: You couldn't have traveled by yourself, Sweetheart. Not at seventeen.

ANYA: It was snowing in Paris, and cold. My French is abominable. Mama lives on a fifth floor. I walk up. The room is full of tobacco smoke, French people, and an old priest with his prayer book. Such a sad atmosphere. When I see Mama, I feel so sorry for her. I kiss her, hold her head in my hands. Then I hold her hands. I can't let go. She holds me, kisses me, and cries.

VARYA: (*almost crying*) Don't tell me more. Don't.

ANYA: She'd already sold her villa near Menton. She has no money left, nothing. And I didn't either. Not a kopeck. We had hardly enough to come home. And Mama doesn't realize. In all the station restaurants she orders what's most expensive, and tips each waiter a ruble. Charlotta does the same. And so does Yasha. He demands whole dinners for himself. It's dreadful. It is. You know, Yasha is Mama's butler now? She brought him home with us.

VARYA: Yes, I saw the scoundrel. I wish I hadn't.

ANYA: And here? Have you managed the mortgage payments?

VARYA: With what?

ANYA: Oh, my God. My God...

VARYA: In August the entire estate will be sold.

ANYA: Oh, my God...

(LOPAKHIN *sticks his head through the door and moos like a cow.*)

LOPAKHIN: Moo... *(He disappears.)*

VARYA: *(through tears)* Oh, I'd like to hit him... *(She shakes her fist toward the door.)*

ANYA: *(embracing* VARYA, *softly)* Varya, did he propose? *(*VARYA *shakes her head, no.)* He loves you. Talk to him. Why wait?

VARYA: Because nothing will come of it, that's why. He's too busy to think of me. He doesn't know I'm alive. Well, so—that's too bad. I don't want to see him anymore. Everyone congratulates me on our marriage, but there's nothing. It's only a fantasy... *(in a different tone)* You're wearing a new brooch. It's a bee, isn't it?

ANYA: *(sadly)* Mama bought it. *(She goes toward her own room now, and speaks happily, like a child.)* You know, in Paris I went up in a balloon!

VARYA: My angel is home. My precious has returned! *(*DUNYASHA *has comes in with a coffee pot, is preparing the coffee.* VARYA *is near the door.)* Every day working, darling, taking care of the estate—I dream, I hope. If only we could marry you to a rich man, I'd feel at peace. I could visit monasteries, go to Kiev... Moscow, travel from one holy place to another... What bliss.

ANYA: The birds are singing in the orchard. What time is it?

VARYA: It must be three. Time for you to go to bed, darling. *(She goes into Anya's room.)* She's home. What bliss.

*(*YASHA *enters with a lap robe and traveling bag. He crosses the stage airily.)*

YASHA: May I pass through, *s'il vous plaît?*

DUNYASHA: One doesn't recognize you, Yasha. You look so European.

YASHA: A-hem. And who might you be?

DUNYASHA: When you left I was no bigger than this. *(She indicates with her hand.)* I'm Dunyasha, Fyodor's daughter. Don't you remember me?

YASHA: A-hem. A little peach. *(He looks around. Then he quickly embraces DUNYASHA who cries out and drops a saucer. YASHA runs out the door.)*

VARYA: *(annoyed, from the doorway)* What's going on in here?

DUNYASHA: *(tearfully)* I broke a saucer...

VARYA: That's a good omen.

ANYA: *(coming out of her room)* We have to warn Mama. Petya's here...

VARYA: I told them not to wake him.

ANYA: *(dreamily)* It's six years since Papa died and Grisha drowned a month later. Grisha—darling baby brother—only seven. Mama couldn't stand it. She left, and never looked back... *(She shivers.)* I know how she feels. She doesn't know I do, but I do. *(pause)* And Petya Trofimov, Grisha's tutor... It'll remind her.

(FIRS enters wearing a jacket and white waistcoat. He busies himself with the coffee urn.)

FIRS: Madame will have coffee here. *(He puts on white gloves.)* The coffee—is it ready? *(to DUNYASHA, sternly)* And you—where's the cream?

DUNYASHA: Oh, my God. *(She hurries out.)*

FIRS: *(fussing with the coffee pot)* Nincompoop. Good for nothing. *(muttering to himself)* The mistress back from Paris. The old master used to go to Paris too, only he went by carriage. *(He laughs.)*

VARYA: What are you laughing at, Firs?

FIRS: Miss? *(joyfully)* My mistress is back. She's home! She's home! I haven't waited for nothing. Now I can die.

(He cries for joy. LYUBOV ANDREYEVNA, GAYEV, SIMEONOV-PISHCHIK and LOPAKHIN enter. PISHCHIK wears a long sleeveless peasant vest of fine cloth, with full Russian trousers tucked into his boots. GAYEV, as he enters, mimes the motions of a billiard player with his hands and elbows.)

LYUBOV ANDREYEVNA: Wait—how does it go? Wait, I remember—yellow into the corner, pot the red.

GAYEV: Cut shot into the corner! Sister, do you remember when we were little we both slept here? And now I'm fifty-one, strange as it seems.

LOPAKHIN: Time flies.

GAYEV: What?

LOPAKHIN: I said time flies.

GAYEV: There's a smell of cheap cologne in here.

ANYA: I'm going to bed. Good night, Mama. *(She kisses her mother.)*

LYUBOV ANDREYEVNA: My darling little girl. *(She kisses her hands.)* Are you glad to be home? I still can't believe it.

ANYA: Good night, Uncle.

GAYEV: *(kissing her face and hands)* May God keep you, bless you. You look just like your mother. Lyubov, you look just like her.
   (ANYA shakes hands with LOPAKHIN and SIMEONOV-PISHCHIK. She goes out, closing the door behind her.)

LYUBOV ANDREYEVNA: She's so tired.

PISHCHIK: It was a long journey.

VARYA: *(to LOPAKHIN and PISHCHIK)* Well, gentlemen, it's after three. It's time to go.

LYUBOV ANDREYEVNA: *(laughing)* Same old Varya. *(She pulls VARYA toward her and kisses her.)* Let me finish my coffee, and then we'll all go to bed. *(FIRS slides a cushion under her feet.)* Thank you, my dear. I drink coffee all the time now. I've become used to it. I drink it day and night. Oh, thank you, dear old soul. Thank you. *(She kisses him.)*

VARYA: I'll see if they've brought in all your things. *(She goes out.)*

LYUBOV ANDREYEVNA: Is this really me sitting here? *(She laughs.)* I want to wave my arms and jump for joy. *(She buries her face in her hands.)* But what if I'm asleep and this is only a dream? Oh, my God, I love my country. I feel such tenderness for it. On the train I was crying so much I could hardly see through the window. *(almost crying)* But I must finish my coffee. Thank you, Firs, thank you, my dear. I'm so happy you're still alive.

FIRS: The day before yesterday...

GAYEV: He's going deaf.

LOPAKHIN: I have to go now. At five this morning I have to leave for Kharkov. Poor me. But I wanted to see you, talk with you again. You're as beautiful as ever.

PISHCHIK: *(breathing heavily)* More. She's more beautiful. And in her Paris dress—I'm hers forever.

LOPAKHIN: Your brother here calls me oaf, peasant, and boor—but I don't care. Let people say what they want. There's only one thing I care about: that you should trust me as you've always trusted me, that your wonderful eyes should look at me as tenderly as they did. Dear God, my father was your grandfather's slave, and your father's—but you did so much for me once that I forget that. And I love you as my own sister, more than my sister.

LYUBOV ANDREYEVNA: I can't sit still. Not now. Not now. It's not possible. *(She jumps up, paces back and forth in the room, very moved.)* This joy, it's too much… Laugh at me if you like. I know I'm foolish. My dear little bookcase. *(She kisses the bookcase.)* My own little table.

GAYEV: While you were gone, Nanny died. *(She sits again and drinks her coffee.)*

LYUBOV ANDREYEVNA: Yes, God rest her soul. They wrote and told me.

GAYEV: Anastasy is dead too. And one-eyed Petrushka left me. He's living in town now, working for the police inspector. *(He takes a box from his pocket and sucks on a candy.)*

SIMEONOV-PISHCHIK: My daughter, Dashenka—says to say hello.

LOPAKHIN: I would like to tell you something that would please you, cheer you up. *(looking at his watch)* But there's no time. I have to go. Well, only two or three words. You know your cherry orchard must be sold to pay your debts, and the auction is set for the twenty-second of August. But don't worry, my dear, you can rest easy. There's a solution. Now listen carefully, here's my plan. Your estate is only thirteen miles from town, right? The railroad passes nearby, so if you divide the cherry orchard and the land along the river into cottage sites, and lease the sites to summer residents— you'll take in a minimum of twenty-five thousand rubles a year.

GAYEV: Forgive me, but that's nonsense.

LYUBOV ANDREYEVNA: What are you saying, Yermolay Alexyevich? It's not clear to me.

LOPAKHIN: Ask at least twenty-five rubles a year for each two-and-a-half acre plot, and if you hurry and advertise now, I'll bet you won't have a single piece of land left by fall. They'll all be taken. You'll see. In brief, I congratulate you. The situation is saved. The site is beautiful, the river deep enough to swim in. Of course, you'll have to rearrange things, tidy up the place. For instance, tear down the old buildings, including this house which isn't worth anything, and cut down the old cherry orchard.

LYUBOV ANDREYEVNA: Cut down the cherry orchard? My dear, excuse me, but you don't understand. If in the entire province there is a single remarkable site, it's our cherry orchard.

LOPAKHIN: It's remarkable only because it's big. In fact, it bears only once in two years, and even then you can do nothing with the cherries. There's no market for them.

GAYEV: But even the encyclopedia talks about our cherry orchard.

LOPAKHIN: (consulting his watch) There's no other way. If you don't decide, the cherry orchard, the whole estate, will be auctioned on the twenty-second of August. Make up your mind. There's no other solution. None. Absolutely none.

FIRS: In the old days, forty, fifty years ago, they picked the cherries— dried, soaked and marinated them, and made them into jam. And sometimes —

GAYEV: Firs, be quiet.

FIRS: Sometimes they sent cartloads of dried cherries to Moscow and Kharkov. And that brought in money. Those cherries then were sweet and juicy, and the smell... They knew how to do it. They had the recipe.

LYUBOV ANDREYEVNA: Well, what is the recipe?

FIRS: It's forgotten. No one remembers.

SIMEONOV-PISHCHIK: (to LYUBOV ANDREYEVNA) And what about Paris? How was it? Did you eat frogs?

LYUBOV ANDREYEVNA: I ate crocodiles.

SIMEONOV-PISHCHIK: Incredible.

LOPAKHIN: Until now there were only landlords and peasants in the country, but summer people are moving in. Already the smallest village is surrounded by summer homes. In twenty years the number of summer people will be greatly multiplied. All they do now, of course, is drink tea on their front porches, but maybe some day they'll cultivate their own acre. Then the cherry orchard will be happy, rich, and productive.

GAYEV: *(indignant)* Ridiculous.

(VARYA *and* YASHA *enter.)*

VARYA: Mama dear, two telegrams came for you. *(With a key from her ring she opens the old bookcase. Her keys jingle.)* Here they are.

LYUBOV ANDREYEVNA: From Paris. *(She tears up the telegrams without reading them.)* It's all over with Paris.

GAYEV: Do you know how old this bookcase is, Lyuba? A week ago I opened the bottom drawer, and saw the date burned into it. It was made exactly one hundred years ago. Isn't that something, hmm? We could celebrate its centennial. I know it's only an inanimate object, but still, it's a bookcase.

SIMEONOV-PISHCHIK: *(surprised)* A hundred years old? Incredible!

GAYEV: *(lightly touching the bookcase)* Yes. Now this is a bookcase. Dear highly esteemed bookcase, I salute you. For a century your existence has turned our minds toward bright ideals of goodness and justice. Your silent call to fruitful work has never faltered. You've upheld our family's courage for generations, our faith in a better future. You've implanted in our hearts a sense of right, a social conscience... *(pause)*

LOPAKHIN: Yes.

LYUBOV ANDREYEVNA: Still the same Leonya. You haven't changed.

GAYEV: *(a little embarrassed)* Cannon off the right. Cut into the side pocket.

LOPAKHIN: *(glancing at his watch)* Well, I must go. It's time.

YASHA: *(handing a pillbox to* LYUBOV ANDREYEVNA) Will you take your pills now, Madame?

SIMEONOV-PISHCHIK: Take no medicine, *chere Madame*. It does neither good nor harm. May I have them please? *(He takes the pill box from her, empties the pills into the palm of his hand, blows on them, swallows them, and washes them down with kvass.) Voilà.*

LYUBOV ANDREYEVNA: *(startled)* You're mad.

SIMEONOV-PISHCHIK: Swallowed them all.

LOPAKHIN: What a digestive system. *(All laugh.)*

FIRS: When His Honor came here during Holy Week, he ate half a bucket of salted cucumbers all by himself. *(FIRS mutters.)*

LYUBOV ANDREYEVNA: What did he say?

VARYA: He's been mumbling like that for three years now. We're used to it.

YASHA: It's age. (CHARLOTTA IVANOVNA, *looking thin, tightly corseted, wearing a white dress with a lorgnette at her belt, crosses the stage.*)

LOPAKHIN: Excuse me, Charlotta Ivanovna. I haven't had a chance to welcome you. (*He tries to kiss her hand.*)

CHARLOTTA: (*pulling her hand away*) If I let you kiss my hand, next you'll want to kiss my elbow, and then my shoulder.

LOPAKHIN: I'm out of luck today. (*All laugh.*) Show us one of your magic tricks.

LYUBOV ANDREYEVNA: Yes, Charlotta, do show us a trick.

CHARLOTTA: No, I'm going to bed now. (*She goes out.*)

LOPAKHIN: We'll see each other then in three weeks. (*He kisses* LYUBOV ANDREYEVNA*'s hand.*) Goodbye 'til then. I have to go. (*to* GAYEV) Goodbye. (*He kisses* PISHCHIK.) Goodbye. (*He shakes hands with* VARYA, *then with* FIRS *and* YASHA.) I don't feel the least desire to go. (*to* LYUBOV ANDREYEVNA) Think it over about the summer cottages. When you've decided, let me know. I can find you a loan of fifty thousand. Think it over seriously.

VARYA: (*angrily*) Well, if you're going, why don't you go?

LOPAKHIN: I'm going, I'm going... (*He goes.*)

GAYEV: Oaf. Oh, I'm so sorry. He's Varya's fiance, isn't he?

VARYA: Don't talk nonsense, Uncle.

LYUBOV ANDREYEVNA: But Varya, dear. I'd be very happy. He's a good man.

SIMEONOV-PISHCHIK: A worthy man. And my Dashenka says—she says many things. (*He snores, but wakes up at once.*) Anyway, dearest lady, would you loan me two hundred and forty rubles? Tomorrow the interest on my mortgage must be paid.

VARYA: (*frightened*) No, no, there's no money.

LYUBOV ANDREYEVNA: That's true. I don't have any.

SIMEONOV-PISHCHIK: We'll find some. I never lose hope. Just when I think it's all over, that I'm ruined, lo and behold the railroad crosses my land and they give me money. Anything can happen from one day to the next. My Dashenka could win two hundred thousand rubles. She has a lottery ticket.

LYUBOV ANDREYEVNA: Well, the coffee's finished. We can all go to sleep now.

FIRS: *(brushing* GAYEV's *clothes, admonishing him)* You've put on the wrong pants again. What am I to do with you?

VARYA: *(softly)* Anya's asleep. *(She quietly opens a window.)* The sun is up. It's getting warm. Look, Mama, how beautiful the trees are. My God, the air... And the starlings are singing.

GAYEV: *(opening another window)* The orchard is all white. You didn't forget it, Lyuba, did you? On moonlit nights that long path stretching out there like a ribbon shining—you remembered it, didn't you? You couldn't forget it.

LYUBOV ANDREYEVNA: *(looking out the window)* Oh, my childhood, my innocence. My room. I slept here. I awoke every morning happy, looking out at the orchard—the orchard exactly as it is now. Nothing has changed. *(She laughs with joy.)* White, all white. Oh, my own dear orchard! After a dark dismal autumn and a freezing winter, here you are young again, full of joy. The holy angels have not abandoned you. Oh, if only I could lift this weight from my heart, forget what's past.

GAYEV: Yes, and now, strange as it may seem, the orchard will be sold to pay our debts.

LYUBOV ANDREYEVNA: Look! Darling Mama. Walking through the orchard in her white dress. *(She laughs with joy.)* It's Mama. There she is!

GAYEV: Where?

VARYA: Oh Mama dear, God protect you.

LYUBOV ANDREYEVNA: There's nobody. I imagined it. Down there on the right—where the path goes to the summer house—that little bent over white tree looked like a woman. *(TROFIMOV enters in a worn student's uniform and glasses.)* Oh, this orchard! This wonderful orchard! Those masses of white flowers, the blue sky...

TROFIMOV: Lyubov Andreyevna! *(She turns around.)*

TROFIMOV: I only want to greet you. Then I'll leave. *(He kisses her hand fervently.)* They told me to wait until morning, but I couldn't. *(LYUBOV ANDREYEVNA looks at him, not recognizing him.)*

VARYA: *(through tears)* It's Petya Trofimov.

TROFIMOV: Petya Trofimov, Grisha's tutor. Have I changed so much? (LYUBOV ANDREYEVNA *embraces him, crying softly.*)

GAYEV: *(embarrassed)* Now, now Lyuba.

VARYA: *(crying)* Petya, I told you to wait until tomorrow.

LYUBOV ANDREYEVNA: My Grisha... my little boy... Grisha... my baby.

VARYA: Nothing we can do, little Mama. It's the will of God.

TROFIMOV: *(gently, almost crying)* Please. It's over now. Enough.

LYUBOV ANDREYEVNA: *(continuing to cry quietly)* My little boy is dead. Drowned. Why? Why, my friends? *(lowering her voice)* Anya's asleep in the next room, and I'm too loud. I'm making too much noise. Well, Petya? You were so handsome. Why have you aged so?

TROFIMOV: On the train a peasant woman said I looked like a shabby moth-eaten student.

LYUBOV ANDREYEVNA: You were a boy then, a sweet little student. And now, where's your hair? And you're wearing glasses. Surely you're not still a student? *(She goes toward the door.)*

TROFIMOV: I'll probably always be a student.

LYUBOV ANDREYEVNA: *(kissing her brother, then* VARYA*)* And now it's time for bed. And you, you've aged too, Leonid.

SIMEONOV-PISHCHIK: So, that's it. Bedtime. Ai, my gout. I'm spending the night. Lyubov Andreyevna, my dear friend, if you could— tomorrow morning, very early—two hundred and forty rubles...

GAYEV: A one-track mind.

SIMEONOV-PISHCHIK: Two hundred and forty rubles to pay the interest on my mortgage.

LYUBOV ANDREYEVNA: I have no money, my dear.

SIMEONOV-PISHCHIK: I'll give it back, *ma chere*. An insignificant sum.

LYUBOV ANDREYEVNA: All right. Leonid will give it to you. Give it to him, Leonid.

GAYEV: *(ironically)* Oh, of course. Leonid will give it to him. Right away. Why not?

LYUBOV ANDREYEVNA: What else can we do? He needs it. Give it to him. He'll pay it back.

(LYUBOV ANDREYEVNA, PISHCHIK *and* FIRS *go out.* TROFIMOV, GAYEV, VARYA *and* YASHA *are still on stage.)*

GAYEV: My sister is still in the habit of throwing her money away. *(to* YASHA*)* Move, my good man, move off—you smell like a brothel.

YASHA: *(smirking)* And you, Leonid Andreyvich, are still exactly the same.

GAYEV: What? *(to* VARYA*)* What did he say?

VARYA: *(to* YASHA*)* Your mother's come from the village. She's in the kitchen, waiting for you since yesterday. She wants to see you...

YASHA: So what? She doesn't interest me.

VARYA: Yasha, you should be ashamed!

YASHA: Who cares? She should have come tomorrow. *(He goes out.)*

VARYA: Mama's just the same. She hasn't changed at all. If she could, she'd give away everything she has.

GAYEV: Yes. *(pause)* If many cures are prescribed, you know the illness is incurable. I think of many cures which means, of course, we don't have any. It would be a good cure if we inherited a fortune, or married our Anya to a rich man, or if one of us went to Yaroslavl to try our luck with our old aunt, the Countess. After all, Auntie is very very rich.

VARYA: *(in tears)* If only God would help us.

GAYEV: Stop crying. Your aunt is rich but she doesn't like us. First of all because my sister married a lawyer who was not a noble. *(*ANYA *appears at the door.)* He was a commoner. And admittedly my sister's conduct hasn't been exactly virtuous either. She's good and kind and I love her—she's lovable, but she's weak. You have to admit she's loose—licentious. It's obvious in her every gesture.

VARYA: *(in a whisper)* Anya's here.

GAYEV: What? *(pause)* That's funny. I have something in my right eye. I can't see very well. As I was saying, last Thursday when I was down at the District Court...

*(*ANYA *enters.)*

VARYA: Why aren't you sleeping, Anya?

ANYA: I can't. I'm restless.

GAYEV: Darling. My own child. *(He kisses* ANYA*'s hands and face.)* Dearest child. *(through tears)* You're not only my niece, you're my angel. You're everything to me. Believe me, believe me...

ANYA: I believe you, Uncle. We all love and respect you, but, dear Uncle, you mustn't talk so much, you simply mustn't. What you just said about Mama—about your own sister—why say that?

GAYEV: I know, I know. *(He covers his face with* ANYA's *hand.)* It's awful. God help me. And tonight—that speech to the bookcase—how stupid. I only realized when I finished—how stupid.

VARYA: It's true, little Uncle. It would be better to keep quiet. Just to say nothing, that's all.

ANYA: If you keep quiet—you'll see, you'll feel better.

GAYEV: I'll keep quiet. *(He kisses* ANYA's *and* VARYA's *hands.)* I'll keep quiet. Only one word—about business. On Thursday I was at District Court. Some of us were talking, about this and that, and from what they say, it might be possible to get a loan to pay the interest.

VARYA: If only God would help us!

GAYEV: Tuesday I go back, and I'll talk to them again. *(to* VARYA*)* Stop crying. *(to* ANYA*)* Your mother will see Lopakhin. He won't refuse to help her, I know. And you, as soon as you're rested you'll leave for Yaroslavl, to see your great aunt the Countess. So we'll attack on three different fronts, and it's in the bag! We'll pay the interest, I know it. *(He puts a candy into his mouth.)* On my honor. I'll swear on anything. The estate won't be sold. *(excitedly)* I swear on my own happiness. Here's my hand. You can call me bad or heartless if I let the estate go to auction. By my life I swear it won't.

ANYA: *(her spirits risen, happy)* How good you are, Uncle, and clever. I feel better now. I'm not worried. I'm happy. *(*FIRS *enters.)*

FIRS: *(reproachfully)* Leonid Andreyevich, aren't you ashamed? When are you going to bed?

GAYEV: I'm coming, I'm coming. Go, Firs. I'll undress alone. Well, little ones, goodnight. Tomorrow is another day. Time for bed. *(He kisses* ANYA *and* VARYA.*)* I'm a man of the eighties. Today we don't think much of those years. I had to suffer then for my opinions, I can tell you. It's not for nothing I'm loved by the peasants. You have to understand the peasant mentality. You have to know how to talk to them, and—

ANYA: You're starting again, Uncle.

VARYA: Dear Uncle, please be quiet.

FIRS: *(angry)* Leonid Andreyevich!

GAYEV: I'm coming. I'm coming. Go to bed now. Double bank shot. Into the side pocket. Pot the white. A clean shot. *(He goes out.* FIRS *hobbles after him.)*

ANYA: I'm not worried anymore, but I don't want to go to Yaroslavl. I don't like Great-aunt. It doesn't matter. I'm not worried anymore, thanks to Uncle. *(She sits.)*

VARYA: We have to go to bed. I'm going. While you were gone, there was some trouble. You know only the old servants live on the estate now Yefimushka, Polya, Yevstignei, and, of course, Karp. Well, they invite all sorts of people to stay with them. All right. I don't say a word. Then someone starts a rumor I ordered the kitchen to serve only dried peas out of stinginess, you understand. Yevstignei started that rumor. All right, I say to myself, if that's your game, we'll see about that. So I send for Yevstignei. *(yawning)* I say—what makes you say such things? You're a fool, Yevstignei. Do you know that? A fool. *(She looks at* ANYA.*)* Anichka. *(pause)* She's asleep. *(She leads* ANYA *by the arm.)* Come to bed, my darling. My little darling is asleep. Come. *(They go toward the door. In the distance a shepherd is playing his pipe.* TROFIMOV *crosses the stage. When he sees* ANYA *and* VARYA, *he stops.)* Shhhhhh. She's asleep, asleep. Come on, darling.

ANYA: *(speaking softly, half-asleep)* I'm so tired. All those little bells... tinkling, tinkling. Uncle darling, and Mama. Uncle...

VARYA: Come, little one. Come, darling. *(They go into* ANYA's *room.)* Come, my precious. Angel, come.

TROFIMOV: *(very moved)* My sunshine! My spring!

Curtain

In a meadow, an abandoned chapel falling over. Next to it a well, some large stones probably once tombstones, and an old bench. We see the road from GAYEV's *house. To one side are several dark poplar trees bordering the cherry orchard. Farther is a row of telegraph poles. In the farthest distance can be guessed the outline of a large town visible on very clear days. The sun will soon set.*

CHARLOTTA, YASHA *and* DUNYASHA *are seated on the bench.* YEPIKHODOV *stands playing the guitar. All look pensive.* CHARLOTTA, *wearing an old cap, has taken a shotgun from her shoulder and is adjusting the buckle on the strap.*

CHARLOTTA: *(musingly)* I don't have a real passport. I don't even know my age. I always feel like a little girl. When I was a child, my father and mother traveled from one fair to another giving performances—very good performances. And I did *salto-mortale*, death-defying leaps and things like that. Then when Poppa and Mama died, a German lady took me in. She raised me. Good. I became a governess. But where am I from, and who am I? I don't know. Who were my parents? Were they even married? I don't know. *(She takes a cucumber from her pocket and munches it.)* I don't know anything. I want to talk to someone. But who? There's no one.

YEPIKHODOV: *(playing guitar, singing)* "Not for me, this noisy world. I care not for friend or foe." Ah, how pleasant to play the mandolin.

DUNYASHA: That's a guitar, not a mandolin. *(She looks at herself in a little mirror, powders her face.)*

YEPIKHODOV: To a fool dying of love, this is a mandolin.

"Oh, if only my heart were enflamed with love requited, oh." *(YASHA sings softly with him.)*

CHARLOTTA: How dreadfully they sing. Faugh! Like shrieking dogs.

DUNYASHA: *(to YASHA)* You're so lucky to have been abroad.

YASHA: Yes, of course. I can't disagree with you. *(He yawns, then lights a cigar.)*

YEPIKHODOV: Abroad everything has reached a state of completion, obviously.

YASHA: Yes.

YEPIKHODOV: I'm a man of culture, I read unusual and exceptionally interesting books. But the trouble is I don't always grasp the intent of my own mind. What do I really want—to live, or to blow my brains out? Therefore, I always carry a revolver. Here it is. *(He shows the revolver.)*

CHARLOTTA: I'm finished. I'm going. *(She slings the gun over her shoulder.)* You're too clever, Yepikhodov. You're dangerous. Women must be crazy about you. Brrr. *(She starts to leave.)* These intellectuals are always so stupid. I have no one to talk to... Alone, alone, I'm always alone... I have no one. And who am I? Why am I here? I have no idea... *(She leaves in a leisurely way.)*

YEPIKHODOV: Truth to tell, apart from anything else, I must confess that as far as I'm concerned, Fate treats me with no pity. I am but a small ship tossed by the waves. If this is not so, then I ask why, upon awakening this morning, did I perceive an enormous spider upon my chest, as big as this? *(He demonstrates with both hands.)* And why, when I'm thirsty and pick up a glass of kvass, do I find an indecent thing in it, like a cockroach? *(pause)* Have you read Buckle? *(pause)* I would like the honor of a few words with you, Avodotya Fydorovna, please.

DUNYASHA: Well, what is it?

YEPIKHODOV: Well—I'd like them in private... *(He sighs.)*

DUNYASHA: *(embarrassed)* Alright... But first fetch me my little cape... It's near the armoire... It's a little damp here...

YEPIKHODOV: Very well. I shall bring it. And now I know what to do with my revolver... *(He takes his guitar and goes out playing it softly.)*

YASHA: Twenty-two misfortunes! Between you and me, I think he's stupid. *(He yawns.)*

DUNYASHA: Still, pray God he doesn't shoot himself. *(pause)* I'm so sensitive. Everything frightens me. I was still little when the masters took me into the house to work. Now I've lost the habit of ordinary living. Look at my hands—white, white as a lady's. I've become so sensitive, so, so refined. Everything frightens me. I'm so frightened. If you deceive me, Yasha, my nerves won't hold out.

YASHA: *(kissing her)* Little cucumber! Young ladies don't lose their heads. And if there's one thing I can't stand, it's a girl who doesn't know how to behave like a lady.

DUNYASHA: You're so educated, Yasha. You can talk about anything. I love you passionately. *(pause)*

YASHA: *(yawning)* Mmmm...A girl who says she's in love is not a lady. *(pause)* I like smoking cigars out here in the open air... *(He listens.)* They're coming. It's them. (DUNYASHA *kisses him effusively.)* Go back toward the house. Pretend you're coming from swimming in the river. Go that way, or they'll think I had a rendezvous with you. I can't stand that.

DUNYASHA: *(with a little cough)* My head is aching from that cigar.
(She goes out. YASHA *remains sitting by the chapel.* LYUBOV ANDREY-EVNA, GAYEV *and* LOPAKHIN *come in.)*

LOPAKHIN: You must make a decision. Time won't wait. The question is very simple. Just tell me—do you or don't you want to sell your land for building summer cottages? You have only to say a single word—yes or no. One single word.

LYUBOV ANDREYEVNA: Who's been smoking those revolting cigars out here? *(She sits down.)*

GAYEV: Convenient now the railroad is so near. Imagine—we had lunch in town. Cannon off the white! I'd like to go back to the house and play a game.

LYUBOV ANDREYEVNA: There'll be time enough for that.

LOPAKHIN: Only one word. *(imploring)* Yes or no? Please tell me!

GAYEV: *(yawning)* What?

LYUBOV ANDREYEVNA: *(looking into her purse)* Yesterday there was money in my purse. Today there's almost none. My poor Varya tries to save. She serves us only milk soup. In the kitchen the old servants get nothing but dried peas—while I waste, I just waste money for no reason... I don't know why. *(She drops her purse. Gold pieces fall. She's annoyed.)* Now look. There they go.

YASHA: Permit me, Madame. I'll pick them up. *(He picks up the gold pieces.)*

LYUBOV ANDREYEVNA: Thank you, Yasha. Why did I go to lunch? That ugly restaurant of yours, that stupid music, and those tablecloths smelling of soap. Why do you drink so much, Leonya? And eat so much? And talk so much? And to whom? To the waiters about the seventies and decadent literature—to the waiters about decadent literature! What for?

LOPAKHIN: Yes.

GAYEV: *(with a gesture of resignation)* I know. I know. I'm hopeless. It's obvious. *(to YASHA, irritably)* Why are you always hanging around bothering us?

YASHA: *(laughing)* I can't hear you speak without starting to laugh...

GAYEV: *(to his sister)* Either he goes, or I go...

LYUBOV ANDREYEVNA: Go now, Yasha. Go away...

YASHA: *(handing her purse to Lyubov Andreyevna)* Right away. I'm going. *(hardly able to repress his laughter)* This minute... *(He goes out.)*

LOPAKHIN: They say the rich Deriganov wants to buy your estate. He's coming in person to the auction.

LYUBOV ANDREYEVNA: How do you know?

LOPAKHIN: I heard it in town.

GAYEV: Our Yaroslavl aunt promised to send money, but when and how much, who knows?

LOPAKHIN: How much? A hundred thousand? Two hundred?

LYUBOV ANDREYEVNA: Oh, no. We're lucky if it's ten or fifteen thousand.

LOPAKHIN: Forgive me, but I have never in my life met people as impractical as you, my friends—so eccentric, so unbusinesslike. I have told you clearly and simply—your estate is about to be sold. But you don't seem to understand.

LYUBOV ANDREYEVNA: Well, what can we do? What? Tell us.

LOPAKHIN: I tell you and I tell you. I tell you every day. You must rent your cherry orchard and lands—divide them into lots for summer cottages. You must do it as soon as possible. The auction is almost here. Try to understand. Once you decide to build summer cottages, you'll have all the money you want. You'll be saved.

LYUBOV ANDREYEVNA: All those little houses and summer people. Forgive me, but it's so vulgar.

GAYEV: I couldn't agree more.

LOPAKHIN: I'm going to cry. I'm going to scream. I'm going to faint. I can't take it any more. You've exhausted me. *(to GAYEV)* You are a silly old woman.

GAYEV: What?

LOPAKHIN: A silly old woman. *(He starts to leave.)*

LYUBOV ANDREYEVNA: *(alarmed)* No, dear friend, please stay. Please. Maybe we'll find a way.

LOPAKHIN: There's only one way.

LYUBOV ANDREYEVNA: Don't leave. I beg you. When you're here everything seems less gray. *(pause)* I keep feeling something awful is about to happen, as if the walls of the house were going to fall on us.

GAYEV: *(in his own world)* Cannon off the middle. Pot the white.

LYUBOV ANDREYEVNA: So many sins in our lives...

LOPAKHIN: You have no sins...

GAYEV: *(putting a candy into his mouth)* They say I ate up my fortune in bon-bons... *(He laughs.)*

LYUBOV ANDREYEVNA: Oh, my sins. I've always been reckless with money, tossed it away like a lunatic. Then I married a man who had a genius for debt. Champagne killed him in the end—he was always drunk. Then, oh Lord—another man. I fell in love, became his mistress. Then—my first punishment came like a blow on the head... My boy Grisha, my beautiful little boy, was drowned, here in this river. I went away... I shut my eyes. I wanted never to come back, never to see this river again... I didn't want to know where I was or what I was doing. I went abroad. But *he* followed me... He was merciless, brutal. He wouldn't leave me alone. I had a villa near Menton. He fell ill there. I nursed him. For three years day and night I had no rest. He exhausted me. He used up my soul. Last year I sold the villa to pay our debts. In Paris he robbed me, and went to live with another woman. I tried to poison myself... So senseless, humiliating. Then suddenly I felt a yearning for Russia, for my homeland and my little girl... *(She wipes away her tears.)* Oh, God have mercy. Forgive my sins. Don't punish me any more. *(She takes a telegram from her pocket.)* This came from Paris today. He begs me to forgive him and come back. *(She tears up the telegram.)* I seem to hear music from somewhere. *(She listens.)*

GAYEV: It's our famous Jewish orchestra. Do you remember? Four violins, a flute and a double bass.

LYUBOV ANDREYEVNA: It still exists? We must have them come one evening.

LOPAKHIN: *(listening)* I don't hear it. *(He sings softly.)* "And for money the Germans will countrify a Russian, ha ha ha!" *(He laughs.)* I saw a play in the theatre last night. It was very funny.

LYUBOV ANDREYEVNA: It probably wasn't funny at all. Instead of going to plays, look at yourselves—how gray your lives are, what useless things you say.

LOPAKHIN: Yes, that's true. I admit it. Our lives are stupid. *(pause)* My father was a peasant, a dumb fool. He knew nothing, so he taught me nothing. He beat me with a stick when he was drunk, that's all. At bottom I'm a fool like him. I know I have an ugly handwriting. I write like a chicken scratching for worms. I'm ashamed of it.

LYUBOV ANDREYEVNA: What? You need a wife, my friend.

LOPAKHIN: Yes. I know you're right.

LYUBOV ANDREYEVNA: Marry our Varya. She's a good girl.

LOPAKHIN: Yes.

LYUBOV ANDREYEVNA: She's a hard worker, and like you she comes from peasant people. But what's most important—she loves you. And you've been fond of her a long time.

LOPAKHIN: Why not? I'm not against it. She's a good girl. *(pause)*

GAYEV: They've asked me to work at the bank, did you know that? Six thousand rubles a year.

LYUBOV ANDREYEVNA: You? In a bank? Don't be ridiculous. *(FIRS enters carrying a coat.)*

FIRS: *(to GAYEV)* It's damp. Please put on your coat, sir.

GAYEV: *(putting on the coat)* You're such an old nuisance.

FIRS: Please. Already this morning you left without telling me. *(He looks GAYEV over carefully.)*

LYUBOV ANDREYEVNA: How old you've become, Firs!

FIRS: What can I get you, Madame?

LOPAKHIN: She says you're very old!

FIRS: It's because I've lived a long time. When your papa wasn't even born, they were already planning a wife for me... *(He laughs.)* When the slaves were freed, I was already head footman here. I didn't want to be freed. I was head footman. I stayed with my masters... *(pause)* They were happy then. Why? I don't know. They didn't know themselves.

LOPAKHIN: Oh, the old days were fine—they could at least flog the peasants then.

FIRS: *(not having heard)* That's right. The peasants took care of the masters, and the masters took care of the peasants. Now everyone goes his own way, and no one understands anything.

GAYEV: That's enough, Firs. Tomorrow I go to town. A certain general might give us a loan.

LYUBOV ANDREYEVNA: He's delirious. There's no such general.

(TROFIMOV, ANYA *and* VARYA *enter.*)

GAYEV: Here come our little girls.

ANYA: Here's Mama!

LYUBOV ANDREYEVNA: *(tenderly)* Come, come here, my sweet ones. *(She kisses* ANYA *and* VARYA.*)* I love you. If you only knew how much. Sit here near me—that's right, like this. *(They all sit.)*

LOPAKHIN: Our eternal student is always with the young ladies.

TROFIMOV: So what?

LOPAKHIN: Almost fifty and still a student.

TROFIMOV: Stop being stupid.

LOPAKHIN: Why are you angry, you funny person?

TROFIMOV: Leave me alone. (LOPAKHIN *laughs.*)

LOPAKHIN: Just one question—what do you think of me?

TROFIMOV: Here's what I think, Yermolay Alexyevich. You're rich—soon you'll be a millionaire. And just as the predator devouring everything in its path is necessary to the balance of nature, so are you. *(Everyone laughs.)*

VARYA: Petya, why don't you tell us about the planets?

LYUBOV ANDREYEVNA: Let's continue yesterday's discussion.

TROFIMOV: What was it about?

GAYEV: Pride—whether Man should be proud.

TROFIMOV: When you say Man should take pride in himself—from a spiritual point of view you may be right. But if we take the question simply, why should Man be so proud? Physiologically, he's pretty poorly put together. And with few exceptions, he's brutal, ignorant, and profoundly miserable. So why admire ourselves? The only thing to do is work.

GAYEV: We're going to die anyway, whatever we do.

TROFIMOV: Who knows? And what does it mean, to die? Maybe Man has a hundred senses. Maybe only the five we know die. Maybe the ninety-five others stay alive.

LYUBOV ANDREYEVNA: Petya, you're so clever!

LOPAKHIN: *(ironically)* It's frightening.

TROFIMOV: Humanity, as it progresses, attempts to perfect itself. What's unattainable now will one day be usual, but not without our working at it. In Russia few do anything worthwhile. Intellectuals look for no truths, do nothing, don't know how to work, call themselves "intelligentsia," while treating their servants with contempt, and peasants like animals. They don't educate themselves or read serious books. They chatter about science, and what do they know about art? Grim-faced, they philosophize while workers are badly nourished, sleep thirty, forty to a room with no real beds, with bedbugs, foul odors, dampness, and in moral degradation. Our fine talk serves to divert and blind us. Where are the child care centers and libraries everyone talks about? In novels, yes—but in life they don't exist. What does exist is dirt, vulgarity, and our medieval ways. I don't trust serious faces. They frighten me. And I don't trust serious conversation. We'd do better to keep silent.

LOPAKHIN: Well, I for one get up at five each morning and work until night. I handle money, mine and others'. I see what people are like. Start to work, do anything, and you'll soon realize how few honest respectable folk there are. Sometimes when I can't sleep, I think— "Lord, you gave us these vast forests, endless fields, wide horizons. We who live here ought to be giants."

LYUBOV ANDREYEVNA: Giants. Why giants? They're fine in fairy tales, but in life they'd be terrifying. *(YEPIKHODOV is passing in the background playing his guitar.* LYUBOV ANDREYEVNA *speaks dreamily.)* There goes Yepikhodov.

ANYA: *(dreamily)* There goes Yepikhodov.

GAYEV: The sun has set, my friends.

TROFIMOV: Yes.

GAYEV: *(quietly, as if reciting)* Oh, glorious Nature, wonderful, gleaming with eternal light, beauteous and indifferent—we call you Mother. You are life, you are death, you give us birth, and you destroy us.

VARYA: *(imploringly)* Uncle, *please!*

ANYA: Uncle, you're at it again.

TROFIMOV: You'd better bank the yellow in the middle pocket.

GAYEV: I'm silent, I'm silent.

(All sit silent, musing. It is quiet. FIRS *mutters softly to himself. The sound of a rope breaking is heard from far off, coming as if from the sky. Gradually the sound fades, leaving traces of sadness.)*

LYUBOV ANDREYEVNA: What is that?

LOPAKHIN: I don't know. Maybe somewhere in a mine shaft a cable broke, a bucket fell. But somewhere very far away.

GAYEV: It might have been a bird, like a heron.

TROFIMOV: Or an owl.

LYUBOV ANDREYEVNA: *(shivering)* It was eerie. *(pause)*

FIRS: It was the same before the disaster. The owl hooted and the samovar sang without stopping—both.

GAYEV: Before what disaster?

FIRS: Before the emancipation. *(pause)*

LYUBOV ANDREYEVNA: You know, my friends, let's go. It's getting dark. *(to* ANYA*)* You have tears in your eyes. What is it, my little one? *(She holds her in her arms.)*

ANYA: Nothing, Mama. Nothing.

TROFIMOV: Someone's coming.

(A VAGRANT *appears in an old white soldier's cap and an overcoat. He's somewhat drunk.)*

VAGRANT: Excuse me. Very sorry to disturb you, but please tell me, can I get to the station this way?

GAYEV: Yes, yes, just stay on this road.

VAGRANT: Thank you very much, sir. *(He coughs.)* Beautiful weather… *(He recites.)* "Oh brother, poor suffering brother, go to the Volga, where your groans …" *(to* VARYA*)* Miss, how about thirty kopecks for a hungry Russian?

*(*VARYA *cries out, scared.)*

LOPAKHIN: *(angrily)* Really. That's enough.

LYUBOV ANDREYEVNA: *(frightened, hurriedly)* Here, this is for you. *(She searches frantically in her purse.)* No silver. Doesn't matter. Take a gold piece.

VAGRANT: Thank you very much, Madame. Much obliged to you. *(He laughs.)*

VARYA: *(frightened)* I'm going. I'm going. Oh, Mama, my poor Mama. We have nothing for the servants to eat, and you give him gold.

LYUBOV ANDREYEVNA: What can I do? I'm too stupid. When we're home, I'll give you everything I have left. Yermolay Alexyevich, you'll advance me more, won't you?

LOPAKHIN: Of course.

LYUBOV ANDREYEVNA: Come along everyone. It's time to go in. And just now, Varya, we've arranged a match for you. We've settled your marriage plans. Congratulations.

VARYA: *(almost crying)* Mama, don't joke about that.

LOPAKHIN: "Get thee to a nunnery, Amelia."

GAYEV: My hands are shaking. They're too long away from the billiard table.

LOPAKHIN: "Amelia, O nymph, in thy horizons be all my sins remembered."

LYUBOV ANDREYEVNA: Come, my friends! It's almost supper time.

VARYA: He scared me. My heart is pounding.

LOPAKHIN: Ladies and gentlemen, allow me to remind you. On the twenty-second of August the cherry orchard will be sold. Bear that in mind. Think. *(They all leave except* TROFIMOV *and* ANYA.*)*

ANYA: *(laughing)* Thank you, stranger, for frightening away Varya. Now we can be alone.

TROFIMOV: Varya's afraid we'll fall in love. That's why she won't leave us alone. She's narrow-minded. She can't see we're above love. We must avoid everything false or unworthy, everything which prevents us from being fully alive and joyous. Onward we march, drawn by our bright shining star. Onward! Keep in step, comrades.

ANYA: *(stretching her arms upward)* How wonderfully you talk! *(pause)* It's so beautiful out today.

TROFIMOV: Yes, the weather's glorious.

ANYA: What have you done to me, Petya? Why don't I love the cherry orchard as I did before? I loved it so tenderly. I thought there was no better place in the world than our orchard.

TROFIMOV: All of Russia is our orchard. The world is vast and beautiful, and there are many marvelous places in it. *(pause)* Think of it, Anya—your grandfather, great grandfather, your family all the way back owned slaves, living souls. Can you hear the voices of those souls? Don't you feel human beings looking at you from every tree in the orchard? To have owned human souls has perverted all of you, your whole family—your ancestors and you who are alive now. Your mother, your uncle, and even you don't realize you're debtors living at the expense of people you wouldn't even allow into your house. We're behind by two hundred years. We've learned nothing yet. We can't even assess the past. We just philosophize, complain of *ennui* and drink vodka. To live in the present we must first redeem our past, atone for it. We can do that only by suffering and work—relentless work. Understand that, Anya.

ANYA: For a long time now our house hasn't really been our house. I'm going to leave it. I swear I will. I'll leave it.

TROFIMOV: If you have the keys to the house, throw them down the well. Leave. Be free as the wind.

ANYA: *(ecstatic)* You said that so beautifully!

TROFIMOV: Believe me, Anya, believe me. I'm not even thirty and I'm still a student, but I've suffered. When winter comes I starve, I'm sick, anxious, poor as a beggar. Where hasn't Fate tossed me, where haven't I been? But always, each moment, day and night, my soul is filled with incredible hope. I feel happiness coming, Anya. I already glimpse it...

ANYA: *(thoughtfully)* The moon is rising.

(YEPIKHODOV is heard playing the same sad song on the guitar. The moon has risen. Somewhere behind the poplars VARYA is looking for ANYA.)

VARYA: *(offstage, calling)* Anya! Where are you?

TROFIMOV: Yes, the moon is rising. *(pause)* Here it is. Happiness. It's coming closer and closer. I can almost touch it. But even if we don't see it, if we can't recognize it— it doesn't matter. Others will see it.

VARYA: *(offstage)* Anya! Where are you?

TROFIMOV: Varya again. *(angrily)* It's torture.

ANYA: Never mind. Let's run down to the river. It's so beautiful there.

TROFIMOV: Let's go. *(They go.)*

VARYA: *(still offstage)* Anya! Anya!

Curtain

Evening. In the drawing room, separated from the ballroom by an arch, a chandelier is lit. In the ballroom they are dancing a Grand Rond. We hear the Jewish orchestra playing.

SIMEONOV-PISHCHIK: *(offstage)* Promenade a une paire.

(The following couples dance through the drawing room—SIMEONOV-PISHCHIK and CHARLOTTA, TROFIMOV and LYUBOV ANDREYEVNA, ANYA and the POST-MASTER, VARYA and the STATION MASTER, and finally DUNYASHA and her PARTNER. As she dances, VARYA is crying quietly and wiping away her tears.)

SIMEONOV-PISHCHIK: *(shouting)* Grand rond, balancez! Les cavaliers a genoux et remerciez vos dames! *(FIRS in a frock coat carries a tray of seltzer water. PISHCHIK and TROFIMOV enter the drawing room.)* I've had two strokes already. It's not good for me to dance. But, "When in Rome..." Anyway—I'm healthy as a horse. My dear departed father—God have mercy on his soul—maintained that the line of Simeonov-Pishchik descends from the horse Caligula made a senator. *(He sits down.)* I have only one trouble—money. Money. And a hungry dog thinks only of meat. *(He goes to sleep and snores, but immediately wakes up.)* Like me—I can only talk of money...

TROFIMOV: It's true, now that you mention it, there is something a little equine about you.

SIMEONOV-PISHCHIK: Well, the horse is not a bad animal... At least you can always sell it...
(From the next room we hear the sound of billiard balls clicking against each other. VARYA appears under the arch.)

TROFIMOV: *(teasing her)* Madame Lopakhin! Madame Lopakhin!

VARYA: *(angrily)* Moth-eaten shabby old student!

TROFIMOV: Yes, moth-eaten, shabby, an old student—and proud of it.

VARYA: *(brooding bitterly)* So we've hired musicians now, and how are we going to pay for them? *(She goes out.)*

TROFIMOV: *(to PISHCHIK)* If you used the energy differently that you spend looking for money to pay interest on your debts—you could turn the world upside down.

SIMEONOV-PISHCHIK: Nietzsche—that famous great philosopher, that gigantic intellect—writes that Man can counterfeit money.

TROFIMOV: You've read Nietzsche?

SIMEONOV-PISHCHIK: No. Dashenka told me. In my situation, counterfeiting may be the only solution… Day after tomorrow I owe three hundred and ten rubles… I've already found a hundred. *(He feels his pockets, alarmed.)* Where is it? I've lost it. *(close to tears)* Where's the money? *(joyously)* I have it. It's in the lining. I'm sweating.

(LYUBOV ANDREYEVNA and CHARLOTTA enter. LYUBOV ANDREYEVNA hums the Lezghinka, a dance.)

LYUBOV ANDREYEVNA: Why hasn't Leonid come home? What can he be doing so long in town? *(to DUNYASHA)* Dunyasha, offer tea to the musicians.

TROFIMOV: There probably wasn't an auction.

LYUBOV ANDREYEVNA: This is not the night for an orchestra. We're giving a party at the wrong time. Well, too bad. *(She sits, hums quietly.)*

CHARLOTTA: *(handing deck of cards to PISHCHIK)* Think of a card.

SIMEONOV-PISHCHIK: I have.

CHARLOTTA: Now shuffle. Very good. Now, give them to me, my dear Monsieur Pishchik. *Eins, zwei, drei.* Now look for it. It's in your coat pocket.

SIMEONOV-PISHCHIK: *(pulling a card out of his pocket)* The eight of spades. That's absolutely right. *(amazed)* Incredible.

CHARLOTTA: *(holding the deck toward TROFIMOV)* Quickly, what's the top card?

TROFIMOV: What? Queen of spades.

CHARLOTTA: Correct. *(to PISHCHIK)* And you? What's the top card?

SIMEONOV-PISHCHIK: Ace of hearts.

CHARLOTTA: Correct! *(She claps her hands. The deck of cards disappears.)* What beautiful weather we're having today.

(The mysterious voice of a woman, seeming to come from under the floor, answers her.)

VOICE: Yes, what beautiful weather we're having today.

CHARLOTTA: You are my ideal. You are beautiful. *Mon bel ideal.*

VOICE: And I admire you, Madame.

STATION MASTER: *(applauding)* Well done, madame ventriloquist. Bravo!

SIMEONOV-PISHCHIK: *(surprised)* Incredible. Charming Charlotta Ivanovna... I am simply in love with you.

CHARLOTTA: In love? *(She shrugs her shoulders.)* How can you possibly be in love? *Guter Mensch, aber schlechter Musicant.*

TROFIMOV: *(slapping* PISHCHIK *on the shoulder)* Good old horse.

CHARLOTTA: Attention please. One more trick. *(She takes a large shawl from a chair.)* Here's a beautiful shawl. I want to sell it. *(shaking it out)* Is there a buyer?

SIMEONOV-PISHCHIK: *(amazed)* Incredible.

CHARLOTTA: *Eins, zwei, drei!*
(She lifts the shawl quickly. Behind it is ANYA *who performs a little curtsy, runs to her mother, kisses her, and runs back into the ballroom. Everyone is delighted.)*

LYUBOV ANDREYEVNA: *(applauding)* Bravo, bravo!

CHARLOTTA: Once more. *Eins, zwei, drei!*
(She lifts the shawl, behind which is VARYA, *who bows.)*

SIMEONOV-PISHCHIK: *(astonished)* Incredible.

CHARLOTTA: That's all. Finished.
(She curtsies and runs out, flinging her shawl at PISHCHIK.*)*

SIMEONOV-PISHCHIK: *(running after her)* Oh, you little rascal. *(chortling happily)* Heinh? Heinh? *(He goes out.)*

LYUBOV ANDREYEVNA: And Leonid still not here. What's he doing in town? I can't understand it. Either the estate is sold, and it's all over—or there hasn't been an auction at all. Why hold us in suspense?

VARYA: *(wanting to comfort her)* Dear Uncle will buy it. I'm sure of it.

TROFIMOV: *(ironic)* Oh, of course.

VARYA: Great-aunt sent him power of attorney to buy it in her name, and she'll assume the debt. She's doing it for Anya. I'm sure God will help us. Uncle will buy it.

LYUBOV ANDREYEVNA: Our great-aunt from Yaroslavl sent only fifteen thousand to buy the estate—in her name. She doesn't trust us. Besides, that amount wouldn't even pay the interest. *(She covers her face with her hands.)* My fate is being decided today, my fate...

TROFIMOV: *(teasing* VARYA) Madame Lopakhin.

VARYA: *(angrily)* Eternal student! You've already been thrown out of the university twice.

LYUBOV ANDREYEVNA: Why are you so angry, Varya? He's teasing you about Lopakhin. So? Why don't you marry Lopakhin? He's a good man, interesting. Of course you don't have to marry him if you don't want to. No one's forcing you, darling...

VARYA: I'm considering it, Mama—seriously. I am. He's a good person. I like him very much.

LYUBOV ANDREYEVNA: So marry him. What are you waiting for? I don't understand.

VARYA: Mama dear, it's not for me to propose to him. For two years now everyone else talks to me about it. But he either says nothing, or he makes a joke of it. I know why. He's busy getting rich—he's involved with his work, he doesn't have time to think about me. If only I had money—not much, even a little—I'd leave everything and go away, the farther the better. I'd enter a convent.

TROFIMOV: How saintly.

VARYA: *(to* TROFIMOV*)* A student is supposed to be clever. *(in a soft tone, tears in her voice)* How ugly you've become, Petya—how old you've grown. *(to* LYUBOV, *no longer crying.)* I can't live without work, Mama. I have to have something to do every minute. *(*YASHA *enters.)*

YASHA: *(tittering)* Yepikhodov broke a billiard cue. *(He goes out.)*

VARYA: What's Yepikhodov doing here? Who asked him to play billiards? I don't understand people like that. *(She goes out.)*

LYUBOV ANDREYEVNA: Don't tease her, Petya. You can see she has enough troubles already.

TROFIMOV: Well, why does she interfere so much? Why does she meddle? She hasn't left Anya and me alone the entire summer. She's afraid we're going to fall in love. What business is that of hers? Besides, there's no reason to worry. We're removed from such trivialities. We're above love.

LYUBOV ANDREYEVNA: And I, I suppose, am below love? *(agitated)* Why hasn't Leonid come home? All I want to know is—has the estate been sold, yes or no? It seems inconceivable to me. I don't know what to think. I'm losing my mind. I could scream, do stupid things. Save me, Petya. Say something.

TROFIMOV: Whether the estate is sold today or not, what's the difference? All that has been over and done with for a long time. You can't turn back the clock. Try to be calm, dearest Lyubov Andreyevna. Don't deceive yourself. For once in your life, face the truth.

LYUBOV ANDREYEVNA: What truth? You, of course, always see what's true and what's not. But I don't, I don't see—I'm blind. You have answers to all the important questions. But, my dear, that's because you're young. Those questions haven't hurt you yet. You haven't suffered. When you look forward, you look boldly—you see nothing frightening. Your young eyes haven't seen life yet. You're stronger and more honest than we are, less superficial—that's true. But stop and think. Be generous, have pity on us. Try to imagine— I was born here, my parents lived here, my grandfather... I love this house. My life makes no sense without the cherry orchard. If it has to be sold, then sell me too—with the orchard. *(She hugs* TROFIMOV, *kisses him on the forehead.)* My little boy drowned here. *(crying)* You have a good kind soul, my dear. Have pity on me, have pity.

TROFIMOV: You know I sympathize with you, with all my heart.

LYUBOV ANDREYEVNA: Ah, but that's not the way to say it—not like that. *(She takes out her handkerchief. A telegram falls from it to the ground.)* My heart is so full today, you can't imagine. There's too much noise here. Each sound makes me jump. I'm trembling, but I can't go up to my room—it's too frightening up there, too silent, too lonely. Don't judge me harshly, Petya. I love you as my family. I'd give you my Anya now, I swear I would. But, my dear, you must work a little, finish your studies. You don't do anything. You live by allowing Fate to fling you from place to place. That's strange, but it's true, isn't it? And then do something about your beard. Train it to grow properly. *(She laughs.)* You're so funny!

TROFIMOV: I don't want to look handsome. *(He picks up the telegram.)*

LYUBOV ANDREYEVNA: A telegram from Paris. There's one every day now. Yesterday, today... That wild man is ill again. Something's wrong with him again. He wants me to forgive him, to come back. It's true—I should go to Paris, stay with him a little. You look disapproving, Petya. But what else can I do, my dear? He's sick and miserable, and alone. Who'll take care of him, stop him from being silly, give him his medicine? And then—why hide it? Why not say it? I love him. It's true. I love him, I love him. He's a millstone around my neck, but I love that stone. He'll drag me down, but I love him. I can't live without him... *(She presses Trofimov's hand.)* Don't judge me, Petya. Don't say anything. Don't speak a word...

TROFIMOV: *(almost crying)* Forgive me, I beg you—but he's stolen from you, he's robbed you!

LYUBOV ANDREYEVNA: No, no, no. You mustn't say that. *(She puts her hands over her ears.)*

TROFIMOV: He uses you. It's obvious. You're the only one who doesn't see it. He's a scoundrel, a nobody.

LYUBOV ANDREYEVNA: *(controlling her anger)* You must be twenty-six now or twenty-seven, but still you think like a schoolboy.

TROFIMOV: So?

LYUBOV ANDREYEVNA: At your age, you ought to be a man. Why don't you fall in love? Learn to understand what that means. Fall in love with someone yourself. *(angrily)* Yes, yes, it's not that you're so pure. You're a prude, that's what it is—a little boy, ridiculous and smug.

TROFIMOV: *(horrified)* What is she saying?

LYUBOV ANDREYEVNA: "I'm above love." You're not above love. You're simply a nincompoop, as Firs would say. When I think that at your age you don't even have a mistress!

TROFIMOV: *(horrified)* This is horrible! What is she saying? *(He goes quickly toward the ballroom, his head in his hands.)* Horrible. I can't stand it. I'm going. *(He goes out, but returns immediately.)* It's over between us! *(He goes out toward the hall.)*

LYUBOV ANDREYEVNA: *(calling after him)* Petya, wait! You're so funny. It was just a joke, Petya! *(We hear steps running up the stairs from the hall, then a rolling sound and a crash. We hear ANYA and VARYA scream, but then immediately we hear them laugh.)* What happened?

(ANYA runs in laughing.)

ANYA: Petya fell down the stairs. *(She runs out.)*

LYUBOV ANDREYEVNA: He's so funny, Petya.

(The STATION MASTER stops in the middle of the ballroom and begins to recite "The Sinner" by Alexei Tolstoy. The others listen, but after a few lines a waltz is heard, and all start to dance again. TROFIMOV, ANYA, VARYA and LYUBOV ANDREYEVNA return.)

LYUBOV ANDREYEVNA: But, Petya—forgive me, my innocent darling, I beg you. Come dance. *(She dances with* PETYA. ANYA *and* VARYA *dance.* FIRS *enters, putting his cane near the door.* YASHA *also comes in and watches the dancers.)*

YASHA: What's the matter, Grandpa?

FIRS: I'm not feeling well. In the old days generals, admirals and barons came to our balls. Now look. We send for the postmaster, the station master—and even they have to be begged. I'm feeling weak. The old master—the grandfather—whenever you felt sick, he'd give you sealing wax. I take it every day now for twenty years—longer. Maybe that's why I'm still alive.

YASHA: You bother me, Grandpa. *(He yawns.)* Why don't you go off and die?

FIRS: You, you... nincompoop—good for nothing. *(He mutters.* TROFIMOV *and* LYUBOV ANDREYEVNA *dance in the ballroom, then in the drawing room.)*

LYUBOV ANDREYEVNA: Merci. I must sit. *(She sits.)* Tired. *(*ANYA *enters.)*

ANYA: *(all excited)* In the kitchen just now a man said the cherry orchard's been sold.

LYUBOV ANDREYEVNA: Sold? To whom?

ANYA: He didn't say. He's gone. *(She dances with* TROFIMOV *into the ballroom.)*

YASHA: Just an old man talking—he's not from around here.

FIRS: And Leonid Andreyevich not home yet, not back. He wore his light-weight coat. He'll catch cold—ach, young people.

LYUBOV ANDREYEVNA: I think I'm dying. Yasha, go quickly. Ask to whom the estate was sold.

YASHA: He left a long time ago, that old man. *(He laughs.)*

LYUBOV ANDREYEVNA: *(annoyed)* What's so funny about that? What's so amusing?

YASHA: *(laughing)* That Yepikhodov—so stupid. No sense. Twenty-two misfortunes.

LYUBOV ANDREYEVNA: Firs, if the estate is sold, where will you go?

FIRS: Wherever you say.

LYUBOV ANDREYEVNA: Why do you look like that? Are you ill? You should go to bed.

FIRS: Yes. *(with an ironic smile)* I go to bed—and who will serve? Who'll keep order? There's only me for the whole house.

YASHA: Lyubov Andreyevna, may I ask you something please—a favor? Would you be kind enough, if you go to Paris, to take me with you? It's impossible here. *(He looks around him, lowers his voice.)* I don't need to tell you—you see for yourself—this country isn't civilized. The population has no idea how to do things, and it's boring. The food in the kitchen is terrible. And old Firs is always wandering about muttering. Please take me with you.

(PISHCHIK enters.)

PISHCHIK: Will you grant me a little waltz, most bountiful lady? *(LYUBOV ANDREYEVNA gets up, goes with him.)* Ma chere, I must still borrow those hundred and eighty rubles from you. *(They dance.)* Just a hundred and eighty little rubles. *(They dance into the ballroom.)*

YASHA: *(singing softly)* "Won't you understand the torments of my heart?" *(In the ballroom a figure in checked pants and a grey top hat waves both hands and jumps around. There are cries of "Bravo, Charlotta Ivanovna.")*

DUNYASHA: *(stopping to powder her nose)* Young mistress ordered me to dance. There are many gentlemen and not enough ladies. But dancing makes my head spin. My heart is pounding. And, Firs Nikolayevich, just now the postmaster said something so nice to me, so nice it simply took my breath away. *(The music plays more softly.)*

FIRS: What did he say?

DUNYASHA: He said, "You're like a flower."

YASHA: *(yawning)* How stupid... *(He goes out.)*

DUNYASHA: Like a flower... I'm so delicate and sensitive. I love tender words.

FIRS: That'll be your downfall.

(YEPIKHODOV enters.)

YEPIKHODOV: You pay no more attention to me now, Avodtya Fydorovna, than if I were an insect. *(He sighs.)* Ah, life.

DUNYASHA: But what can I do about it?

YEPIKHODOV: Of course—you're probably right, of course. *(He sighs.)* Nonetheless, from my point of view, if I may mention it—you put me in an odd position. Of course, I'm accustomed to my fate—

each day a new misfortune—I'm accustomed to that, and I greet life with a smile. Nonetheless, you gave me your word, and I'm—

DUNYASHA: Please, let us discuss it another time. At this moment, please leave me to myself—I'm dreaming. *(She plays with her fan.)*

YEPIKHODOV: Each day—a new misfortune. But I just smile. Sometimes I even laugh.

(VARYA enters from the ballroom.)

VARYA: *(to YEPIKHODOV)* Haven't you gone yet? You're really impossible. *(to DUNYASHA)* Dunyasha, leave us. *(to YEPIKHODOV)* First you play billiards and break a cue, and now you're standing around the drawing room as if you were a guest.

YEPIKHODOV: You have no right to speak to me in that tone, if I may say so.

VARYA: I'm not speaking "in that tone." I'm telling you. You never do any work. I don't know why we employ a clerk at all.

YEPIKHODOV: *(offended)* Whether I work, eat, wander about or play billiards concerns only people of quality. I may be judged only by my peers.

VARYA: How dare you say that to me? *(getting very angry)* How dare you? I'm not a person of quality? Get out of here. Now! This instant.

YEPIKHODOV: *(alarmed)* I beg you to express yourself with more delicacy.

VARYA: *(beside herself)* Get out! Clear out. Now. Out. Out! *(He goes toward the door. She follows him.)* Twenty-two misfortunes! Out. I don't want you here anymore. Out!

(YEPIKHODOV goes out. We hear his voice.)

YEPIKHODOV: *(offstage)* I'm going to file a complaint against you.

VARYA: What! Are you trying to come back? *(She grabs the cane forgotten by FIRS.)* Just try it. Go ahead. Try it. You'll see. Come in now, come in. This is for you. *(She swings the cane the moment LOPAKHIN enters.)*

LOPAKHIN: Thank you.

VARYA: *(angrily and ironically)* I'm terribly sorry.

LOPAKHIN: It's nothing. Thank you for your warm welcome.

VARYA: Don't mention it. *(She moves off, then turns around and asks him gently.)* Did I hurt you?

LOPAKHIN: No, not really. There'll be a big bump.

(voices in the ballroom)

VOICES: Lopakhin is here! Yermolay Alexyevich!

(PISHCHIK enters.)

SIMEONOV-PISHCHIK: He's back. You can see him! You can touch him! *(He kisses LOPAKHIN.)* You smell of brandy, dear heart. We've been having a good time too.

(LYUBOV ANDREYEVNA enters.)

LYUBOV ANDREYEVNA: Yermolay Alexyevich. Where were you? Where's Leonid?

LOPAKHIN: Leonid Andreyevich came back with me. He's coming.

LYUBOV ANDREYEVNA: *(agitated)* Well? What happened? Was there an auction? Say something.

LOPAKHIN: *(embarrassed, afraid of showing his joy)* The auction was over at four... We missed the train. We had to wait until 9:30. *(sighing heavily)* Unh, my head is spinning.

(GAYEV comes in. With his right hand he holds his purchases, with his left he wipes away his tears.)

LYUBOV ANDREYEVNA: What happened? Quick! Tell us, Leonya. *(passionately, with tears)* For God's sake!

(GAYEV gestures helplessly, not answering her. Crying, he speaks to FIRS.)

GAYEV: Here, take these... Anchovies and herrings... I've had nothing to eat all day... Oh, what I've been through.

(The door of the billiard room is open. We hear the sounds of billiard balls clicking and of YASHA's voice.)

YASHA: *(offstage)* Seven and eighteen.

(GAYEV's face changes. He stops crying.)

GAYEV: I'm tired. Firs, come help me change.

(He goes to his room through the ballroom, FIRS following.)

SIMEONOV-PISHCHIK: What about the auction? Speak up. What happened?

LYUBOV ANDREYEVNA: Is the cherry orchard sold?

LOPAKHIN: Sold.

LYUBOV ANDREYEVNA: Who bought it?

LOPAKHIN: I bought it. *(A pause. LYUBOV ANDREYEVNA is overcome. She would fall if she weren't near an armchair and table. VARYA undoes the ring of keys from her belt, throws the keys on the drawing room floor and goes out.)* I bought it. Yes. Wait, my friends, please. Please wait a moment. Everything is spinning in my head. I can't speak. *(He laughs.)* All right. We get to the auction. Deriganov is already there. Leonid Andreyevich has only fifteen thousand, and right away Deriganov goes up to thirty thousand plus the mortgage. I see what's happening. I jump in and bid forty thousand. He, forty-five. Me, fifty-five. He goes up by five thousand. I go up by tens. In the end I bid ninety thousand plus the mortgage, and I get it. The cherry orchard is mine! Mine! *(He bursts out laughing.)* Dear Lord, my God—the cherry orchard is mine. Tell me I'm drunk, tell me I'm crazy, that I'm dreaming... *(He reels.)* Don't laugh at me. If my father and grandfather could only rise from their graves and see me now—me, their ignorant little Yermolay, almost illiterate, their Yermolay who was beaten, who went without shoes in winter. Now that same little Yermolay has just bought the most beautiful estate in the world! I bought the estate where my father and grandfather were slaves, where they weren't even allowed into the kitchen. I must be dreaming, asleep, imagining. This only seems like its happening. It can't be true! *(He picks up the keys, speaks with a little childlike smile.)* She's thrown down the keys to show she's not mistress here any more. *(He jingles the keys.)* So it must be true. *(We hear the musicians tuning their instruments.)* Hey, musicians, play. I want to hear you. Come, come everyone, see how Yermolay Lopakhin is going to take an ax to the cherry orchard— how the trees are going to fall! We're going to build new houses, and our grandchildren and all our descendants are going to know a new life here. Music! Play! *(The music plays.* LYUBOV ANDREYEVNA *falls into a chair, crying bitterly.* LOPAKHIN *speaks remorsefully.)* But why, why didn't you listen to me, my dear friend? My poor friend. It's too late now. *(through tears)* Oh, if only all this would be over soon, soon. If only our absurd, unhappy lives would change soon!

*(*PISHCHIK *takes* LOPAKHIN *by the arm, speaks in a low tone.)*

SIMEONOV-PISHCHIK: She's crying. Come. Come into the ballroom. We'll leave her alone... Come. *(He leads* LOPAKHIN *into the ballroom.)*

LOPAKHIN: What's the matter? Come on, music, play louder! Let everything be as I want it. *(ironically)* Here he is, the new master—the owner of the cherry orchard. *(He accidentally bumps into a small table, nearly knocks over some candlesticks.)* It's alright. I'll pay for everything!

(He goes out with PISHCHIK. *There's no one left in the ballroom or the drawing room except* LYUBOV ANDREYEVNA *who sits in a chair crying bitterly. The music plays quietly.* ANYA *and* TROFIMOV *enter quickly.* ANYA *goes to her mother, and kneels in front of her.* TROFIMOV *remains standing in the entrance to the ballroom.)*

ANYA: Mama! Mama, are you crying? My dear, good, sweet Mama, my beautiful Mama—I love you, I bless you. The cherry orchard is sold, no more cherry orchard—it's true. It's true, but you mustn't cry, Mama. You have life in front of you and your soul, good and pure. Come with me, my darling, let's leave here. We'll plant a new orchard, more beautiful than this one—you'll see. Then you'll know, you'll know a joy—a deep, calm joy will come into your heart, like sunset light. And you'll smile, Mama. Come, darling! Come!

Curtain

The scene is the same as Act I, but there are no curtains on the windows, or pictures on the walls. What little furniture is left is piled in one corner, as if for sale. There's a feeling of emptiness. Near the outside door, at the back of the stage, are suitcases, traveling bags, etc. The door on the left is open. From it are heard ANYA's *and* VARYA's *voices.* LOPAKHIN *is standing, waiting.* YASHA *holds a tray of champagne glasses. In the entrance hall* YEPIKHODOV *is tying a box with a string. From offstage there is the sound of people talking—peasants who have come to say goodbye. We hear* GAYEV's *voice speaking to them.*

GAYEV: *(offstage)* Thank you, brothers, thank you.

YASHA: The peasants have come to pay their last respects. In my opinion, Yermolay Alexyevich, peasants are not bad people, but they're ignorant.

(The sound of the voices subsides. LYUBOV ANDREYEVNA *and* GAYEV *enter from the hall. She is not crying, but she's pale. Her face quivers. She's unable to speak.)*

GAYEV: You gave them your purse, Lyuba. You mustn't do things like that. You mustn't!

LYUBOV ANDREYEVNA: I couldn't help it. I couldn't help it.

(They go out.)

LOPAKHIN: *(at the door, calling after them)* Please have some champagne before you go. I forgot to get some in town, but I found one bottle at the station. So please, have some. *(pause)* No? You don't want any? *(He comes back from the door.)* If I had known—I wouldn't have bought it. Alright then—I won't have any either. *(YASHA carefully puts the tray on a chair.)* You have some at least, Yasha.

YASHA: Good health to those who are leaving. Good health to those who are staying. *(He drinks.)* This isn't French champagne, I can tell you.

LOPAKHIN: Eight rubles a bottle. *(pause)* Colder than hell here.

YASHA: They didn't light the fires today, since we're leaving. *(YASHA laughs.)*

LOPAKHIN: What's so funny?

YASHA: Just laughing for joy.

LOPAKHIN: It's October, but it's sunny, and no wind. It's like summer. Good building weather. *(He looks at his watch and calls toward the door.)* Ladies and gentlemen, your train leaves in forty-seven minutes. You must leave for the station in twenty minutes. Better hurry up.

(TROFIMOV enters from outside in an overcoat.)

TROFIMOV: Is it time to go? The horses are ready. Where are my galoshes? I've lost them. *(calling through the door)* Anya, where are my galoshes? I can't find them.

LOPAKHIN: I go to Kharkov on the same train as you, to spend the winter there. I've been wasting time gossiping with you all. I'm sick of doing nothing. I can't stand being without work. I don't know what to do with my hands. They start to droop somehow, as if they weren't mine.

TROFIMOV: Well, we're leaving now. So you can get back to your useful occupations.

LOPAKHIN: Have a glass of champagne.

TROFIMOV: I don't want one.

LOPAKHIN: So, are you going to Moscow?

TROFIMOV: Yes. I accompany them to town, and tomorrow I go to Moscow.

LOPAKHIN: Yes. Well, I suppose all the professors are waiting for you.

TROFIMOV: Mind your own business.

LOPAKHIN: How long have you been at the university?

TROFIMOV: Try another joke. That one has gone stale. *(He looks for his galoshes.)* Listen, we may never see each other again, so let me give you some advice. Stop making those grand sweeping gestures. Lose the habit of throwing your arms about. And all that talk about building villas, believing summer people will till the land—those are grand gestures too. But—in spite of everything—I like you, you know. You have fine, sensitive hands—artist's hands. And a fine sensitive soul.

LOPAKHIN: *(embracing him)* Goodbye, dear friend. Thank you. If you need money for the trip—I'll give you some, happily.

TROFIMOV: Why? It's not necessary.

LOPAKHIN: But you don't have any.

TROFIMOV: Yes I have, thanks. I just received some for a translation. I have it in my pocket, here. *(anxious)* But I can't find my galoshes.

VARYA: *(from the next room)* Here are your filthy galoshes. *(She throws them into the middle of the stage.)*

TROFIMOV: Why are you so angry, Varya? And these aren't my galoshes.

LOPAKHIN: I planted three thousand acres of poppies this spring—cleared forty thousand rubles. Poppies are beautiful when they bloom—they make a beautiful picture. I cleared forty thousand, so I'm offering because I can afford it. Why be proud? I'm just a peasant. I say what I mean.

TROFIMOV: Your father was a peasant, and mine was a pharmacist. What does that prove? *(LOPAKHIN takes out his wallet.)* Put it away. You could offer me two hundred thousand—I wouldn't take it. I'm free. Money, which you rich value so highly—as do the poor—has no power over me. It's just feathers in the wind. I don't need you, I pass you by—I'm strong, I'm proud. Humanity marches toward a higher truth, toward the greatest possible happiness on earth, and I'm in the front ranks.

LOPAKHIN: And will you reach your goal?

TROFIMOV: I will. *(pause)* Or I'll teach others how to reach it.

(From a distance we hear axes striking the trunks of trees.)

LOPAKHIN: Well, dear friend, goodbye. Time to go. We have our pride, we show off to each other— while life goes on, paying us no mind. When I've been working a long time without stopping then my thoughts are lighter, and I feel I too know why I'm alive. But in Russia, brother, how many of us know why we live? Well, never mind. Why dwell on it? Doesn't pay the rent. It seems Leonid Andreyevich has accepted a position in a bank—six thousand a year. He won't last long there. Too lazy.

ANYA: *(at the door)* Mama asks would you not cut down the trees before she goes.

TROFIMOV: It's true. You might have the tact... *(He goes out through the hall.)*

LOPAKHIN: Of course, of course... Those workers, really. *(He follows TROFIMOV out.)*

ANYA: Did they take Firs to the hospital?

YASHA: I told them to this morning. One assumes they did.

ANYA: *(to YEPIKHODOV)* Please go ask if Firs has been taken to the hospital.

YASHA: *(offended)* I told Egor this morning. Why ask ten times?

YEPIKHODOV: The venerable Firs, in my opinion, has already lived too long. He's past mending. He should join his ancestors. And I can only envy him. *(He puts a suitcase on a hat box which he crushes.)* There. Naturally. Of course. *(He goes out.)*

YASHA: *(making fun of him)* Twenty-two misfortunes…

VARYA: *(from behind the door)* Did they take Firs to the hospital?

ANYA: Yes.

VARYA: Then why didn't they take the letter for the doctor?

ANYA: *(as she goes out)* We'll have to send it right away.

VARYA: *(from behind the door)* Where's Yasha? Tell him his mother's here. She wants to say goodbye.

YASHA: *(with a gesture of annoyance)* So exasperating.

(DUNYASHA, who has been busy with the baggage, goes up to YASHA as soon as they're alone.)

DUNYASHA: Look at me, at least once, Yasha. You're leaving, you're abandoning me. *(She throws herself on his neck, crying.)*

YASHA: What's the use of crying? *(He drinks some champagne.)* In six days, Paris! Tomorrow the express, and poof—we're gone. You'll never see us again. I can hardly believe it. *Vive la France!* I don't feel good here. I can't get used to it. There's nothing to do all day. And I'm sick of all this stupidity. I've had enough. *(He drinks some champagne.)* What's the use of crying? If you were a real young lady, you wouldn't cry.

DUNYASHA: *(powdering her nose, looking into her small pocket mirror)* Write to me. I loved you so much, Yasha. So much! I'm so delicate and sensitive.

YASHA: They're coming.

(He busies himself with the baggage, humming. LYUBOV ANDREYEVNA, GAYEV, ANYA and CHARLOTTA enter.)

GAYEV: We should go. It's almost time. *(looking at YASHA)* Who smells of herring here?

LYUBOV ANDREYEVNA: In another ten minutes, we climb into the carriage. *(She looks around.)* Goodbye, my dear house, my old ancestor. Winter will end, and in spring—you'll no longer exist. Demolished.

Dear old walls, how much you've seen. *(She kisses her daughter warmly.)* My little treasure, you're beaming. Your eyes are like two diamonds. Are you happy? Very happy?

ANYA: Very. I'm happy. A new life is beginning, Mama.

GAYEV: *(happily)* Yes, everything's going to be all right now. Before the cherry orchard was sold, we worried and suffered. But now that everything's settled, we're calm, calm and happy. Here I am a banker, a financier. Yellow ball to the side pocket. And you look better, Lyuba. You do.

LYUBOV ANDREYEVNA: Yes. My nerves are calmer. They are. *(She is brought her coat and hat.)* I sleep better now. My things, Yasha. It's time. *(to ANYA)* My little girl. We'll see each other soon. I must go back to Paris. I'll live on the money your great-aunt from Yaroslavl sent to buy the estate. God bless dear Auntie! But the money won't last long.

ANYA: Come back soon, Mama—soon, won't you? I'll study and pass my exams. Then I'll work. And I'll help you. We'll read many books together—won't we, Mama? *(She kisses her mother's hands.)* In the long autumn evenings we'll read books. And a new world, a wonderful world, will open for us. *(daydreaming)* You will come back, won't you, Mama?

LYUBOV ANDREYEVNA: I'll come back, my treasure.

(She embraces her daughter. LOPAKHIN *enters.* CHARLOTTA *quietly hums a little song.)*

GAYEV: Lucky Charlotta—she's singing.

(CHARLOTTA picks up a bundle that looks like a baby wrapped in swaddling clothes.)

CHARLOTTA: Hush-a-bye, baby. *(We hear the baby crying: "Oh ah.")* Hush, hush, little baby, poor little baby, sweet little baby. Bye, bye, baby. *("Oh, ah, oh, ah.")* I'm so sorry for you. You break your Mama's heart. *(She throws the bundle down.)* Will you find me another job, please. I need one.

LOPAKHIN: We'll find you a job, Charlotta Ivanovna. Don't worry. We'll find you a job.

GAYEV: Everyone's abandoning us. Varya's leaving. Suddenly no one needs us.

CHARLOTTA: I have no place to live in town. I have to go somewhere else. *(She hums.)* Well, so what?

(PISHCHIK enters.)

LOPAKHIN: Here's our miracle of nature.

SIMEONOV-PISHCHIK: *(out of breath, panting)* Ouf! Have to catch my breath... I'm worn out. I salute you all... Give me some water.

GAYEV: He's come for money again. *(bowing.)* Your humble servant. Time to make myself scarce. It's safer. *(He goes out.)*

SIMEONOV-PISHCHIK: I haven't been to see you for a long time... Most beautiful lady... *(to LOPAKHIN)* And you're here too... Good to see you, you clever man. Here... Take this... *(He gives LOPAKHIN a bundle of bills.)* Four hundred rubles—I still owe you eight hundred and forty.

LOPAKHIN: *(shrugging his shoulders, amazed)* I must be dreaming... Where'd you get this?

SIMEONOV-PISHCHIK: Wait... I'm too hot... An amazing occurrence... Some Englishmen came, discovered white clay on my land... *(to LYUBOV ANDREYEVNA)* Here's four hundred for you, my most beautiful and *charmante amie*. *(He gives her the money.)* The rest will come later. *(He drinks a glass of water.)* A little while ago on the train, a young man told me a great philosopher said: "Everyone should dare to jump off a roof." "Jump," he said, "and that'll settle everything." *(amazed)* Incredible. Water, please.

LOPAKHIN: What about the Englishmen?

SIMEONOV-PISHCHIK: I rented them the land with the white clay for twenty-four years. Now, forgive me, but I have to go to the next house—to Znoikov's, then to Kardamanov's. I owe everyone money. *(He drinks.)* Good health to you all. I'll come by again on Thursday.

LYUBOV ANDREYEVNA: We're moving to town today. Tomorrow I'm going abroad.

SIMEONOV-PISHCHIK: What? *(alarmed)* To town? So that's it... Furniture, suitcases... Well, that's all right. *(almost crying)* Remarkably intelligent, those Englishmen. That's all right. Be happy. God will help you. That's all right. Everything ends in this world. *(He kisses LYUBOV ANDREYEVNA's hand.)* And if one day you should hear I'm dead, think of Caligula's horse, and say: "Once upon a time there lived a certain Simeonov-Pishchik, God have mercy on his soul." Wonderful weather we're having. Yes. *(He goes out, obviously shaken, but returns immediately and speaks from the door.)* Dashenka says to say hello. *(He goes out.)*

LYUBOV ANDREYEVNA: Now we leave... But I still have two worries. The first is Firs, who is ill. *(She looks at her watch.)* We have five minutes...

ANYA: They took Firs to the hospital, Mama. Yasha had him go this morning.

LYUBOV ANDREYEVNA: My second worry is Varya. She's used to getting up early and working hard. Now with nothing to do, she's like a fish out of water. She's thin and pale—she cries, poor dear. *(pause)* You know as well as I, Yermolay Alexyevich, I've always dreamed of her marrying you. And there's been every sign you would marry her. *(She whispers to ANYA who nods to CHARLOTTA, and they both go out.)* She loves you, you like her. I don't know, I don't understand why you seem to run away from each other.

LOPAKHIN: I don't understand it either... It's peculiar. But if there's still a little time, I'm ready—this very minute. Let's finish this business once and for all. Because when you're gone, I know I won't be able to ask her.

LYUBOV ANDREYEVNA: Good! After all, one minute is enough. I'll call her...

LOPAKHIN: There's even champagne. That's lucky. *(He looks at the glasses.)* Someone's drunk it all. *(YASHA laughs.)* You could call that guzzling it down.

LYUBOV ANDREYEVNA: *(decisively)* Good! We'll leave you alone together. Yasha, *allez!* I'll call her... *(calling through the door)* Varya, come here a moment—alone. Come here! *(She goes out with YASHA.)*

LOPAKHIN: *(looking at his watch)* Yes...

(A pause. From behind the door stifled laughs, whispering. Finally VARYA enters.)

VARYA: *(carefully examining the baggage)* That's funny. I can't find it anywhere.

LOPAKHIN: What are you looking for?

VARYA: I packed it myself, but I don't know where. *(pause)*

LOPAKHIN: Where will you go now, Varvara Mikhailovna?

VARYA: Me? To the Ragoulines. We've arranged—I'm going as their housekeeper, I think.

LOPAKHIN: To Yashnevo? That's about seventy miles from here. *(pause)* Well, life in this house seems to be over...

VARYA: *(examining the baggage)* Where did I put it? Unless it's in a trunk... Yes, life in this house is over. There won't be any more...

LOPAKHIN: And me, I'm off to Kharkov in a little while. Taking the same train. I've got work to do. I'm leaving Yepikhodov here. I've hired him.

VARYA: Have you?

LOPAKHIN: Last year at this time, if you remember, it was already snowing. Now it's quiet and sunny. But there's frost... It's three degrees.

VARYA: I haven't checked the thermometer. *(pause)* Anyway—ours is broken.

(A pause. A voice from the courtyard is heard calling: "Yermolay Alexyevich!")

LOPAKHIN: *(as if he'd been expecting this call)* Coming!

(He goes out quickly. VARYA, sitting on the floor, her head on a bundle, sobs softly. The door opens. LYUBOV ANDREYEVNA enters cautiously.)

LYUBOV ANDREYEVNA: Well? *(pause)* We have to go.

VARYA: *(no longer crying, wiping her eyes)* Yes, Mama dear, it's time. I'll reach the Ragoulines today, if we don't miss the train.

LYUBOV ANDREYEVNA: *(calling toward the door)* Anya, put on your coat. *(ANYA enters, then GAYEV and CHARLOTTA. GAYEV wears a winter coat with a hood. The servants and drivers enter. YEPIKHODOV fusses with the baggage.)* And now, we start our travels.

ANYA: *(joyfully)* On our way!

GAYEV: My friends, my dear good friends, now—when leaving this house forever—how can I be silent? How can I not express the profound feelings with which my entire being—

ANYA: *(pleading)* Uncle!

VARYA: Uncle dear, you mustn't.

GAYEV: *(dejectedly)* Double off the white. Yellow to the side pocket. I'm silent.

(TROFIMOV enters, and then LOPAKHIN.)

TROFIMOV: Well, my friends—time to go.

LOPAKHIN: Yepikhodov, my coat!

LYUBOV ANDREYEVNA: Let me sit here just another moment. It's as if I'd never seen the walls of this room before, or the ceiling. I look at them so greedily now, with such love.

GAYEV: I remember when I was six, a day after Easter, I sat by that window watching Father leave for church.

LYUBOV ANDREYEVNA: Have they taken all our things?

LOPAKHIN: I think so, yes. (*putting on his coat, speaking to* YEPIKHODOV.) Keep things in order here, Yepikhodov.

YEPIKHODOV: (*his voice hoarse*) You don't need to worry, Yermolay Alexyevich.

LOPAKHIN: What's the matter with your voice?

YEPIKHODOV: I drank some water a little while ago. I must have swallowed wrong.

YASHA: (*with contempt*) Hopeless.

LYUBOV ANDREYEVNA: We're going, and not a soul will live here anymore.

LOPAKHIN: Until spring.

(*From a parcel* VARYA *pulls out her umbrella with a sharp gesture, as if she were going to hit someone with it.* LOPAKHIN *pretends to be frightened.*)

VARYA: What's the matter with you? It didn't even occur to me.

TROFIMOV: My friends! The carriage! It's time. The train won't wait.

VARYA: Petya, here are your galoshes. Behind this suitcase. (*almost crying*) They're so worn and dirty.

TROFIMOV: (*putting on his galoshes*) Let's go, my friends. Ladies and gentlemen, let's go.

GAYEV: (*extremely troubled, afraid of crying*) The train... The station... *Croisez* to the middle. Double the white into the corner.

LYUBOV ANDREYEVNA: Come, let's go!

LOPAKHIN: Everyone here? No one in there? (*He locks a door on the right.*) Have we left anything? Have to lock up! Let's go.

ANYA: Goodbye, house! Goodbye, our old life.

TROFIMOV: Long live our new life.

(TROFIMOV *and* ANYA *go out.* VARYA *glances around once more, and goes out unhurriedly.* YASHA *and* CHARLOTTA *with her little dog follow her.*)

LOPAKHIN: Until spring. Come, friends. Til we meet again.

(He goes out. LYUBOV ANDREYEVNA *and* GAYEV *are left alone. As if they had waited for this moment, they throw themselves into each other's arms. They sob, but restrainedly, afraid of being heard.)*

GAYEV: *(in despair)* My sister, my sister!

LYUBOV ANDREYEVNA: Oh, my orchard. My dear, sweet beautiful orchard! My life, my youth, my happiness. Farewell. Farewell!

*(*ANYA*'s voice is heard calling joyfully.)*

ANYA: *(offstage)* Mama!

TROFIMOV: *(offstage, gay and animated.)* Auuu, auuu.

LYUBOV ANDREYEVNA: One last look at these walls, these windows... How dear mama used to love to walk around this room...

GAYEV: My sister, my sister!

ANYA: *(offstage)* Mama!

TROFIMOV: *(offstage)* Auuu, auuu.

LYUBOV ANDREYEVNA: We're coming.

(They go out. The stage is empty. We hear doors being locked, and the carriages leaving. It becomes quiet. There is only the muffled sound of an ax hitting a tree, a sad lonely sound. Some steps. FIRS *appears at a door on the left. He is dressed as usual in a frock coat, white vest, and slippers. He is sick. He goes to the main door, turns the handle.)*

FIRS: It's locked. They're gone. *(He sits on the couch.)* They've forgotten me... Doesn't matter... Rest here... I know Leonid Andreyevich didn't wear his fur coat... He's gone out in his light-weight coat... *(He sighs anxiously.)* And I wasn't watching—ach, he's such a child. *(He mutters some words we can't understand.)* So life has gone by... And it seems I still haven't lived. *(He lies down on the couch.)* Lie down for a while. You have no strength left—nothing... Ach, go on—you... Nincompoop, good for nothing.

(He remains lying down, not moving. From a distance, as if from the sky, comes the sound of a snapped string, a melancholy sound. It gradually dies away. Then silence. We hear only the sound of axes on trees far away in the orchard.)

Curtain

1903